On Cultural L

The rise of non-Western great powers, the spread of transnational religiously justified insurgencies, and the resurgence of ethno-nationalism raise fundamental questions about the effects of cultural diversity on international order. Yet current debate – among academics, popular commentators, and policymakers alike – rests on flawed understandings of culture and inaccurate assumptions about how historically cultural diversity has shaped the evolution of international orders. In this path-breaking book, Christian Reus-Smit details how the major theories of international relations have consistently misunderstood the nature and effects of culture, returning time and again to a conception long abandoned in specialist fields: the idea of cultures as coherent, bounded, and constitutive. Drawing on theoretical insights from anthropology, cultural studies, and sociology, and informed by new histories of diverse historical orders, this book presents a new theoretical account of the relationship between cultural diversity and international order: an account with far-reaching implications for how we understand contemporary transformations.

CHRISTIAN REUS-SMIT is Professor of International Relations at the University of Queensland and a Fellow of the Academy of the Social Sciences in Australia. Among his previous books, he is the author of *Individual Rights and the Making of the International System* (2013), *American Power and World Order* (2004), and *The Moral Purpose of the State* (1999); coauthor of *Special Responsibilities: Global Problems and American Power* (2012); and editor of *The Politics of International Law* (2004).

LSE INTERNATIONAL STUDIES

SERIES EDITORS

George Lawson (Lead Editor)
Department of International Relations, London School of Economics
Kirsten Ainley
Department of International Relations, London School of Economics
Ayça Çubukçu
Department of Sociology, London School of Economics
Stephen Humphreys
Department of Law, London School of Economics

This series, published in association with the Centre for International Studies at the London School of Economics, is centred on three main themes. First, the series is oriented around work that is transdisciplinary, which challenges disciplinary conventions and develops arguments that cannot be grasped within existing disciplines. It will include work combining a wide range of fields, including international relations, international law, political theory, history, sociology and ethics. Second, it comprises books that contain an overtly international or transnational dimension, but not necessarily focused simply within the discipline of International Relations. Finally, the series will publish books that use scholarly inquiry as a means of addressing pressing political concerns. Books in the series may be predominantly theoretical, or predominantly empirical, but all will say something of significance about political issues that exceed national boundaries.

On Cultural Diversity

International Theory in a World of Difference

CHRISTIAN REUS-SMIT
University of Queensland

 CAMBRIDGE
UNIVERSITY PRESS

CAMBRIDGE
UNIVERSITY PRESS

University Printing House, Cambridge CB2 8BS, United Kingdom

One Liberty Plaza, 20th Floor, New York, NY 10006, USA

477 Williamstown Road, Port Melbourne, VIC 3207, Australia

314–321, 3rd Floor, Plot 3, Splendor Forum, Jasola District Centre, New Delhi – 110025, India

79 Anson Road, #06–04/06, Singapore 079906

Cambridge University Press is part of the University of Cambridge.

It furthers the University's mission by disseminating knowledge in the pursuit of education, learning, and research at the highest international levels of excellence.

www.cambridge.org
Information on this title: www.cambridge.org/9781108473859
DOI: 10.1017/9781108658058

© Christian Reus-Smit 2018

First published 2018

Printed and bound in Great Britain by Clays Ltd, Elcograf S.p.A.

A catalogue record for this publication is available from the British Library.

ISBN 978-1-108-47385-9 Hardback
ISBN 978-1-108-46274-7 Paperback

For my parents
Janet and Karel

Contents

Preface

The question of how culture conditions international relations has stalked my work from the outset, but until now I have shied away from confronting it directly. As a graduate student at Cornell University I toyed with several dissertation topics that engaged questions of global community, but after an intense but brief interest in claims to justice in the emerging climate change regime, I set out to explain why historical societies of states – which scholars thought exhibited very similar political dynamics – nonetheless developed very different fundamental institutions. This was eventually published as *The Moral Purpose of the State*, and while culture appeared in the subtitle, it appeared in the standard constructivist guise: as social norms, in this case deep and structural. This was in part a methodological strategy: it gave me discrete cultural variables to process trace. But it was also safe: it was a way to study culture without ever confronting its nature and complexity. In the years since that project I have worked on hegemony, international law, special responsibilities, legitimacy, and individual rights, always stressing how social meanings and practices shape international politics. It was not until current debates about the rise of non-Western great powers, the resurgence of the politics of religion, the return of xenophobic nationalisms, and the implications of all of these for the future of the modern international order that I was finally ready to address the question of culture squarely. Culture features prominently in these debates, but in an anachronistic form, radically at odds with what anthropologists, cultural studies scholars, and sociologists have been telling us about culture for at least three decades. And as international relations (IR) scholars parry their way through these debates, their propositions about culture and international order appear largely untouched by a new wave of historical research that highlights the heterogeneous cultural contexts in which diverse international orders have evolved. This book, and the trilogy of which it is a part, builds on these neglected insights to rethink the relationship between cultural diversity and international order.

I dedicate the book to my parents, Janet and Karel, whose unusual choices for their young family sparked the interests that animate this study. In the early 1970s they bucked the trend and moved us from Melbourne's outer suburbs to inner city Fitzroy, buying a dilapidated Victorian terrace in a once grand avenue, then home to a mix of Greek and Italian migrants and itinerant 'Anglo' labourers. They sent me and the elder of my two sisters, Saskia, to a radical experimental high school in the neighbouring suburb of Brunswick, where the anarchic offspring of successive waves of postwar migration ran a merry circle around a courageous group of young educational innovators. The notorious 'White Australia Policy' had been abandoned a decade earlier, and the government was busy instituting a new policy of multiculturalism, shifting Australia from an overtly racist way of ordering cultural difference to a more pluralist, if equally structured, one. In late 1975 my parents set off on another adventure, loading us in a Peugeot 504 Familiale wagon and taking us on a road trip – from Paris to India. For fifteen months we followed the hippie trail from Europe, around the Mediterranean, through Iran and Pakistan, and down to Madurai in the south of India, ticking off as many of the world's great archaeological sites as we could.

This journey had a profound effect on me. It sparked my lifelong fascination with world politics and left me determined to study politics and history at university. More than this, it added a global layer to my inner-city appreciation of the beauty, complexity, and ubiquity of cultural diversity. As we traversed a large swath of Eurasia, the colours, contours, and textures of culture changed, but we didn't step from one hermetically sealed cultural unit to another and we crossed no civilizational border posts. Culture had a topography but no territoriality.

I have been fortunate over the years to collaborate with outstanding scholars from across IR's varied theoretical spectrum, from critical theorists to rational choice scholars. I turned to this group for feedback on the project, and I thank these friends for their penetrating and enormously helpful comments: Emanuel Adler, Michael Barnett, Maria Birnbaum, Roland Bleiker, Ian Clark, Tim Dunne, Robyn Eckersley, Evelyn Goh, Ian Hall, Emma Hutchison, John Ikenberry, Peter Katzenstein, Andrew Phillips, Heather Rae, Elizabeth Shakman Hurd, Duncan Snidal, Maja Spanu, Andrea Warnecke, Nicholas Wheeler, and William Wohlforth. As with my previous projects, I have benefitted from taking my ideas on the road, and I greatly appreciate the comments I received from audiences at these institutions: the Australian National University, the University of Cambridge, the Goethe University Frankfurt, the London School of Economics, the University of Melbourne, Princeton University, the University of Sydney, the University of Toronto, and the 2016 Oceanic International Studies Conference in Brisbane. I also presented several chapters to the wonderful IR Theory and History group at the University of Queensland, and in addition to those already mentioned, I thank Lorenzo Cello, David Duriesmith, Jacinta O'Hagan, Sarah Percy, and Neil Renic for their immensely helpful comments.

This book is the first of three volumes on cultural diversity and international order, and while writing the following chapters, I have also been collaborating with Andrew Phillips on the second volume: an interdisciplinary dialogue between leading theorists of international order and prominent specialists of cultural diversity from anthropology, history, international law, political theory, and sociology. I cannot express how much I have learned from this group, and I commend to others the huge gains that come from embedding your evolving thought within a structured dialogue with others, especially those who come from other disciplines. For their contributions to our collaborative volume, and their less direct but no less important contributions to my thinking in following chapters, I thank Michael Barnett, Ellen Berrey, Maria Birnbaum, Victoria Tin-bor Hui, Andrew Hurrell, John Ikenberry, Arnulf Becker Lorca, James Millward, Anne Norton, Ann Towns, Ann Swidler, and Ayse Zarakol. Andrew and I also thank the Social Trends Institute in Barcelona for generously funding and hosting this group's first workshop on 30 March–1 April 2017. We also greatly appreciate Patrick Herron's and Elif Kalaycioglu's contributions as workshop respondents and participants.

Peter Katzenstein advised me years ago that when embarking on a new research area I should always find a way to teach on it. One way or another I have done this with all of my projects, and in this case it has been through a series of master classes. The first, in October 2016, was with the University of Queensland's masters and PhD students; the second, a year later, was with a small group of our honours students. Both of these classes were teaching at its best – super smart, highly engaged students; a discrete but intense time cloistered together; and a highly topical issue, curiously neglected in contemporary IR. I thank all of the students who participated in these classes: I learnt an enormous amount from our discussions.

This project would not have been possible without the support I have received from the University of Queensland. Generous funding was provided jointly by the Vice-Chancellor, the Faculty of Humanities and Social Sciences (HASS), and the School of Political Science and International Studies (POLSIS). I have also been given the time to pursue such an ambitious project, and I express my enormous appreciation to the former Executive Dean, Tim Dunne (now Pro-Vice-Chancellor at the University of Queensland), and the Head of POLSIS, Richard Devetak, for backing my curiosities, stoking them with ongoing feedback and debate, and leavening it all with friendship and support. I also thank Peter Harrison, Director of the University of Queensland's Institute for Advanced Studies in the Humanities, for welcoming me to the Institute's immensely stimulating community.

Excellent research assistance was provided by Ryan Smith and Eglantine Staunton. Without their enthusiasm for the project, creative detective work, and attention to detail I would still be chasing the wide-ranging literatures that inform the following discussions. I also thank Ryan for his work compiling the Bibliography.

Earlier rehearsals of parts of argument advanced here were published in a number of journals, and I thank their publishers for permission to draw on these works, and their editors and reviewers for their extraordinarily helpful feedback. See 'International Law and the Mediation of Culture', *Ethics and International Affairs*, 28.1 (2014), 1–18; and 'Cultural Diversity and International Order', *International Organization*, 71.4 (2017), 851–885. I also tested the structure of the book in an essay for the Normative Orders Cluster of Excellence at Goethe University, Frankfurt. See 'Seeing Culture in World Politics', in Gunther Hellmann (ed.), *Theorizing Global Order* (Frankfurt: Campus Publishers, 2018), pp. 65–89.

The book's cover features an image by the outstanding Iranian-Australian artist Hoda Afshar. An abiding theme of Hoda's work is the complex processes of cultural negotiation, adaptation, and reconstitution that define the migrant experience. This photograph, titled 'We Didn't Grow Here, We Flew Here', from her 2010 series 'In-Between Spaces', captures the complexity of migrant identities, blending traditional Persian representational forms with contemporary 'Aussie' cultural symbols and imagery. This is more than simple hybridity: Hoda reveals, in a striking way, the structuring effects of dominant cultural constructions and the persistence of gendered cultural hierarchies in seemingly transformative processes of cultural change. Often art reveals these complexities far better than words, and I thank Hoda for allowing me to use her beautiful, intriguing, and confronting work.

My greatest thanks go to my partner, Heather Rae, and my teenage children, Sam and Lili, for their love and support, as well as their engagement with the ideas and issues explored in these pages. When I was busy skirting the issue of culture, Heather was confronting it head-on in her early work on ethnic cleansing and genocide in international history, *State Identities and the Homogenization of Peoples* (Cambridge University Press, 2002). She showed how these practices were related to processes of state-building: to the construction and legitimation of national political orders. I suggest here that analogous, if less extreme, practices of organizing cultural difference also feature in the construction of international orders, and my journey to this argument has been deeply influenced by my conversations with Heather.

A final word of thanks goes to my Sicilian-born Weimaraner, Manuel, who is everything a faithful canine companion should be: sitting under my desk as I wrote almost every word, and never failing to leap up and follow me as I chased another coffee or stretched my legs. *Grazie mille*!

Introduction

Cultural diversity is inherent to the human condition. Humans live in webs of intersubjective meanings, expressed through, and embedded within, language, images, bodies, practices, and artefacts. These meanings shape our identities (and vice versa), inform our interests, and provide powerful resources that can be mobilized to realize diverse goals. Yet even in local contexts, the topography of culture is far from uniform. Individuals inhabit multiple, often contradictory identities – religious, ethnic, class, gender, professional, sexual, even transnational – and these become more or less salient as we move from one context to another. Culture also sends mixed messages. Individuals don't encounter one cultural script or a single neatly ordered repertoire of practices. Instead, they navigate diverse, often discordant, meanings. Added to this, individuals interpret these meanings differently. Religious meanings are a prime example. Christianity, Judaism, and Islam – all are systems of meaning, but all are subject to disparate interpretations.

If this is true of local contexts, it is an existential reality of global life. Cultural diversity is a given, just like unequal material capabilities. But while we are told repeatedly to stare material power in the face, to see it, and its implications, in the cold light of day, we either ignore culture or view it through worn and distorted lenses. This has left us profoundly ill-equipped to understand current transformations in world politics. Power is shifting to non-Western states, diffusing to non-state actors (including transnational insurgents), and undergoing a significant reconfiguration within liberal-democratic polities. Yet this redistribution of power is deeply entangled with culture. Rising states, such as China and India, bring to the stage their own cultural values, practices, and histories (contradictory and contested as these might be); transnational insurgents justify violence not in the name of national liberation or political ideology, but religious identity,

1

grievance, and change; and ethno-nationalism and civilizational chauvinism are the preferred garb of the West's far right.

If there was ever a time when international relations (IR) scholars needed to look squarely at culture, and to think clearly and systematically about the nature and implications of cultural diversity, it is now. IR scholars have, of course, looked at culture before, even if the field has been focused elsewhere. Samuel Huntington's 'clash of civilizations' is perhaps the most prominent example, but others include realist arguments about nationalism and strategic culture, English School writings on the civilizational foundations of international society, constructivist research on norms, rationalist work on how cultural symbols communicate the common knowledge that facilitates coordination, postcolonial writing on culture and imperialism, and normative theory on universalism and cultural particularism. Even materialist claims that culture is epiphenomenal or causally irrelevant, and rationalist moves to reduce culture to preferences, are, in some sense, arguments about the nature, place, and significance of culture. Yet all of these ways of seeing culture are problematic, amounting in the end to different forms of blindness to culture's nature and complexity.

This book is the first of three volumes on cultural diversity and international order. Debate rages today about the future of the modern 'liberal' international order, with widespread concern that civilizational, ethno-national, and religious differences are eroding an order built by the West, for the West. Others counter that the modern order, undergirded by norms of sovereign equality, non-intervention, and self-determination, is uniquely capable of accommodating states and peoples of diverse cultural backgrounds. Yet the truth is that we know very little about the relationship between cultural diversity and international order, and what we think we know rests on dubious assumptions about the nature of culture or simplistic, untested propositions about the adaptive capacities of modern institutions. My goal for these volumes is to place debate on more robust foundations, to understand, in a more systematic way, the nature of cultural diversity, how it affects international order, and how orders, in turn, condition diversity.

Such a project relies heavily on the insights of specialists in other fields: most notably anthropology, history, and sociology, as well as comparative politics and political theory. Volume II, written alongside this volume, presents a collaborative engagement between leading scholars of international order and prominent specialists on cultural diversity, in part designed to engineer a new cross-disciplinary conversation, but also to enrich my own thinking by identifying key ideas from diverse fields and bringing them into systematic dialogue. What follows here has been greatly influenced by this engagement, and I thank my co-editor, Andrew Phillips, and our stellar collaborators for their intellectual aid.

Volume III will be a work of comparative historical sociology, similar in approach to my previous books on fundamental institutions and individual rights.[1] Much of today's debate about cultural diversity and international order has a 'shock of the new' quality, as though we have been living in a culturally homogeneous order and are only now beset by newly emergent (or salient) cultural differences. Yet like many of the truisms that persist in IR, this sits uncomfortably with history. New histories of the most important international orders of the past – the Chinese, the Ottoman, and the early modern – show that these orders emerged in heterogeneous, not homogeneous, cultural contexts, and that the governance of diversity was a key imperative of order building. Even a cursory reading of the history of the modern order reveals something very similar. From its origins in the nineteenth century, the modern order has been deeply conditioned by global cultural interactions, structured by civilizational hierarchies, wracked by nationalist conflicts, and has undergone a dramatic global expansion, encompassing in time the full complexity of the human cultural condition. The history of the modern order is punctuated by grand attempts to govern this diversity. The notorious 'standard of civilization', the granting of sovereignty, first, to ethnically defined nations and, later, to civic nations, and the propagation of international norms of multiculturalism are all examples. Getting a proper grasp on what new axes of cultural diversity, entangled with shifting configurations of power, mean for the future of the modern international order requires that we understand not only how diversity has shaped the order in the past (and how it has in turn conditioned diversity) but also how the modern experience compares with that of past orders. How was cultural diversity manifest and governed in these orders? How did this affect social hierarchies and stability? And what does this tell us

---

[1] Christian Reus-Smit, *The Moral Purpose of the State* (Princeton, NJ: Princeton University Press, 1999); and Christian Reus-Smit, *Individual Rights and the Making of the International System* (Cambridge: Cambridge University Press, 2013).

about the modern order, its distinctiveness, its capacity to adapt to shifting configurations of power and difference, and its relative cultural toleration?

Before we can get to this, though, considerable theoretical groundwork is required. Writing anything on culture in our field, let alone three books, immediately meets with scepticism. Culture is the home turf of other disciplines: a deeply unstable terrain on which IR scholars should tread warily. It is, first of all, a deeply contested concept, with struggles over its nature and meaning consuming generations of fine anthropological and sociological minds. More importantly, for a field with an energetic positivist core, culture is intangible and thus unmeasurable. This is partly because of its definitional ambiguity: if we can't define it, we can't measure it. A more significant reason, however, is that whichever definition you choose, it invariably involves intersubjective meanings. As critics of norms research ask repeatedly, how do we know an intersubjective meaning (or norm) when we see one, how do we measure it, and how do we weigh its causal effects (as if meanings were any more intangible or methodologically challenging than interests, or power for that matter)? Stepping from the study of single norms – the focus of much constructivist scholarship – to the level of culture, which invariably involves larger complexes of meanings, only compounds this problem.

Yet despite this scepticism IR scholars make assumptions about culture all the time, especially when thinking about international order. I am not referring here to the diverse literatures that examine culture and particular issue areas, such as culture and diplomacy, culture and foreign policy, culture and globalization, the culture of internationalism, or culture and normative theory.[2] Rather, I am concerned with the deeper understandings of culture, and in turn of cultural diversity, that often undergird these and other literatures. A central claim of this book is that IR scholars return time and again to a single, deeply problematic understanding, which I term the *default conception*. Different schools

---

[2] See, for example, Iver Neumann, *At Home with the Diplomats* (Ithaca, NY: Cornell University Press, 2012); Valerie M. Hudson, *Culture and Foreign Policy* (Boulder, CO: Lynne Rienner, 1997); Mike Featherstone (ed.), *Global Culture* (London: Sage, 1990); Akira Iriye, *Cultural Internationalism and World Order* (Baltimore, MD: Johns Hopkins University Press, 1997); Chris Brown, *Practical Judgment in International Relations* (London: Routledge, 2010); and Toni Erksine, *Embedded Cosmopolitanism* (Oxford: Oxford University Press, 2008).

of thought come at culture from different directions as they wrestle
with their own distinctive questions and problematics. Yet despite
their different approaches, they arrive at essentially the same conceptual destination. This default conception treats cultures as coherent
entities: bounded, integrated, and distinct wholes. It imagines them as
autogenous – products of their own internal processes. And it sees
them as analytically distinct from society, but nonetheless deeply
constitutive of social institutions and practices.

Identifying, explicating, assessing, and moving beyond this stub-
bornly recurrent understanding of culture are the tasks of this first
book, *On Cultural Diversity*. The first three of these tasks are commonly dispensed with in a discrete literature review, a minor antece-
dent to the main game. The default conception is so deeply engrained
in how we think about culture and international relations, however,
that it demands sustained engagement. Moreover, the argument about
cultural diversity I advance in these three volumes, and that unfolds
first in Chapter 6, differs markedly from the common view, insisting
that culture is always heterogeneous and contradictory, that social
institutions play a key role in its patterning, and that culture, so
understood, shapes political orders not as a deeply constitutive or
corrosive force but as a governance imperative. Before readers will
engage this new argument they will need persuading that their deeply
engrained assumptions, and the established parameters of debate, are
problematic and worth transcending. Sustained engagement with
existing ways of seeing culture in IR has the side benefit of also
providing, in a single volume, a critical survey of these approaches,
offering a standalone resource for students and scholars interested in
culture and IR theory.

Having said this, the following chapters make no pretence of providing a comprehensive survey of all conceptions of culture to be found
in IR. Choices had to be made, and instead of going 'broad but thin'
I have opted for 'narrow but thick'. This is partly because of the
aforementioned need to subject the principal ways of seeing culture
in IR to sustained critique, thus creating space for my alternative
perspective. Such critique is possible only if attention is focused on a
small number of key perspectives. The principal reason, however,
relates to the larger purpose of these volumes – to understand, in a
more sophisticated and systematic way, the relationship between cultural diversity and international order. This purpose has narrowed my

gaze, focussing attention on four perspectives that have been central to debates in IR about cultural diversity and order, that have been poles in broader debates about culture and world politics, or that have provided ideas I later enlist in the development of my new theoretical account. These perspectives are proffered by realists, the English School, constructivists, and rational choice theorists. Several other perspectives have insights that complement my own line of argument, most notably strands of feminism, poststructuralism, postcolonialism, and normative IR theory. I discuss these in Chapter 1, and enlist them later as either critical resources or theoretical building blocks.

Some books give their theoretical punch line early, say in the second or third chapter, and spend the remaining chapters providing an empirical or theoretical defence. Other books reason their way to a punch line that comes late in the piece, in the final substantive chapter perhaps. This book takes the second form. Chapter 1 surveys the evolution of ideas about culture in anthropology and sociology, locates IR's default conception within this evolution, and sets out a series of propositions about the nature of culture that serve as critical reference points in following chapters. Chapters 2 to 5 provide the detailed analyses of realist, English School, constructivist, and rational choice perspectives on culture. It is not until Chapter 6 that I set out my alternative theoretical perspective on cultural diversity and inter-national order, wrapping up this book, offering some conceptual reference points for the interdisciplinary discussion in Volume II, and laying out, in preliminary form, a theoretical framework for Volume III's comparative historical sociology.

Raymond Williams famously observed that culture 'is one of the two or three most complicated words in the English language'.[3] It has a meandering genealogical history, still has multiple meanings, and has long been subject to vigorous theoretical debate, yielding contending schools of thought across anthropology, cultural studies, and sociology (the 'specialist' disciplines or fields, as I shall call them). I make no claim to simplify this complexity or resolve these debates, especially as an IR scholar (a rank outsider if there ever was one). Chapter 1 does offer a working definition of culture that incorporates much that is common across contending schools of thought. Its main purposes,

---

[3] Raymond Williams, *Keywords: A Vocabulary of Culture and Society* (London: Fourth Estate, 2014), p. 84.

however, are twofold. The first is to locate IR's default conception of culture within the long history of anthropological and sociological debates about the concept, showing how IR's understanding is marooned in debates that last thrived in the 1930s–1950s. The second purpose is to draw out two key insights from more recent work in anthropology, history, and sociology, insights that inform the critiques I advance in Chapters 2–5, and that I enlist when building my own perspective in Chapter 6. The first insight is that, contrary to the default conception, cultures are not homogeneous or unified entities, tightly integrated, neatly bounded, or coherently constitutive. The dominant view today is that culture is highly variegated, often contradictory, only loosely integrated, and fluidly and porously bounded. The second insight concerns social institutions. If culture is always heterogeneous, what gives it any form? Culture is not just a grab bag of atomized meanings, symbols, and practices for strategic use: it is patterned and structured, its contradictions bind as much as they divide. A key specialist insight is that social institutions play a crucial role in this patterning. Institutions are themselves cultural artefacts, but once established – once they take a structural form, reproduced through routinized practices – they channel 'the cultural flow'.[4]

These insights are not only alien to most IR scholarship, they challenge directly the default conception to which IR scholars routinely return, a view that would warm the heart of a 1930s anthropologist. Whether at the systemic level or at the level of the state, culture is seen as a coherent thing: a foundational substratum, deeply constitutive of political life. Institutions, from this perspective, are unproblematic cultural artefacts, their form determined by underlying cultural values, their efficacy sustained by cultural consensus. These views also inform much of the anxiety in Western capitals about the future of the modern order, as diversity is seen as threatening the cultural foundations of its institutions. The principal counter to such views comes from liberal pluralists, who grant institutions far more power. For some, the core institutions of sovereignty, non-intervention, and self-determination provide a framework that enables states and peoples of different cultures to coexist; for others, the open, rules-based nature of the post-1945 American-led order gives these states and peoples

---

[4] Ulf Hannerz, *Cultural Complexity* (New York: Columbia University Press, 1992), p. 14.

unprecedented opportunities to pursue their interests, much as the liberal polity accommodates individuals with different purposes. Both views see institutions as neutralizing culture, as rendering cultural difference politically irrelevant. This misses, however, the key specialist insight – that institutions don't neutralize cultural difference, they organize it. They take extant cultural heterogeneity and construct authorized forms of difference.

Read from the perspective of these insights, the four approaches to culture considered in the following chapters amount, in the end, to different forms of blindness to culture. This is a bold claim, as at least three of these perspectives are explicitly concerned with culture or cultural phenomena. There are different ways to be conceptually, theoretically, or analytically blind, though. A perspective can be blind to culture because culture has no place in its ontology: its assumptions about the nature of the international universe do not include culture as a causally significant element. This is the blindness of heavily materialist versions of realism, discussed in Chapter 2. Blindness can also take a second form, though. A perspective can be blind to culture by not seeing it for what it is: by looking, but not seeing – much like teenagers searching for things in their bedrooms. This is the blindness of the default conception, manifest in realist discussions of groups, strategic culture, and order and legitimacy (Chapter 2), in culturalist strands of the English School (Chapter 3), in constructivist accounts of international order (Chapter 4), and in rationalist arguments about culture and common knowledge (Chapter 5).

Some might find it strange that I include a chapter on realism at all, as its blindness to culture appears so complete, rendering it largely irrelevant to a project concerned with cultural diversity and international order. Beyond telling us that culture matters little to the cut and thrust of real world politics, what resources can it possibly offer? Yet, as Chapter 2 explains, realism is a complicated beast, with at least two faces. On the one hand, its default view of the world is materialist: realists stress guns and money first, and ask questions about other factors later. On the other hand, there are certain issues that draw realists inexorably onto the cultural terrain. Groupism, for example, is a core realist assumption: IR is a realm of organized conflict groups, principally states. But when realists unpack the nature of these groups, their arguments become strongly cultural. Similarly, in order to explain why different states respond differently to the same security imperatives, realists, along with others, have turned to the study of strategic culture, invoking again a version of the default conception. Most importantly for this project, when classical and neoclassical realists probe the foundations of international order, culture enters as a key source of legitimacy. Henry Kissinger has long argued that legitimacy is essential to a stable international order.[5] In his recent work he stresses how essential a shared civilization is for such legitimacy, highlighting the common culture that undergirded the European order, and fearing that a 'generally accepted legitimacy'[6] will be impossible in today's culturally divided world.[7]

No school of thought has devoted more attention to the relationship between culture and international order than the English School. It evinces two very different positions, though: one culturalist, the other pluralist. As Chapter 3 explains, the first is exemplified by Martin Wight's writings, the second by Robert Jackson's, while Hedley Bull's thought contains elements of both. Wight presented a quintessential expression of the default conception of culture, holding that international orders emerge only in unified cultural contexts, common values inform the nature of international institutions, cultural consensus bolsters normative compliance, and diversity undermines order. Jackson's pluralism could not be more different. In response to the religious turmoil of the Thirty Years' War, states instituted a unique solution to the problem of order in diversity. Norms of sovereign equality and non-intervention allowed states of diverse cultural complexions to coexist, effectively transferring culture as an issue from the international to the domestic arena. Bull's position was more complex. Like Wight, he saw a common culture as an important basis of international order, but ultimately he stressed the elementary interests that drive states to construct a pluralist international society. Where Wight feared for the future of order in a multicultural world, and Jackson discounts such concerns, Bull's writings vacillate between a confidence in underlying pluralist interests and anxiety about anaemic global culture. As we shall see, these contrasting positions supervene on other aspects of the English School's thought: producing, most notably,

---

[5] Henry Kissinger, *A World Restored: Metternich, Castlereagh and the Problems of Peace: 1812–1822* (Boston: Houghton Mifflin, 1957).

[6] Ibid., p. 1.

[7] Henry Kissinger, *World Order: Reflections on the Character of Nations and the Course of History* (London: Allen Lane, 2014), p. 8.

conflicting narratives of international history. What matters for the larger project, though, is that the School is torn between two equally unsatisfying views of culture. Wight's conception of culture is vulnerable to all of the aforementioned criticisms of the default conception, and his widely quoted claim that the best historical examples of systems of states have all emerged in unified cultural contexts is belied by a wealth of new histories.[8] Jackson's conception suffers from precisely the opposite problem: religious conflict spurred the Westphalian solution, but after the Westphalian settlement institutes a pluralist international society, culture drops out of his account, offering us no resources with which to understand the complex cultural politics that has actually shaped the modern order.

Constructivists treat cultural phenomena, if not culture, as foundational. Ideational structures are privileged; their intersubjective meanings determining how, among other things, actors understand material structures – 'anarchy is what states make of it', as Alexander Wendt famously argues.[9] Meanings are also said to constitute actors' social identities, a primary source of their interests. And, last, rules and norms are seen as providing reasons for action, justificatory resources that actors conscript to realize their interests. Not surprisingly, constructivists often cast what they study as 'culture'; Peter Katzenstein's landmark collection, *The Culture of National Security*, is a case in point.[10] Yet constructivism evinces two, equally unsatisfactory, treatments of culture. The first disaggregates culture into individual norms, and then studies their emergence, reproduction, and causal effects. However productive this project has been, it obscures how individual norms, or normative dyads, sit within wider complexes of diverse and often discordant meanings and practices. Not only does this pay

[8] See, for example, Karen Barkey, *Empire of Difference: The Ottomans in Comparative* Perspective (Cambridge: Cambridge University Press, 2000); Jane Burbank and Frederick Cooper, *Empires in World History: Power and the Politics of Difference* (Princeton, NJ: Princeton University Press, 2010); Euan Cameron, *The European Reformation*, 2nd edn. (Oxford: Oxford University Press, 2012); Pamela Kyle Crossley, *A Translucent Mirror: History and Identity in Qing Imperial Ideology* (Berkeley: University of California Press, 2002); Lisa Lowe, *The Intimacies of Four Continents* (Durham, NC: Duke University Press, 2015).
[9] Alexander Wendt, 'Anarchy Is What States Make of It: The Social Construction of Power Politics', *International Organization*, 46.2 (1992), 391–426.
[10] Peter J. Katzenstein (ed.), *The Culture of National Security: Norms and Identity in World Politics* (New York: Columbia University Press, 1996).

insufficient attention to the fact that actors always navigate complex intersubjective terrains; it misses the highly complex cultural contexts in which international orders evolve. The second approach treats culture as deep structure, as a coherent set of constitutional norms, social epistemes, or collective mentalities that determine the institutional architectures of international orders. Here the problem is not atomism but undifferentiated holism, and it is in this work that we see one of the most pronounced expressions of the default conception of culture.

Rationalists offer the fourth way of approaching culture. Many assume that they have nothing to say on the subject (or, more critically, nothing to contribute). By focusing on the strategic, utility-maximizing behaviour of individuals, bracketing interest formation, and discounting the constitutive role of institutions, rationalists are seen as fencing off culture, treating it as ontologically irrelevant. Yet these criticisms miss the now well-developed rationalist accounts of culture, accounts that grant significant weight to intersubjective meanings, albeit within a choice-theoretic framework. Rationalists have long argued that their focus on individual preferences accommodates cultural phenomena, as nothing in their theory requires interests to be material, and cultural values are most saliently expressed through individual preferences. As Chapter 5 shows, however, this is now complemented by an argument about the structural significance of intersubjective meanings. For individuals to coordinate their actions they need common knowledge – knowledge that everyone knows, and everyone knows that everyone knows.[11] Culture provides this knowledge, rationalists argue. Rituals and practices, which instantiate intersubjective meanings, reproduce and communicate the information individuals need to coordinate. As Chapter 6 explains, this insight helps explain why order-builders routinely seek to organize and discipline the complex cultural environments they encounter, channelling culture in ways that facilitate control through coordination. It is limited in two important respects, though. It does nothing, first of all, to counter the long-standing criticism that rationalists ignore the constitutive power of intersubjective meanings: how they shape actors' identities and interests before issues of coordination ever arise. More importantly for this project, it is

---

[11] Michael Suk-Young Chwe, *Rational Ritual: Culture, Coordination, and Common Knowledge* (Princeton, NJ: Princeton University Press, 2001), p. 3.

not clear that the rationalist view captures the complexities of culture, the fact that in any given cultural context individuals have to navigate multiple, often conflicting values and practices, and that this complexity has its own implications for the development of political orders. Indeed, unamended, the rationalist thesis that shared rituals and practices are needed to generate the common knowledge that enables coordination can be read as supporting the problematic Wightian thesis that a unified culture is necessary for the emergence of an international order (qua system of states).

As this brief survey indicates, all four ways of seeing culture circle back, through one path or another, to some version of the default conception of culture. Cultures – whether strategic mindsets, nations, civilizations, or collective mentalities – are imagined as coherent things: integrated, differentiated, and strongly constitutive in their effects.

The argument I advance in Chapter 6, and summarize here, starts from a very different position.[12] We should begin by assuming existential cultural diversity, by assuming that the cultural terrain in which politics plays out is polyvalent, multilayered, riven with fissures, often contradictory, and far from coherently integrated or bounded. As Andrew Hurrell argues, 'it is precisely *differences* in social practices, values, beliefs, and institutions that represent the most important expression of our *common* humanity. What makes us different', he insists, 'is precisely what makes us human'.[13] Elements of unity, strands of commonality, and patches of homogeneity do exist, of course, but we learn more about politics, I suggest, especially the politics of international orders, if we treat these as things to be explained, not assumed. It would be tempting at this point to accept the fact of diversity but adopt the standard practice of norms research: locate key constitutive norms within the heterogeneous mix and trace how they shape or sustain an international order. Again, my approach is different. My previous work shows how hegemonic beliefs affect the nature of an order's basic institutions.[14] I now think that cultural

---

[12] This argument was first elaborated in Christian Reus-Smit, 'Cultural Diversity and International Order', *International Organization*, 71.4 (2017), 851–885.

[13] Andrew Hurrell, *On Global Order: Power, Values, and the Constitution of International Society* (Oxford: Oxford University Press, 2007), p. 40.

[14] Reus-Smit, *Moral Purpose of the State*; and Christian Reus-Smit, 'The Constitutional Structure of International Society and the Nature of Fundamental Institutions', *International Organization*, 51.4 (1997), 555–589.

diversity itself has an effect, above and beyond the constitutive effects of any particular meanings.

I argue elsewhere that international orders are best conceived as systemic configurations of political authority,[15] and like all authority structures they require legitimation. This is always a complex affair, but involves two principal challenges. The first, which has received considerable attention, requires inequalities of material power to be converted into political authority: might has to become right, so to speak. The second challenge, which has been largely neglected, is to turn extant cultural heterogeneity into authorized forms and expressions of difference. Three imperatives drive order-builders to so organize diversity. Control is number one. In heterogeneous cultural environments multiple opportunities exist for the construction of identities, mobilization of meanings, and the harnessing of both to diverse political projects, which can be either order sustaining or order threatening. By organizing diversity, order-builders seek to institutionalize preferred meanings and identities, engineer consent for these institutions, and limit the scope for innovation. The second imperative is self-location: the placing of one's identity, as an order-builder, within the cultural terrain one seeks to organize. This involves the cultural narration of identity; the crafting of the broader landscape of identities, meanings, and practices; and the choreographing of hierarchical relations within this landscape. The third imperative is social and political coordination. By privileging and structuring meanings, licensing and ordering forms of identification, and authorizing certain practices, order-builders generate the common and collective knowledge needed for such coordination. In all of this, order-builders are not animated solely by strategic calculation, but are commonly informed by their own beliefs about what constitutes a legitimate cultural order.

Meeting these legitimation challenges has had a significant affect on the institutional architectures of international orders. Although largely ignored by IR scholars, all international orders have developed what I term 'diversity regimes': systemic norms and practices that legitimize

---

[15] See Reus-Smit, 'Cultural Diversity and International Order'; Christian Reus-Smit, 'The Concept of Intervention', *Review of International Studies*, 39.4 (2013), 1057–1076; and Christian Reus-Smit, 'The Liberal International Order Reconsidered', in Rebekka Friedman, Kevork Oskanian, and Ramon Pacheco-Pardo (eds.), *After Liberalism* (London: Palgrave Macmillan, 2013), pp. 167–186.

certain units of political authority (states, empires, etc.), define recognized categories of cultural difference (religion, civilization, nation, etc.), and relate the two (civilization and empire, nation and state, etc.). All of the great moments of order building that have occupied IR scholars – Westphalia, Vienna, Versailles, San Francisco, and post-1945 decolonization – involved the construction of such regimes, and the same is true of the great non-Western orders. The Ottomans instituted the Millet system, for example, and the Qing Chinese established the Lifanyuan and Eight Banners systems: all marrying particular configurations of political authority with distinctive organizations of cultural difference. Built in response to prevailing distributions of material capabilities and articulations of cultural difference, these regimes have historically faced two pressures for change: shifts in the underlying distribution of material power, and the expression and mobilization of new cultural claims, often animated by grievances against the exclusions and hierarchies of prevailing or past diversity regimes.

This argument about diversity and order takes seriously the insistence by anthropologists, cultural studies scholars, and sociologists that cultural complexity and heterogeneity are the norm. It also builds on their instructive insight about the structuring effects of institutions. From studies of how 'diversity' policies adopted in multiple institutional contexts have restructured the racial order in the United States,[16] through analyses of contrasting national multicultural policies and their effects on patterns of ethnic identification,[17] to research on how the legal institution of marriage conditions the culture of love,[18] scholars have shown how institutions give culture form. My own work on international law shows that the same dynamics are at work at the international level, with the institutional norms and practices of international law structuring global cultural interaction around human rights.[19] Chapter 6 applies this insight to international orders, arguing

---

[16] Ellen Berrey, *The Enigma of Diversity: The Language of Race and the Limits of Racial Justice* (Chicago, IL: University of Chicago Press, 2015).

[17] Kenan Malik, 'The Failure of Multiculturalism', *Foreign Affairs*, 94.2 (2015), 21–22.

[18] Ann Swidler, *Talk of Love: How Culture Matters* (Chicago, IL: University of Chicago Press, 2001).

[19] Christian Reus-Smit, 'International Law and the Mediation of Culture', *Ethics and International Affairs*, 28.1 (2014), 1–18.

that the very fact of cultural heterogeneity drives order-builders to construct diversity regimes, institutional norms and practices designed to authorize particular axes of cultural difference and link these to structures of political authority.

Thinking about diversity and order in this way has several implications, two of which are taken up in the Conclusion. The first concerns how we should think about the future of the modern international order. As noted earlier, debate is presently polarized between two positions. Culturalists see the modern order as a Western cultural artefact, and fear for the order's survival under conditions of heightened cultural diversity. Institutionalists, by contrast, place faith in the modern order's distinctive institutions, claiming that they can accommodate states and peoples of diverse cultural backgrounds. The first of these fails to understand that cultural diversity has been a constant in the history of the modern order, and the second misses the recognition function of international institutions: how they organize, not neutralize, cultural diversity. From the perspective advanced here, both positions fail to grasp the key question for the future of the modern order: Can the prevailing diversity regime accommodate new conjunctions of power and articulations of difference? The second implication of my argument is normative. Until recently, normative debate in IR has been pulled between cosmopolitan universalism, which discounts the moral significance of cultural differences, and communitarian relativism, which sees discrete cultural communities as the primary sources of moral values and obligations. The argument advanced here challenges both of these positions, holding (against cosmopolitans) that culture matters, but (against communitarians) that its diversity is not that of cultural billiard balls. Moreover, while cultural landscapes are always highly varied, they are also institutionally structured. Political theorists have long been attuned to this institutional ordering of diversity, subjecting the assimilation and multicultural policies of states to sustained normative scrutiny. Normative IR theorists have largely ignored the international analogues of these policies and practices, and taking them seriously, I suggest, requires an institutional turn.

1 | *The Road Not Taken*

In 2014 I was fortunate enough to join an academic delegation to Israel and the Occupied Territories. The organizers' goal was to foster among IR scholars a greater appreciation of the complexities of the Israeli-Palestinian conflict, conveyed through meetings with experts, leaders on both sides, civil society actors, and community representatives, including Jewish settlers and Palestinians living in both Israel and the Territories. Like a good student, I got the complexity message. I was just beginning this project, and visiting the region seemed like a good way to further my thinking on the nature of culture and its implications for political orders. This is, after all, a place where national and religious identities are starkly pronounced and cultural differences run deep, profoundly affecting the nature and stability of political institutions. Yet the more people I met, and the more I saw and heard, the less straightforward culture and its effects appeared. Not all Israelis are Jews, and not all Israeli Jews understand their faith in the same way. Some of the deepest political cleavages in Israel run between secular and orthodox religious Jews, who differ not only over the meaning of their Judaism but also over the proper relationship between religion and the state. The Palestinians are similarly divided: some are Christians, some Muslims; some are secular, some religious; and some are Israeli citizens, while most live a liminal political existence in the Occupied Territories or exiled in neighbouring states. This is not a place of singular identities or stable meanings, but one where religious and national identities are multiple, fluid, and contested, and where the politics of competing narratives dominates, as cultural and historical meanings are mobilized for contending political purposes. There are no neat religious divides here, no neat national divides, and no neat or singular fit between religious and national identities.

All of this resonates with what anthropologists, cultural studies scholars, and sociologists have been telling us about culture for at least three decades. Culture is always highly variegated, often contradictory,

16

and frequently contested. In Ann Swidler's words, 'all real cultures contain diverse, often conflicting symbols, rituals, stories, and guides to action'.[1] As noted in the Introduction, this view is often accompanied by the argument that social institutions play a key role in structuring culture. This chapter examines these propositions in greater detail, as they constitute key reference points and building blocks for what follows. I begin by tracing, however briefly, the development of the now outdated conception of culture as an integrated system of meaning, and the associated view of a world divided into multiple but distinct cultural units, ideas still alive in the unexamined assumptions of much IR. This discussion serves not only to locate prevailing assumptions in IR – to give the default conception a home – but as a background for a more detailed discussion of current understandings of the complexity, contradictions, and tangled interconnections of all cultural forms. The final section acknowledges theoretical strands of IR where this understanding of culture is already well established (particularly feminism, postcolonialism, and poststructuralism), notes key projects on civilizations and religion where it has been deployed to great effect, and differentiates all of these from the perspective I advance here and in subsequent volumes.

A Brief History of 'Culture'

Williams's observation that culture is one of the 'most complicated words in the English language'[2] is borne out in its multiple everyday uses. Terry Eagleton highlights four of these. The first refers to 'a body of artistic or intellectual work', the use that informs the idea of the cultural arts – the ballet, symphony, painting, poetry, and the novel, for example. The second describes 'a process of spiritual or intellectual development', becoming 'cultured'. George Bernard Shaw's *Pygmalion* is tale of culture in this sense, where Professor Henry Higgins wagers he can train a flower girl, Eliza, to pass as a duchess.[3] The third treats culture as 'the values, customs, beliefs and symbolic practices by which men and women live', the intersubjective environment in which we evolve as social agents and go about our varied purposes. The fourth,

---

[1] Ann Swidler, 'Culture in Action: Symbols and Strategies', *American Sociological Review*, 51.2 (1986), 277.
[2] Williams, *Keywords*, p. 84.
[3] George Bernard Shaw, *Pygmalion* (Harmondsworth: Penguin, 2001).

and final, usage presents culture as a 'whole way of life', encompassing everything from 'poetry, music and dance' to a society's 'transport network, system of voting and methods of garbage disposal'.[4]

These contrasting uses intersect and impinge on one another in complex ways. Culture as artistic or intellectual work might be the goal of culture as a process of development, and such work may be integral to the symbolic practices that shape individuals' lives or a vital part of culture as a whole way of life. These intersections will reappear as our discussion proceeds. My main concern, however, is with the third and fourth uses: culture as values, beliefs, and practices, and culture as social life in its entirety. Not only are these the uses that feature most prominently in anthropological and sociological debates about the nature of culture, they are the uses most readily invoked within IR, especially in debates over the relationship between cultural diversity and international order.

In the following pages I trace the shifting ways in which these two conceptions of culture have been understood, concentrating on debates in anthropology and sociology from late nineteenth century until the 1970s. The discussion is by no means comprehensive; my purpose is simply to show the gradual movement from a conception of culture tightly bound to ideas of a uniform human history to one in which cultures are seen as autogenous, integrated wholes. In this transition, three ideas were gradually abandoned. The first held that all cultures exhibited similar traits, and that these traits had common causes. Cultures, wherever they were, had recognizable kinship structures, for example, and these arose for similar reasons. Because of this, the second idea proposed, all cultures were part of a single, uniform human history, and differed only in their levels of development within this history. These similarities *and* differences could be attributed, the third idea insisted, to the psychological unity of humankind, and to variations in experiential learning under unequal material conditions.

A Uniform Human History

Most surveys of the concept of culture begin with Edward Tylor's 1871 definition. 'Culture or Civilization', Tylor wrote, 'is that complex whole which includes knowledge, belief, art, morals, law, custom, and

---

[4] Terry Eagleton, *Culture* (New Haven, CT: Yale University Press, 2016), p. 1.

any other capabilities and habits acquired by man as a member of society'.[5] Commentators rightly take this as a classic statement of the 'culture as a whole way of life' view, noting how it encompasses ideas, values, institutions, and practices (qua 'habits'), and how the limits of culture are coterminous with the limits of social interaction and existence.

Less commonly discussed, however, is where Tylor went after setting out this definition. Culture, he held, was amenable to scientific study, understood, first, as investigation guided by general principles and, second, as the formulation of 'laws of human thought and action'.[6] This was possible, Tylor and his Victorian counterparts believed, because all cultures exhibit common traits – because of the 'uniformity which so largely pervades civilization'.[7] Buried within this argument were two interrelated propositions. The first is that individual societies have a high degree of cultural homogeneity. There is, Tylor argued, a 'remarkable tacit consensus or agreement which so far induces whole populations to unite in the use of the same language, to follow the same religion and customary law, to settle down to the same general level of art and knowledge'.[8] The second proposition is that across all societies there are cultural similarities that permit generalization. These similarities are revealed, Tylor argued, through systematic processes of classification and comparison. Weapons, arts, myths, and rites could be differentiated, for example, and each broken down into subcategories. This would reveal not only traits common across cultures but also different levels of cultural development: savage, barbarian, and civilized. For Tylor this was a matter of science: observation, not valuation. 'The connection which runs through religion', for example, 'from its rudest forms up to the status of an enlightened Christianity, may be conveniently treated with little recourse to dogmatic theology'.[9]

Not only were cultures thought to exhibit common traits, Tylor attributed these to common causes: 'In studying both the recurrence of special habits or ideas in several districts, and their prevalence within each district, there comes before us ever-reiterated proofs of regular causation producing the phenomena of human life, and of the laws of maintenance and diffusion according to which these

---

[5] Edward B. Tylor, *Primitive Culture*, vol. 1 (Boston: Estes and Lauriat, 1874), p. 1.
[6] Ibid. [7] Ibid. [8] Ibid., p. 10. [9] Ibid., p. 23.

phenomena settle into permanent standard conditions of society, at definite stages of culture'.[10] This worked at two levels for Tylor. There were, first of all, standard causes operating in diverse societies that led to a 'geographical distribution' of traits: 'In district after district, the same causes which have introduced the cultivated plants and domesticated animals of civilization, have brought in with them a corresponding art and knowledge ... Experience leads the student after a while to expect to find that the phenomena of culture, as resulting from widely-acting similar causes, should recur again and again in the world.'[11] At a second level, Tylor identified causal mechanisms within individual cultures that drove processes of cultural development. He argued, for example, that higher-level cultural beliefs and practices developed out of lower-level traits, and that this process was driven by collective learning.[12] This informed Tylor's belief that 'the main tendency of culture from primeval up to modern times has been from savagery towards civilization'.[13]

Nineteenth-century anthropologists were deeply divided over whether racial differences explained different levels of cultural development. Tylor, for his part, explicitly denied the importance of race. It is 'both possible and desirable', he wrote, 'to eliminate considerations of hereditary varieties or races of man, and to treat mankind as homogenous in nature, though placed in different grades of civilization'.[14] Those holding this view tended to stress the psychological unity of humankind, the notion, as Lewis Henry Morgan expressed it, 'that the operations of the mental principle have been uniform in virtue of the specific identity of the brain of all the races of mankind'.[15] These views challenged directly those of prominent physical anthropologists, particularly in the United States. Strong advocates of polygenism – the theory that different races were different species, and that their evolutionary paths were unconnected – these scholars saw race as foundational, their ideas widely enlisted in the defence of slavery and segregation. Samuel George Morton's 1839 comparison of human skulls is emblematic. Rejecting the idea that humans had common evolutionary origins, Morton identified five races, each constituting a

---

[10] Ibid., p. 13.   [11] Ibid., p. 10.   [12] Ibid., p. 16.   [13] Ibid., p. 21.
[14] Ibid., p. 7.
[15] Lewis H. Morgan, *Ancient Society* (New York: Henry Holt and Company, 1877), p. 8.

separate species with distinct intellectual, physical, and social attributes. On the 'Negros', a family of the Ethiopian race, Morton wrote:

[T]heir institutions are not unfrequently characterized by superstition and cruelty. They appear to be fond of warlike enterprises, and are not deficient in personal courage; but, once overcome, they yield to destiny, and accommodate themselves with amazing facility to every change of circumstance. The Negros have little invention, but strong powers of imitation, so that they readily acquire the mechanical arts. They have a great talent for music, and all their external senses are remarkably acute.[16]

A finer rationalization of slavery could hardly be found, and by emphasizing fundamental differences of race, and using these to explain cultural differences, Morton denied the very things Tylor, Morgan, and others later asserted – the uniformity of human history, and the location of all cultures on a single developmental path.

A World of Autogenous, Integrated Cultures

The thesis that all cultures have similar characteristics, that these result from common causes, and that, as a consequence, they all form part of a uniform human history was subjected to sustained critique in the first half of the twentieth century. The critique was not that racial differences made uniform history a nonsense, as physical anthropologists had argued a century earlier, but that the common cultural traits evident across cultures might have different causes – that the 'ever-reiterated proofs of regular causation' claimed by Tylor simply did not exist.[17]

Leading the attack was Franz Boas, whose thought had a profound impact on an extraordinary interwar generation of American anthropologists, including Ruth Benedict, Margaret Mead, and Edward Sapir. Boas agreed that there were cultural traits that reappeared across cultures, that '[w]hen studying the culture of any one tribe, more or less close analoga of single traits of such a culture may be found among a great diversity of peoples'.[18] He vigorously denied,

[16] Samuel George Morton, *Crania Americana* (Philadelphia: J. Dobson, 1839), p. 88.
[17] Tylor, *Primitive Culture*, p. 13.
[18] Franz Boas, *Race, Language, and Culture* (Chicago, IL: University of Chicago Press, 1940), p. 271.

however, that such traits necessarily had the same causes. Indeed, he argued that when common traits were identified, the starting assumption should be that they had different causes. '[W]hen we find analogous single traits of culture among distant peoples', he wrote, 'the presumption is not that there has been a common historical source, but that they have arisen independently'.[19] As an example, he cited the common use of geometrical patterns in textiles. Sometimes these reflect natural forms, but they could also express symbols or be the product of technical imperatives.[20]

Because of this causal variation, Boas challenged two of Tylor's cardinal propositions. The fact that humans could develop similar cultural beliefs and practices but for different reasons meant that any notion of the psychological unity of humankind was nonsense. 'We cannot say', he argued, 'that the occurrence of the same phenomenon is always due to the same causes, and thus that it is proved that the human mind obeys the same laws everywhere'.[21] This was reinforced by his critique of environmental determinism. 'A hasty review of the tribes and peoples of our globe', he insisted, 'shows that people most diverse in culture and language live under the same geographical conditions'.[22] These views led Boas to reject outright the notion of a uniform human history. We should 'consider all the ingenious attempts at constructions of a grand system of the evolution of society as of very doubtful value, unless at the same time proof is given that the same phenomena must always have the same origin. Until this is done, the presumption is always in favour of a variety of courses which historical growth may have taken.'[23]

If common cultural traits could have different causes, then the prevailing comparative method in anthropology was deeply problematic, Boas held. This method, energetically pursued by the likes of Tylor and Morgan, involved the classification of standard cultural forms, their identification in different cultural settings, the plotting of variations in a universal developmental schema, and the attribution of commonalities to a common psychological cause. For Boas, this was the worst kind of theoretical determinism, '[f]orcing phenomena into the strait-jacket of a theory'.[24] Instead, he called for an inductive mode of inquiry, in which fine-grained ethnographic research revealed the

---

[19] Ibid.   [20] Ibid., p. 274.   [21] Ibid., p. 275.   [22] Ibid., p. 278.
[23] Ibid., p. 276.   [24] Ibid., p. 277.

actual sources of cultural beliefs and practices, as well as their diffusion in local geographical contexts. Comparisons of different cultures should be undertaken only, Boas argued, when the cases were
genuinely comparable, when it had been clearly established that
common traits derived from common causes. 'In short, before
extended comparisons are made, the comparability of the material
must be proved.'[25]

Broad ranging as Boas's critique was, he departed little from
Tylor's conception of culture as a whole way of life, as coextensive
with social life itself. His crucial innovation, however, was to par-
ticularize culture, to conceive it in the plural, as 'cultures'.[26] So long
as all societies were thought to exhibit common cultural traits derived
from common causes, culture could be treated in the singular. But as
soon as these commitments were abandoned, and cultural forms
rooted in local sources, 'culture' became 'cultures'. Physical anthropologists like Morton made this move a century earlier, holding that
different races had different cultures. Boas, however, rejected racial
determinism as much as he rejected the psychological unity of humankind. Culture had its own dynamics, and its manifestations were
highly particularistic.

The shift from culture to cultures was a logical consequence of Boas's
emphasis on the local causes of cultural traits. What was missing,
however, was a clear sense in his writings that cultures were entities –
tightly integrated, organic wholes. This crucial move was made most
famously by his renowned student Ruth Benedict.

Boas's approach to culture started with the identification and
explanation of particular traits, and then moved out to plot local
patterns of diffusion. Benedict rejected this approach, calling for a
holistic method that began with culture as a whole, and then sought
to understand particular traits in relation to this whole. 'The whole',
she argued, 'determines its parts, not only their relation but their very
nature'.[27] Like Boas, Benedict held that culture was 'local and man-
made and hugely variable', but she went well beyond this, arguing that
cultures were also integrated:

---

[25] Ibid., p. 275.

[26] George W. Stocking made this point in 'Franz Boas and the Culture Concept in
Historical Perspective', *American Anthropologist*, 68.4 (1966), 871.

[27] Ruth Benedict, *Patterns of Culture* (Boston: Houghton Mifflin, 1959), p. 32.

A culture, like an individual, is a more or less consistent pattern of thought and action. Within each culture there come into being characteristic purposes not necessarily shared by other types of society. In obedience to these purposes, each people further and further consolidates its experience, and in proportion to the urgency of these drives the heterogeneous items of behaviour take more and more congruous shape.[28]

Notable here is Benedict's emphasis on collective purposes driving integration. 'All the miscellaneous behaviour directed toward getting a living, mating, warring, and worshipping the gods, is made over into consistent patterns in accordance with unconscious canons of choice that develop within a culture.'[29] Cultures integrate more or less successfully, she argued, realizing or failing to realize their animating purposes. She insisted, though, that 'cultures of every complexity, even the simplest, have achieved it. Such cultures are more or less successful attainments of integrated behaviour, and the marvel is that there can be so many of these possible configurations.'[30]

For Benedict, cultures, as integrated wholes, were strongly constitutive, producing individuals as knowledgeable social actors. 'The life history of the individual', she wrote, 'is first and foremost an accommodation to the patterns and standards traditionally handed down in his community. From the moment of his birth the customs into which he is born shape his experience and behaviour. By the time he can talk, he is a little creature of his culture, and by the time he is grown and able to take part in its activities, its habits are his habits, its beliefs his beliefs, its impossibilities his impossibilities.'[31] Just as particular cultural traits derive their nature from the cultural whole, so too does the individual. Indeed, '[n]o man can thoroughly participate in any culture', Benedict claimed, 'unless he has been brought up and has lived according to its forms'.[32]

Like Boas, Benedict rejected the idea of a uniform human history, in which diverse cultures were woven into a single developmental schema. This was partly because she too emphasized the particularity of cultural forms, their origin in local causes. But where Boas agreed with Tylor that there were traits common to different cultures, albeit resulting from different causes, Benedict went further, arguing that different cultures displayed different traits. Adolescence, for example,

[28] Ibid., p. 46.   [29] Ibid., p. 48.   [30] Ibid.   [31] Ibid., pp. 2–3.
[32] Ibid., p. 37.

meant different things in different cultures, engendering very different cultural practices.[33] Her rejection of a uniform history also stemmed from her critique of biological determinism. 'Not one item of his tribal organization, of his language, of his local religion', she argued, 'is carried in his germ cell'.[34] Any attempt to attribute culture to race was thus a nonsense. Indeed, Benedict went further to argue that racial prejudice was itself a cultural phenomenon, a fact in desperate need of recognition in Western civilization of the 1930s.[35] Given this, she was highly critical of prevailing attempts to rank cultures in civilizational hierarchies, holding that 'Anthropology was by definition impossible as long as these distinctions between ourselves and the primitive, ourselves and the barbarian, ourselves and the pagan, held sway over people's minds.'[36]

Distinguishing Culture and Society

Despite seeing cultures as autogenous, integrated entities, Benedict held onto the earlier idea of culture as a whole way of life, the sum total of a people's collective beliefs, practices, and institutions. After the Second World War, this view was subjected to sustained critique, as anthropologists and sociologists sought a more scientific conception with greater heuristic power. If culture encompassed all social belief and action, not only was it was difficult to operationalize, cultural explanations were circular – culture caused culture.

Talcott Parsons cast a long shadow over efforts to formulate a narrower conception of culture. In a grand attempt to develop a general theory of action, Parsons argued that action took place within, and itself constituted, three interrelated 'action systems': the personality, social, and cultural. The personality system consists of the non-sociocultural sources of human motivation, the ego prior to interaction.[37] The social system comprises interactions among individuals, or in more complex terms, it 'is a mode of organization of action elements relative to the persistence or ordered processes of change of the interactive patterns of a plurality of individual actors'.[38] And, finally, the cultural system encompasses the 'symbolic elements of the

---

[33] Ibid., p. 25.   [34] Ibid., p. 12.   [35] Ibid., p. 11.   [36] Ibid., p. 3.
[37] Talcott Parsons, *The Social System* (London: Routledge, 1991), pp. 9–10.
[38] Ibid., p. 15.

cultural tradition, ideas or beliefs, expressive symbols or value patterns'.[39] Parsons insisted that theoretically and analytically these contrasting systems had to be understood as distinct. 'Each of the three', he wrote, 'must be considered to be an independent focus of the organization of the elements of the action system in the sense that no one of them is theoretically reducible to terms of one or a combination of the other two'.[40] He was equally adamant, however, that the three were deeply entwined. Importantly, for example, he held that culture 'is on the one hand the product of, on the other hand a determinant of, systems of human social interaction'.[41]

These ideas had a profound effect on post-1945 understandings of culture and society, as well as the division of labour between anthropology and sociology. Much of this had to do with the nature of Parsons's project, which was both theoretical and institutional. In 1946 he founded a new Department of Social Relations at Harvard, the aim of which was to bring anthropologists, sociologists, and psychologists together in pursuit of a holistic and scientific understanding of human action. Such understanding was possible, however, only if there was a clear division of labour: the anthropologists focusing on the cultural system, the sociologists on the social, and the psychologists on personality. This meant that anthropologists had not only to embrace the project of a general theory of action but also to accept a narrower definition of culture.

This acceptance came in 1952, when Clyde Kluckhohn, a close associate of Parsons at Harvard, and Alfred Kroeber at Berkeley, published a major review of anthropological writings on culture. While they were uncomfortable framing the study of culture in terms of action, and thought Parsons had classified some things as social that were rightly cultural, they embraced the need for a narrower, more scientific conception of culture and, like Parsons, drew a line around values and symbols.[42] 'Culture', they argued, 'consists of patterns, explicit and implicit, of and for behaviour acquired and transmitted by symbols ... [T]he essential core of culture consists of traditional (i.e., historically derived and selected) ideas and especially their

---

[39] Ibid., p. 2.   [40] Ibid., p. 3.   [41] Ibid., p. 9.
[42] Adam Kuper, *Culture: The Anthropologists Account* (Cambridge, MA: Harvard University Press, 1999), pp. 55–59.

attached values'.[43] Further aligning themselves with Parsons, they insisted that 'culture must be regarded as an autonomous system or category and indeed ... can be treated quite frankly in relative abstraction from both personalities and societies'.[44] The disciplinary implications of this were spelled out in a joint 1958 article by Kroeber and Parsons. Old conflations of culture and society, they claimed, had left anthropology and sociology without clear conceptual rationales – the only thing that distinguished them was their differing 'operational' concerns with 'primitive' and 'modern' societies. To give their disciplines clear and distinct conceptual foundations, they separated culture and society. Culture, they held, is 'patterns of values, ideas, and other symbolic-meaningful systems', and society is 'the specifically relational system of interaction among individuals and collectivities'.[45]

Clifford Geertz is the most famous doctoral graduate of the Harvard Department of Social Relations, and while he bucked against the scientific pretensions and theoretical ambitions of Parsons's project, it left an indelible imprint on his approach to culture. He too was unsatisfied with Tyloresque treatments of culture as a whole way of life, which he thought to 'have reached the point where it obscures a good deal more than it reveals'.[46] And in seeking to define it more narrowly, he gave new voice to the view that culture was the realm of meanings and symbols. His conception was 'semiotic', asserting famously 'that man is an animal suspended in webs of significance he himself has spun'.[47] Geertz rejected the notion that cultures were superorganic, evident in Benedict's claim that they had animating purposes, and denied that culture existed in the minds of individuals.[48] Culture was public, operating at the level of intersubjective meanings, and it was produced and reproduced by human actions. He held on, however, to the view of cultures as more or less coherent systems. 'Cultural systems must have a minimal degree of coherence', he argued, 'else we would not call them systems; and, by observation, they normally have a great

---

[43] A. L. Kroeber and Clyde Kluckhohn, *Culture: A Critical Review of Concepts and Definitions* (Cambridge, MA: Peabody Museum, Harvard University, 1952), p. 181.

[44] Ibid., p. 186.

[45] A. L. Kroeber and Talcott Parsons, 'The Concepts of Culture and of Social System', *American Sociological Review*, 23.5 (1958), 583.

[46] Clifford Geertz, *The Interpretation of Cultures: Selected Essays by Clifford Geertz* (New York: Basic Books, 1973), p. 4.

[47] Ibid., p. 5.   [48] Ibid., pp. 10–12.

deal more'.[49] He also accepted the Parsonian distinction between cultural, social, and psychological systems. 'No matter how deeply interfused the cultural, the social, and the psychological may be in the everyday lives of houses, farms, poems, and marriages, it is useful', he wrote, 'to distinguish them in analysis, and, in so doing, to isolate the generic traits of each against the normalized background of the other two'.[50] Geertz deployed this distinction to great effect in his studies of post-independence Java, where communal upheaval resulted from 'an incongruity between the cultural framework of meaning and the patterning of social interaction, an incongruity due to the persistence in an urban environment of a religious symbol system adjusted to peasant social structure'.[51]

This echoed Parsons's understanding of the nature and sources of social order. For Benedict, as we have seen, social order was the product of cultural integration, the degree to which underlying purposes produced a convergence of beliefs and practices. Well-integrated societies were ordered; poorly integrated were not. Because Parsons and others rejected the notion of culture as a whole way of life, their conception of order had to be more complex. An order, Parsons held, was a stable system of social interaction. He was not, however, using order as a synonym for stability – social orders were culturally structured institutional complexes. Not only did cultural symbols enable the communication so essential to stable interaction, the 'normative pattern-structure of values' produces an integration of individuals' motivations.[52] 'In other words the basic condition on which an interaction system can be stabilized is for the interests of the actors to be bound to conformity with a shared system of value-orientation standards.'[53] It is the cultural system, for Parsons, that does this work.

The principal innovations of the Parsonian project were, first, to differentiate the cultural realm from the social and psychological and, second, to give these distinct realms particular content. Importantly, culture became the realm of values and, increasingly, symbolic meanings, and society became the realm of human interaction. This latter realm was seen as including communication, exchange, and, importantly, institutions. Parsons identified a variety of such institutions, including property, marriage, and parenthood, but it is his typology

---

[49] Ibid., pp. 15–16.   [50] Ibid., p. 92.   [51] Ibid., p. 169.
[52] Parsons, *The Social System*, p. 23.   [53] Ibid., p. 24.

that has proven most influential. In a classification many IR scholars will recognize, he differentiated between 'relational' institutions, which define the statuses and roles of individuals, and 'regulatory' institutions, which define 'the limits of the legitimacy of "private" interest-pursuit with respect to goals and means'.[54] Despite these innovations, however, the Parsonian project had one leg in the past. While rejecting the idea of culture as a whole way of life, and abandoning Benedict's notion of cultures as individuals writ large, Parsons, Kluckhohn, Kroeber, Geertz, and others still saw cultures as autogenous, coherent systems. Furthermore, the cultural system remained a crucial determinant of social order. Gone was Benedict's equation of order with cultural integration, but cultural coherence remained essential to communication and value convergence, and order depended on the synchronization of cultural and social systems.

Culture without Cultures

By the 1950s the core elements of Tylor's conception of culture had been abandoned. The claim that all societies had similar cultural traits, rooted in common causes, gave way first to the idea that cultural similarities could have different causes, and eventually to the view that societies had different cultural traits generated by local phenomena. Not only did this undercut the project of constructing a uniform human history, in which all societies could be plotted on a single developmental trajectory, it encouraged the view of a world populated by distinct, self-generating cultural groups. This was accentuated by the claim that cultures were integrated or coherent wholes, a claim that persisted even after culture and society were differentiated. Cultures came to be understood as coherent systems, sustaining stable social interaction by facilitating communication and normative convergence. At the beginning of the story, the assumption that all societies had common cultural traits with common causes focused attention on the cultural (and historical) unity of humankind. By the mid-twentieth century, this unity had been conceptually fragmented into a global mosaic of autogenous, coherent cultural units.

This is the point, I suggest below, where most discussions of culture in IR today are stuck. All four of the approaches discussed in following

---

[54] Ibid., p. 37.

chapters circle back to some version of this 'default' conception, and it reappears time and again in contemporary discussions of civilization, non-Western states as cultural actors, and religion. These discussions continue as though anthropologists, cultural and political theorists, and sociologists had nothing further to say on the topic, as though scholarship in that period between Boas and Geertz discovered essential truths about the nature and effects of culture that warrant little questioning. Yet this ignores the revolution in thinking about culture that has occurred over the past three decades. Two features of this revolution are of particular interest here: the near consensus rejection of the idea that cultures are coherent entities, and the idea that social institutions play a key role in giving culture whatever form it does display. As noted in the Introduction, culture remains a hotly contested concept, but within this contestation few if any specialists accept the 'Benedictine' notion of cultures as integrated wholes. And while the idea that institutions give culture form is not a consensus position, it appears with striking regularity, in both anthropology and sociology.

Against Essentialism

The critique of cultures as coherent entities has three dimensions. The first challenges the idea of cultures as clearly bounded, as neatly fenced off from other cultures. To this point, understandings of culture were founded on a distinctive set of spatial assumptions. As Akhil Gupta and James Ferguson explain, '[t]he distinctiveness of societies, nations, and cultures is based upon a seemingly unproblematic division of space, on the fact that they occupy "naturally" discontinuous spaces. The premise of discontinuity forms the starting point from which to theorize contact, conflict, and contradiction between cultures and societies.'[55] In reality, though, the boundaries of cultures defy definition – all cultural formations are marked by cross-fertilization, interpenetration, and co-constitution. For some, this is the only way to understand culture in a postcolonial, globalized world, one in which material and cultural dynamics of modernity, inextricably tied to the rise and decline of European imperialism, have obliterated whatever boundaries

---

[55] Akhil Gupta and James Ferguson, 'Beyond "Culture": Space, Identity, and the Politics of Difference', *Cultural Anthropology*, 7.1 (1992), 6.

once existed.[56] For others, however, the idea of cultural boundedness was always a myth: 'interstitiality' and 'hybridity' are not just artefacts of modernity. In an early expression of this argument, Alexander Lesser called on anthropologists to assume 'the universality of human contact and influence', to 'conceive of human societies – prehistoric, primitive, or modern – not as closed systems, but as open systems', and to 'think of any social aggregate not as isolated, separated by some kind of wall, from others but as inextricably involved with other aggregates, near and far, in weblike, netlike connections'.[57]

The second critique of cultures as coherent entities confronted the assumption of cultural integration, strongly articulated by Benedict, but enduring in the Parsonian conception of a cultural system. In Benedict's original formulation, integration was tied to purposiveness: a hidden hand of unconscious collective choices drove an ever-greater convergence of belief and practice. By the time we get to Geertz, the purposiveness is gone but the emphasis on systemic coherence remains. But like the assumption of boundedness, this is now seen as deeply problematic. Far from tightly integrated and coherent, cultures are now seen as heterogeneous, even contradictory, and where a person stands within society – their class, gender, or political location and status – affects not only the regime of meanings and practices in which they are embedded but also their interpretive and symbolic resources. In the search for generalization, Lila Abu-Lughod argues, 'anthropologists have flattened out cultural differences, smoothing over contradictions, conflicts of interest, doubts, and arguments, not to mention changing motivations and historical circumstances'.[58] Against generalization, she calls for a focus on the lived experiences of differently located individuals. Her work with Bedouin women shows how in 'the face of the complexity of individual lives even in a single family, a term like "Bedouin culture" comes to seem

---

[56] James Clifford, *The Predicament of Culture* (Cambridge, MA: Harvard University Press, 1988).

[57] Alexander Lesser, 'Social Fields and the Evolution of Society', *Southwestern Journal of Anthropology*, 17.1 (1961), 42. Also see Eric R. Wolf, *Europe and the People without History* (Berkeley: University of California Press, 1982), pp. 13–19.

[58] Lila Abu-Lughod, *Writing Women's Worlds: Bedouin Stories* (Berkeley: University of California Press, 1993), p. 9.

meaningless, whether in the sense of rules that people follow or of a community that shares such rules'.[59]

The final line of critique – well anticipated above – concerns the connections between culture and power. The issue of power had to date been a shadowy figure in conceptions of culture. Early rejections of racial determinism were driven in part by an understanding of how particular conceptions of culture and its roots helped sustain social and political hierarchies – the cultural relativism of Boas and Benedict was, in this sense, a power critique. Yet the flattening-out of the cultural terrain within supposedly bounded cultural groups obscured the complex interconnections between cultural complexity, the varied social locations of individuals, and the dynamics and topographies of power. From the 1960s onward, anthropologists sought not only to deessentialize culture but also to connect the study of complexity to patterns and practices of domination and hegemony. Indeed, Sally Engle Merry argues that *the* 'important question about culture is, therefore, how cultural practices are introduced, appropriated, deployed, reintroduced, and redefined in a social field of power over a historical period'.[60]

Together these three lines of critique informed a new conception of culture, one now shared across a range of disciplines, most notably anthropology, sociology, and political theory. Cultures are no longer understood as bounded, integrated entities; indeed, the idea of 'cultures' has become increasingly difficult to sustain. Now culture is seen as multifaceted and contested. In the words of John and Jean Comaroff:

> Culture always contains within it polyvalent, potentially contestable meanings, images, and actions ... Some of these, at any moment in time, will be woven into more or less tightly integrated, relatively explicit world views; others may be heavily contested, the stuff of counterideologies and 'subcultures'; yet others may become more or less unfixed, relatively freefloating, and indeterminate in their value and meaning.[61]

---

[59] Ibid., p. 14.
[60] Sally Engle Merry, 'Changing Rights, Changing Culture', in Jane W. Cowan, Marie-Benedicte Dembour, and Richard A. Wilson (eds.), *Culture and Rights: Anthropological Perspectives* (Cambridge: Cambridge University Press, 2001), p. 46.
[61] John Comaroff and Jean Comaroff, *Ethnography and the Historical Imagination* (Boulder, CO: Westview Press, 1992), p. 27.

The same conception is expressed in Swidler's oft-quoted article, 'Culture in Action'. IR scholars cite Swidler because her emphasis on the strategic use of cultural resources seemingly supports rational-ist arguments about the instrumental use of norms. Yet her more fundamental point – cited earlier – is that cultures are not seamless wholes: 'all real cultures contain diverse, often conflicting symbols, rituals, stories, and guides to action'.[62] Political theorists were quick to embrace this understanding, especially those working on issues of multiculturalism. In his study of the constitutional challenges posed by cultural difference, James Tully describes culture as 'strange multi-plicity', a 'tangled labyrinth of intertwining cultural differences *and* similarities'.[63]

Social Institutions

This move to (dis)integrate culture – to stress its complex and contested nature – raised a crucial question. What, if anything, gives culture any form? Culture may well be variegated, fragmented, and contradictory, and different individuals may exist in different symbolic universes, but culture is not a mess of atomized meanings, symbols, and practices. All cultural contexts exhibit continuities, linkages, and structures; even their contradictions bind as much as they divide. While there are several possible explanations for these formations – from underlying functional logics to the patterning engendered by routinized practices – one argument reappears across a range of disciplines: that social insti-tutions shape and condition culture.

It is worth noting here that those who make this argument reject the idea of cultures as coherent entities but hold onto the distinction between the cultural and the social. While stressing the interconnect-edness of these two realms, as well as their mutual constitution, they accept not only their substantive differences but also the analytical value of conceiving them as distinct. Culture is understood in the now conventional sense of intersubjective meanings embedded in, and expressed through, symbolic forms and practices. Society, by contrast, is seen as a realm of structured human interactions, characterized by

[62] Swidler, 'Culture in Action', p. 277.
[63] James Tully, *Strange Multiplicity: Constitutionalism in an Age of Diversity* (Cambridge: Cambridge University Press, 1995), p. 11.

divisions of labour, market exchanges, and inequalities of power, all sustained by institutional rules and practices.

Advancing a 'distributive' theory of culture, Ulf Hannerz attributes the heterogeneous but patterned nature of cultural landscapes, as well as the different locations of individuals within these landscapes, to the structuring effects of the prevailing social order. 'The social structure of persons and relationships', he writes, 'channels the cultural flow at the same time as it is being, in part, culturally produced'.[64] Central to this structure are social institutions, which work to 'organize' cultural diversity. As we shall see in the following chapters, if IR scholars think at all about the relationship between culture and institutions, they do so in either of two ways. In the first, culture constitutes institutions, informing the nature and content of institutional norms and practices and providing the normative consensus required for rule negotiation and compliance. In the second, institutions neutralize culture, removing it as a politically salient factor from the international arena. Anthropologists like Hannerz challenge both of these positions. Instead of culture constituting institutions, institutions condition culture. This is not a process of neutralization, however: institutions affect the 'flow' of culture, distributing meanings and practices and organizing diversity.

Two examples illustrate this understanding of institutions and culture. As noted above, in 'Culture in Action' Swidler stresses the complex and contradictory nature of culture, rejecting older notions of a coherent, thickly constitutive realm of values and practices. In her more recent work on the sociology of love, she addresses the question of what, in an inherently diverse and conflicting world of symbolic meanings and practices, gives culture form. Love, she argues, is a quintessential cultural phenomenon: a personal emotion, yes, but stimulated and shaped by intersubjective meanings embedded in, and communicated through, literature, music, social media, television, and movies, and enacted and performed through fashion, bodily expressions, and collective rituals. Yet her Californian interviews revealed strikingly different, often contradictory, understandings of love. Even the same individual could see love as a free choice, a commitment,

---

[64] Ulf Hannerz, *Cultural Complexity: Studies in the Social Organization of Meaning* (New York: Columbia University Press, 1992), p. 14.

and a growing organism, irrespective of the tensions between these.[65] Consistencies were apparent, though. Her respondents at times invoked 'mythic' conceptions of love, at other times 'prosaic': the former highly romantic, the latter distinctly realist.[66] The key to explaining this, Swidler argues, is the social and legal institution of marriage, a structure all of her respondents had to negotiate. 'One is either married or not (however ambivalent the underlying feelings might be); one cannot be married to more than one person at a time; marrying someone is a fateful, sometimes life-transforming choice; and despite divorce, marriages are still meant to last.'[67] This institutional reality encourages both the mythic and prosaic conceptions of love, as the first provides a reason for 'decisive choice', the second 'an ethic about *being* married'.[68] An institutional focus, Swidler concludes, gives 'one answer to the question of why culture might develop coherent patterns even though individuals operate quite happily with diffuse, often incomplete and internally contradictory cultural resources'. '[C]ultural structuring by institutions', she writes, 'might be thought of as operating from the outside in, organizing dispersed cultural materials the way the field surrounding a magnet links iron filings or the way the gravity of the sun orients the planets'.[69]

A second example is Ellen Berrey's recent study of how institutionalized policies and practices of 'diversity' have restructured the racial order in the United States.[70] 'A racial order', Berrey explains, 'establishes boundaries around groups based on their phenotype and ancestry (real or assumed) – classifications such as white, black, Latino, Asian, Native American – positions those groups on a hierarchy, and structures their relations to each other'.[71] Prior to the civil rights movement of the 1950s and 1960s, the racial order in the United States secured white racial domination through 'a rigid and oppressive racial order established by state-sponsored white supremacy and institutionalized through the economic system of slavery, government

---

[65] For example, as Swidler observes, 'free choice implies that one could cease to prefer the person to whom one is already committed'. Ann Swidler, *Talk of Love: How Culture Matters* (Chicago, IL: University of Chicago Press, 2001), p. 26.
[66] Ibid., pp. 111–115.   [67] Ibid., p. 117.   [68] Ibid., p. 118.
[69] Ibid., p. 158.
[70] Ellen Berrey, *The Enigma of Diversity: The Language of Race and the Limits of Racial Diversity* (Chicago, IL: University of Chicago Press, 2015).
[71] Ibid., p. 15.

sanctioned extermination, property law, physical and social segregation, and discriminatory political representation'.[72] After the 1960s,
political and legislative changes prompted organizations in the key
government, business, and education sectors to embrace the discourse
of diversity, and to institutionalize policies and practices in its name.
While acknowledging the benefits of such developments, Berrey
details how they have served to reimagine and reconfigure the racial
order, rather than eradicate it. Selective inclusion has been central to
institutionalized diversity. 'Cultural value is placed on the so-called
diverse people who are most easily incorporated into a setting and
who enhance institutional objectives such as prestige, distinction, or
profit making.'[73] This has increased the percentage of previously
underrepresented groups in elite institutions, but also deflected attention away from underlying structural inequalities and power dispar-
ities. 'It is a mechanism', Berrey writes, 'of containing and co-opting
racial justice, as it largely leaves untouched persistent racial inequalities and the gulf between rich and poor'.[74] Institutionalized diversity
has thus replaced the pre–civil rights racial order with one that
enables persistent racial inequality by subsuming race within 'a cele-
bratory American multiculturalism'.[75]

The Default Conception

IR is the disciplinary equivalent of a magpie – we constantly enlist
concepts and theories from other disciplines to better understand
world politics. Sometimes we do this well, engaging in sophisticated
ways with conceptual debates in another field, and adapting and
applying these in illuminating ways to international questions. IR's
engagement with international law is one example, perhaps, with IR
scholars demonstrating, over a considerable period, a strong and
evolving grasp of legal debates, and an ability to blend these with
discipline-specific ideas to fashion a rich body of scholarship on the
politics of international law. Our engagement with specialist debates
about the nature of culture is not so edifying. IR's neglect of culture is
itself a sorry story – a field that claims special insights into politics
beyond the state, but has little to say about cultural diversity, as
ubiquitous a feature of the global landscape as the unequal distribution

---

[72] Ibid., p. 16.   [73] Ibid., p. 8.   [74] Ibid., p. 9.   [75] Ibid., p. 5.

of material resources. Worse than this, perhaps, when IR scholars do speak of culture – often invoking it as a causal variable – they show none of the currency and nuance that characterizes their engagement with international law. Indeed, as noted above, they enlist conceptions of culture advanced between the 1930s and 1950s, displaying little awareness of the post-1960s developments discussed above. IR appears, in this respect, like a zoo for the conservation of conceptual understandings long dead in their original habitats.

In following chapters, I examine realist, English School, constructivist, and rational choice approaches in IR to the study of culture. Despite their differences, all four circle back to some version of what I term the 'default conception'. This conception has five elements, all familiar from earlier discussions. First, cultures – whether understood in ethnic, national, or civilizational terms – are conceived as coherent entities: bounded, integrated, and distinct wholes. Second, such cultures are considered autogenous, products of their own internal processes of cultural development. With boundedness assumed, this conception is blind to cultural and civilizational cross-fertilization, mutual constitution, and hybridization. Third, culture and society are differentiated, making this conception more Parsonian than Benedictine. Culture has explanatory power only if it stands in a causal relationship of some kind with phenomena in the realm of social interaction, particularly patterns of cooperation and conflict. Fourth, and following from this, culture is seen as constitutive of society: the causal arrow, in this view, seldom points in the other direction. Culture facilitates the growth and stability of institutions; and if institutions are thought to have any affect on culture, it is to neutralize its political effects. Finally, cultural diversity is imagined principally as an absence: a lack of unity, coherence, and integration. Moreover, diversity has only one effect: it undermines social order, impeding communication, eroding common institutional rationality, and preventing value convergence.

As we shall see, this default understanding of culture takes different forms in our chosen theories. Sometimes these differences distinguish one theory from another, but more often different forms straddle theoretical divides. Three differences stand out. The first concerns the unit of culture. For a surprising range of constructivists, English School theorists, and select realists, the units are civilizations. For most realists, however, the units are nations, which in the form of nation-states constitute the principal 'conflict groups'. In rational choice theory, the cultural units are less well defined, largely because of its focus on the individual as the principal unit of analysis. However, when rationalists proffer arguments about the necessity of common knowledge, often mobilized through cultural rituals, to social coordination, they imply, at the very least, the existence of localized cultural units. A second difference concerns how finely grained is the specification of the cultural unit. For example, both Martin Wight and John Ruggie discuss culture at a civilizational level, but where Wight makes broad, holistic claims about Western Christendom, Ruggie is concerned with very specific collective mentalities, just as Andrew Phillips focuses on specific, but civilization-wide, social imaginaries. The third difference concerns how, and the degree to which, favoured cultural units relate to international order (the main interest of this trilogy). In debates about international order, the default conception of culture appears most commonly in a civilizational guise. The modern international order, for example, is presented as a product of a coherent Western civilization. At the other extreme, rationalists have not yet connected their arguments about culturally generated common knowledge to questions of international order, largely because of their focus on localized cultural units. However, the proposition that social coordination depends on common knowledge has clear implications for such questions (which I explore in Chapter 5).

Shadowing this default conception of culture is an idea rejected in the anthropology and sociology of the 1930s to the 1950s: the notion of civilizational hierarchy. Recall that, prior to Boas, cultures were thought to exhibit common traits resulting from common causes, and they differed simply in the degree to which they had developed these traits. All cultures could thus be woven into a single, uniform human history, and cultures could be placed within this history according to their relative development. When these ideas were supplanted by the idea that cultures had different traits, arising from different causes, the notion of a uniform history was jettisoned, and efforts to plot all cultures on a single developmental trajectory were replaced by a new cultural relativism. While IR scholars made Ruth Benedict's move of seeing cultures as autogenous entities, and followed Parsons in distinguishing the cultural from the social, assumptions of civilizational hierarchy persist. These are most pronounced in arguments about the Western cultural foundations of the modern international order, and in the anxieties about cultural diversity that frequently accompany such arguments. The West is given a unique civilizational history in these accounts, one that provided the conditions not only for the rise of capitalism and the sovereign state but also for a pluralist international order that acknowledges, if not protects, the rights of individuals. While this and other civilizations are no longer plotted on single developmental path, civilizational comparison and chauvinism remain (especially in current discussions of Islam). Echoes of the distinctions Benedict berated anthropology for – 'between ourselves and the primitive, ourselves and the barbarian, ourselves and the pagan' – thus still resonate in IR.[76]

Cognate Arguments

Although mainstream IR discussions of culture are stuck in the past, and scholars with seemingly very different approaches return time and again to some version of the default conception, this is not the first study to point this out, or call for a more nuanced understanding. Two decades ago, Yosef Lapid and Friedrich Kratochwil noted a resurgence of interest in culture and identity in IR, but stressed the need to abandon 'categorical, essentialist, and unitary understandings of these concepts',[77] and to grasp instead 'their socially constructed (as opposed to primordially given) nature; their optional (as opposed to deterministic) dimensions; their fragmenting and diversifying (as opposed to integrating/homogenizing) implications; and their multidimensional/dynamic (as opposed to unidimensional/static) features'.[78] Despite the heightened prominence of cultural issues in world politics since this call, the following chapters show just how tenaciously IR scholars have held onto old conceptions. There are, however, important bodies of scholarship in IR that have long employed more complex

---

[76] Benedict, *Patterns of Culture*, p. 3.
[77] Yosef Lapid, 'Culture's Ship: Returns and Departures in International Relations Theory', in Yosef Lapid and Friedrich Kratochwil (eds.), *The Return of Culture and Identity in IR Theory* (Boulder, CO: Lynne Rienner, 1996), p. 8. Jacinta O'Hagan levels a similar caution in 'Conflict, Convergence or Co-Existence – The Relevance of Culture in Reframing World Order', *Transnational International Law and Contemporary Problems*, 9.1 (1999): 537–567.
[78] Ibid., p. 7.

understandings of culture, and notable recent studies of civilization
and religion draw on, and speak to, these understandings.

Critical and Normative Theories

As we saw above in Abu-Lughod's critique of the coherence of Bedouin
culture, it is feminist scholars, excavating the complex intersections
between gender and cultural discourses and practices, who have
revealed most strikingly the complexity of all cultural formations, the
entanglements of power and culture, and the relationship between
gendered subject positions and cultural experience. These insights echo
through feminist IR scholarship, as two examples illustrate. The first is
Ann Tickner's classic critique of how hegemonic conceptions of masculinity inform national security discourses and practices, in which she
highlights not only the relationship between power and cultural meanings but also the multiplicity of sexual identifications these discourses
marginalize. Indeed, '[h]egemonic masculinity is sustained through its
opposition to various subordinated and devalued masculinities, such as
homosexuality, and, more important, through its relation to various
devalued femininities'.[79] Ann Towns provides a second example in her
draft chapter for Volume II of this project. Taking aim at recent
attempts to cast Western civilization as the sole bastion of progressive
gender norms, she insists that 'cultural differences on gender equality
do not align neatly along ethnic, national or civilizational lines.
Instead, support or opposition to gender equality cuts across presumed
national or civilizational boundaries.'[80]

The idea that culture is inherently diverse and socially ordered
also finds expression in the work of poststructural theorists of IR,
where their distinct epistemological position leads to an emphasis on
multiple, often contradictory, discursive constructions of cultural
forms. Poststructuralists begin by denying that there are natural, social,
or cultural phenomena that exist prior to, or independent of, language.
Language does not just render these phenomena meaningful, as

[79] J. Ann Tickner, *Gender in International Relations* (New York: Columbia
University Press, 1992), p. 6.
[80] Ann Towns, 'Contesting the Liberal Order: Gender and the Generation of
Cultural Cleavages across "the West"' (unpublished manuscript), p. 3.

ontological realists hold; it constitutes their reality.[81] Critics commonly point to material entities and processes, claiming that these have a manifest reality regardless of any discursive framing. It is easier to comprehend when applied to cultural phenomena, however. Holding that the West and Islam are not natural forms – that they are constituted and sustained by language and practice – is hardly controversial. 'Language is the medium of culture', Anne Norton argues. It 'is not only the means by which things are named but the schema in which things are placed in relation, and the medium in which those names and those relations are changed'.[82] The crucial point for our purposes is that the discourses that constitute culture are never singular: they are multiple, interwoven, and often contradictory, producing a highly complex cultural universe. Most importantly, these discourses are inherently political. As Lene Hansen explains, they are central to 'the production and reproduction of particular subjectivities and identities while others are simultaneously excluded'.[83] Hansen's study of the Danish 'Muhammad cartoon crisis' offers a powerful illustration, showing how discursive contests over civilizational identities, epistemic certainty, and the salience of law and religion produced hierarchized subjectivities and a highly securitized political crisis.[84]

These arguments resonate with postcolonial critiques of culture as singular and objective. 'All cultures are involved in one another', Edward Said wrote, 'none is single and pure, all are hybrid, heterogeneous, extraordinarily differentiated, and unmonolithic'.[85] The task of the scholar is to understand how axes of cultural difference are constructed. 'What is theoretically innovative, and politically crucial', Homi Bhabha contends, 'is the need to think beyond narratives of originary and initial subjectivities and to focus on moments or processes that are produced in the articulation of cultural differences'.[86] What distinguishes postcolonialism is its focus on European

---

[81] Lene Hansen, *Security as Practice: Discourse Analysis and the Bosnian War* (London: Routledge, 2006), p. 16.

[82] Anne Norton, *95 Theses on Politics, Culture, and Method* (New Haven, CT: Yale University Press, 2004), p. 12.

[83] Hansen, *Security as Practice*, p. 16.

[84] Lene Hansen, 'The Politics of Securitization and the Muhammad Cartoon Crisis: A Post-Structural Perspective', *Security Dialogue*, 45.4–5 (2011), 357–369.

[85] Edward W. Said, *Culture and Imperialism* (New York: Alfred A. Knopf, 1993), p. xxv.

[86] Homi K. Bhabha, *The Location of Culture* (London: Routledge, 2004), p. 1.

imperialism as 'a critical historical juncture in which postcolonial national identities are constructed in opposition to European ones, and come to be understood as Europe's "others"'.[87] Or in Julian Saurin's words, 'It is imperialism … that produces international polities and organizations and that in turn pitches the social world into dyadic oppositions.'[88] We see in these arguments not only a rejection of essentialist conceptions of culture but also the idea that institutions – in this case European imperialism – construct and order axes of cultural identification and difference. Postcolonialism in IR goes beyond this, however. IR is criticized not only for ignoring the impact of imperialism on the nature and organization of global politics and culture but for being epistemologically incapable of comprehending this impact.[89]

The final literature to engage contemporary understandings of culture sits within the broad field of international political theory (IPT), a field that 'studies the "ought" questions that have been ignored or sidelined by the modern study of International Relations, and the "international" dimension that Political Theory has in the past neglected'.[90] For too long IPT was polarized between cosmopolitan and communitarian positions, the former stressing the moral equality of all humans and denying the moral significance of cultural differences, and the latter casting discrete cultural communities as the principal source of moral values and discounting universal moral claims. While early cosmopolitans had little to say about culture, communitarians advanced an understanding very close to the default conception detailed above. Cultures appeared as coherent systems of meaning, constituting members with distinct role identities that informed their conceptions of the good. Without such culturally grounded identities,

---

[87] Geeta Chowdhry and Sheila Nair, 'Introduction: Power in a Postcolonial World: Race, Gender, and Class in International Relations', in Geeta Chowdhry and Sheila Nair (eds.), *Power, Postcolonialism and International Relations* (London: Routledge, 2002), p. 2.

[88] Julian Saurin, 'International Relations as Imperial Illusion; or, the Need to Decolonize IR', in Branwen Gruffydd Jones (ed.), *Decolonizing International Relations* (Lanham, MD: Rowman and Littlefield, 2006), p. 30.

[89] Siba Grovogui, *Beyond Eurocentrism and Anarchy: Memories of International Order and Institutions* (Houndmills: Palgrave, 2006).

[90] Chris Brown and Robyn Eckersley, 'International Political Theory in the Real World', in Chris Brown and Robyn Eckersley (eds.), *The Oxford Handbook of International Political Theory* (Oxford: Oxford University Press, 2018), p. 3.

Charles Taylor argues, individuals 'would be at sea, as it were; they wouldn't know anymore, for an important range of questions, what the significance of things was for them'.[91] Recent developments in IPT have seen a relaxation in both the cosmopolitan and communitarian positions. Cosmopolitans now attribute greater significance to national communities as sites for the cultivation of wider moral obligations,[92] and communitarians are starting to conceive constitutive communities in more varied, multilayered ways.[93] Chris Brown's critique of Huntington's *Clash of Civilizations* is emblematic of the latter. '[C]ivilizations are not monolithic entities occupying ground', Brown argues, 'but systems of ideas which have always coexisted in time and space: indeed, the "clash of civilizations" quite frequently takes place within particular individuals'.[94]

Religion and Civilization

In addition to the understandings found in these broad theoretical perspectives, culture is receiving a more sophisticated reading in specific research projects.[95] The argument of this book about the

[91] Charles Taylor, *Sources of the Self* (Cambridge, MA: Harvard University Press, 1989), p. 27.
[92] See, in particular, Toni Erskine, *Embedded Cosmopolitanism: Duties to Strangers and Enemies in a World of 'Dislocated Communities'* (Oxford: Oxford University Press, 2008); Robyn Eckersley, 'From Cosmopolitan Nationalism to Cosmopolitan Democracy', *Review of International Studies*, 33.4 (2007), 675–692.
[93] For a good discussion of these relaxations, see Peter Sutch, 'The Slow Normalization of Normative Political Theory', in Chris Brown and Robyn Eckersley (eds.), *The Oxford Handbook of International Political Theory* (Oxford: Oxford University Press, 2018), pp. 35–47.
[94] Chris Brown, *Practical Judgement in International Political Theory* (London: Routledge, 2010), p. 102.
[95] In addition to the examples discussed here, see Jutta Weldes, Mark Laffey, Hugh Gusterson, and Raymond Duvall (eds.), *Cultures of Insecurity: States, Communities, and the Production of Danger* (Minneapolis: University of Minnesota Press, 1999); Roxanne Lynn Doty, *Imperial Encounters: The Politics of Representation in North-South Relations* (Minneapolis: University of Minnesota Press, 1996); Ann Towns, *Women and States: Norms and Hierarchies in International Society* (Cambridge: Cambridge University Press, 2010); Tarak Barkawi, *Orientalism and War* (Oxford: Oxford University Press, 2013); Stephan Chan, *Plural International Relations in a Divided World* (Cambridge: Polity Press, 2017); and John Hobson, *The Eastern Origins of Western Civilization* (Cambridge: Cambridge University Press, 2004).

complexity of culture and the structuring effects of institutions echoes Elizabeth Shakman Hurd's work on religious freedom. After the terrorist attacks of 9/11, the United States, its major liberal allies, leading international organizations, and a myriad of transnational advocacy groups instituted sustained campaigns to promote freedom of religious belief and practice, assuming that moderate and tolerant religion could 'take the wind out of the sails of extremist movements by offering a viable alternative to radicalization'.[96] At the heart of this project lies a central contradiction, however. The very notion of moderate and tolerant religion means that only some forms of belief and practice are legitimate: freedom has its bounds. Central to the project is thus the definition of what constitutes legitimate religion, a necessary precursor to fostering the moderate and tolerant over the radical and intolerant. But as Shakman Hurd explains, religion, like culture more generally, is not a coherent entity:

Neither religions nor religious actors are singular, agentive forces that can be analysed, quantified, engaged, celebrated or condemned – and divided into good or bad ... There is often no agreement within any religious tradition on who speaks authoritatively on behalf of that tradition, who is in and who is out, which texts and practices represent the core of the tradition, and so forth. There is no single Judaism or Christianity. There are many. There are no neat lines between believers and nonbelievers, or between the world of the sacred and everyday life.[97]

In the face of such complexity, political and religious elites have long sought to institutionalize legitimate forms of faith and expression, seeking to structure the religious 'flow', to paraphrase Hannerz. The Westphalian authorization of Catholicism, Lutheranism, and Calvinism over heretical Christian sects, and Christianity over Islam and Judaism, is a prominent example, but so too is the current practice of championing good over bad religion. Indeed, Shakman Hurd argues that '[a] novel combination of global political will, shifting patterns of religious governance, accelerating legal globalization, unparalleled financial resources, and historical contingencies such as 9/11 and the rise of counterterrorism have led to a global field of religious and social engineering that is unprecedented in size, scope, and reach'.[98] A key

---

[96] Elizabeth Shakman Hurd, *Beyond Religious Freedom: The New Global Politics of Religion* (Princeton, NJ: Princeton University Press, 2015), p. 3.
[97] Ibid., p. 19.   [98] Ibid., p. 16.

element of this engineering has been the promotion and institutionalization of religious rights. But as Shakman Hurd explains, distributing
rights according to religion 'funnels individuals into discrete faith
communities, empowers those communities and their spokespersons,
and marginalizes other modes of solidarity'.[99] 'Governing through
religious rights', she argues, 'over-codes the boundaries between religions, and naturalizes the line between religion and non-religion'.[100]

Peter Katzenstein's writings on civilizations also challenge the essen-
tialism of recent debates. Although widely critiqued, Samuel Huntington's *The Clash of Civilizations* resuscitated and empowered old ideas
about civilizations as coherent units of world politics, civilizational
boundaries as key axes of difference, and civilizational chauvinism as
a legitimate marker of identity. While joining the debate only recently,
Katzenstein's trilogy is among the most sustained attempts to counter
Huntington's claims while taking civilizations seriously. Like Shakman
Hurd's argument about religion, Katzenstein rejects Huntington's portrayal of civilizations as coherent entities with agential capacities. To
begin with, 'civilizational constellations', as he terms them, are internally pluralistic, characterized by multiple actors (principally states,
polities, and empires), multiple traditions (they 'are not static and
consensual but dynamic and politically contested'), and multiple
processes.[101] Equally importantly, civilizations are deeply interrelated,
shaped by centuries of 'intercivilizational encounters and transciviliza-
tional engagements'.[102] 'To regard Greece, Europe, and the West as set
apart from their Islamic, Semitic, African, and Orthodox-Christian
roots strains the historical record', Katzenstein notes by way of
example. 'For almost a millennium, Islam's contribution to science,
technology, and the arts were more important than that of Western
Europe. Much of Aristotle's work, for example, would have been lost
without the Islamic scholars who transmitted, preserved, and
developed it.'[103] Within this complex, highly fluid cultural domain,

---

[99] Ibid., p. 48.   [100] Ibid.
[101] Peter J. Katzenstein, 'A World of Plural and Pluralist Civilizations: Multiple
Actors, Traditions, and Practices', in Peter J. Katzenstein (ed.), *Civilizations in
World Politics* (London: Routledge, 2010), pp. 23–36.
[102] Ibid., p. 7.
[103] Peter J. Katzenstein, 'Many Wests and Polymorphic Globalism', in Peter
J. Katzenstein (ed.), *Anglo-America and Its Discontents: Civilizational
Identities beyond East and West* (London: Routledge, 2012), p. 207.

continuities, structured relations, and symbols of commonality do exist. But these are accomplishments of power and practice, institutionalized for particular ends. 'Where civilizations appear to cohere around uncontested core values', Katzenstein holds, 'we are witnessing political and intellectual innovations created for particular purposes, rather than inherent cultural traits of unchanging collective identities and practices'.[104] This is true both of projects to construct singular civilizational identities and of the more varied patterning that all constellations exhibit. For example, while Katzenstein rejects the myth of a unified Anglo-American core of 'the West', he shows how three different multicultural patterns have been institutionalized: the racial divide that persists across Anglo-America, New Zealand's transition from biculturalism to triculturalism, and the multiculturalism of Australia and Canada. Each of these is an institutionalized practice to govern the cultural complexity that characterizes 'the West'.[105]

How culture is understood by these authors, and in the critical perspectives discussed above, has greatly informed my own thinking. My project differs from theirs in important respects, though. First, while some of these perspectives are clearly concerned with international order and cultural diversity – postcolonial arguments about culture and imperialism being a good example – they are not seeking broader insights into the relationship between diversity and international orders in general. Indeed, a good number of these scholars would likely reject such a project. Second, although we are all concerned with culture as a highly variegated, politically structured phenomenon, most of the above perspectives hone in on particular aspects, expressions, or discursive constructions, such as gender, religion, civilization, or even securitized cartoons. But as we shall see in Chapter 6, I am interested in cultural diversity more broadly, as a structural condition that shapes the evolution of international orders. Again, some of my fellow travellers may want to get off the train at this point, worrying that I am abstracting away from the micro expressions and politics of difference. This move is merited, however, because it brings into focus the macro-ordering of diversity, and ties this to imperatives of large-scale rule (themes present, if insufficiently developed, in the

---

[104] Ibid., p. 213.
[105] Peter J. Katzenstein, 'The West as Anglo-America', in Peter J. Katzenstein (ed.), *Anglo-America and Its Discontents: Civilizational Identities beyond East and West* (London: Routledge, 2012), pp. 20–26.

above literatures). Finally, the idea that mainstream IR theories ignore or misunderstand culture is implied in all of these perspectives, and sometimes addressed explicitly. This book is unique, however, in detailing this misunderstanding across four of our most prominent theories. Some might argue that this gives them far too much attention, that their deficiencies are easily dispensed with, and that they already consume more airspace than they deserve. My view is different, though. It is the very prominence of these perspectives, especially in debates over international order, that warrants their critical engagement. Moreover, buried within them are often surprising, well-developed arguments about culture that deserve systematic excavation (as in the cases of realism and rational choice), even if ultimately these arguments reiterate some version of the default conception. Only by engaging these theories and their entrenched understandings of culture can we persuade the field – and the policymakers and political commentators who echo the same ideas – that we need to think about diversity and order differently.

Conclusion

Like all concepts, 'culture' is an abstraction intended to clarify and make sense of certain features and dynamics of human existence. And like all such abstractions, no conception of culture can be proven empirically, as that conception will necessarily define what counts as evidence. Conceptions of culture stand or fall in the arguments we have about their logical coherence and heuristic value, arguments wrestled out in particular communities of scholarship and interest. Over the past century and a half debates within specialist disciplines such as anthropology and sociology have pushed the concept of culture from a whole way of life, embedded in a uniform human history, and rankable on a single developmental scale to a highly complex, often contradictory, realm of symbolic meanings and practices, analytically distinct from, but structured by, social processes and structures. Somewhere in the midst of this transition, in the period from the 1930s to 1950s, cultures were imagined as neatly bounded, tightly integrated, quasi-organic entities, a view that persisted even after the notion of culture as a whole way of life was replaced by the idea of a cultural system, distinct but intertwined with the social system. It is here, at this way station in the long evolution of ideas about culture, that IR got stuck.

Explaining why it got stuck is beyond the scope of this book, but several reasons suggest themselves. The first has to do with the growing positivism, materialism, and rationalism of mainstream American IR from the 1950s onward, none of which left much room for the study of culture, let alone engaging with ongoing anthropological or socio-logical debates. In this respect, the story of culture in IR – the stubborn persistence of the outdated default conception – bears some resem-blance to Louis Hartz's fragment thesis of settler societies, where the nature of a society's political culture is determined by the moment it broke free from long-term processes of European political develop-ment.[106] IR, on this reading, is stuck with the conception of culture that prevailed when it disconnected from specialist debates. The story is complicated, however, by the renewed interest IR scholars have displayed in cultural phenomena over the past two decades, interest that suggests reengagement. Yet as we shall see in the following chap-ters, in each of the four approaches to culture considered, IR scholars start out from preexisting theoretical commitments – epistemological, ontological, methodological – and they assimilate cultural phenomena within these frames. In some cases, like the English School, this leads to the immediate invocation of the default conception. In others, the default conception appears as a solution to a step in a preexisting theoretical problem, as in rationalist claims that culture provides the common knowledge needed for collaboration. And in others, the default conception enters the picture only when an otherwise antithet-ical body of thought seeks to address particular questions, for example, in realist arguments about the legitimacy of international orders.

This chapter has laid two foundations for what follows. It has plotted the broad development of ideas about culture from the 1870s to the last three decades, enabling us to locate IR's default conception and define the principal elements of that conception – cultures are autogenous, integrated entities, distinct from but constitutive of society, and cultural diversity is a lack of unity, corrosive of social order. Chapters 2 to 5 detail the stubborn persistence of these views across otherwise very different theoretical perspectives. More than this, though, the chapter has drawn out two features of more recent specialist understandings of culture: the idea that culture is always

[106] Louis Hartz, *The Founding of New Societies* (New York: Houghton, Mifflin, Harcourt, 1969).

heterogeneous, contradictory, and contested, and diffuse, not bounded; and the proposition that social institutions play a key role in organizing cultural diversity. At a historical juncture where IR scholars need to think seriously about the implications of cultural diversity for international order, the tragedy is not only that our mainstream theories have ignored these insights but that properly understood and enlisted they have the potential to inform a very different way of thinking about diversity and order, an alternative I develop in Chapter 6.

2 | *Cultured Realism*

Realists are materialists at heart; they understand the international system as a configuration of material power, and their starting assumption is that states are driven, first and foremost, by material interests: guns, money, and territory, most prominently. In its most extreme form, this is an ontological position – material forces make the world go around, international relations included. More commonly, however, it is an argument about causal primacy. Of course the world consists of cultural stuff – values, practices, artefacts, etc. – but the principal determinants of political behaviour are material: the systemic distribution of capabilities, innate human nature, and the egoistic pursuit of geostrategic and economic interests. Materialism is the default assumption in realism, and in the relationship between the material and the cultural, it is always 'primitive'.

This default materialism is deeply unstable, though. Regardless of how confidently it is expressed, realists are drawn nonetheless onto the cultural terrain. Implicitly, as Alexander Wendt has shown, cultural assumptions underlie some of the most fundamental realist propositions: that anarchy necessarily generates competitive, self-help behaviour, for example, and that states are security egoists.[1] Explicitly, realists invoke cultural arguments when seeking to address key questions, of which three stand out. First, as William Wohlforth argues, realists are 'groupists': they are concerned with relations between collectivities.[2] But when pressed on the nature of these groups, sometimes they are presented as societies of competing interests, mediated and channelled by the institutions of the state, but often they are treated as cultural communities with a hierarchy of interests. Second,

---

[1] Alexander Wendt, *Social Theory of International Politics* (Cambridge: Cambridge University Press, 1999), pp. 92–138.

[2] William C. Wohlforth, 'Realism', in Christian Reus-Smit and Duncan Snidal (eds.), *The Oxford Handbook of International Relations* (Oxford: Oxford University Press, 2008), p. 133.

when structural determinants fail to explain why states behave the way they do, realists (like others) have to probe the nature and origin of state motivations. But as the literature on strategic culture shows, this often leads to essentialist arguments about national cultural predispositions. Third, and most importantly for this study, whenever realists treat international order as an institution, and not merely an unintended consequence of competition, they often attribute the origins and stability of an order to an underlying common culture.

My point here is not to criticise realists for their default materialism; much has been said on this score already. Nor is it to criticise them for smuggling in culture through the back door or for invoking cultural arguments when probing collectivities, motivations, or orders, all of which should make a constructivist happy. Rather, my concern is with how culture is understood in these moves. Sometimes cultures – whether they are strategic communities, nations, or civilizations – appear as coherent entities that condition the play of politics. At other times, the political construction of such cultures is considered essential to successful international competition. In both cases, however, realists adopt versions of the default conception of culture critiqued in Chapter 1.

The following discussion is divided into four main sections. The first section explores the nature of realism as a diverse tradition of thought, and the second section examines its abiding materialist predisposition. Realists come in all stripes. Some emphasize human nature, some system structure; some black-box the state, others open it up; some are 'offensive', others 'defensive'. Realism is not a single theory of international relations, therefore; it is, as many have observed, an evolving tradition with distinctive characteristics. One of these, I shall argue, is default materialism. Irrespective of whether their materialist propositions are sound, realists start with these and work outwards from this point. As I will explain, material forces and factors are primitive in realist thought.

The third and fourth sections examine the instability of this default materialism. I begin by revisiting Wendt's argument that many core realist propositions hold only in particular, unrecognized or unacknowledged, cultural contexts, that the effects of anarchy depend on its intersubjective framing, for example. My principal focus, however, is on the more explicit invocations of culture that recur in realist thought, and on the nature of these invocations. As signalled above, culture appears in realist thought whenever groupism, strategic choice, and orders as institutions are addressed, and it always appears in essentialized form. These are far from side issues, however. Groupism is a fundamental assumption of realism, distinguishing it most starkly from varieties of liberalism. No theory of international relations can stand without an account of state motivations, and strategic choice is central to the security behaviour of states. And realists are no less interested in sources of international order than other scholars; in fact, order is a cardinal, if at times shadowy, value for realists, closely related to the prudent pursuit of the national interest.

Realism as a Tradition

It is common today for realism to be described as a 'tradition' of thought, but the term is used in at least two ways. The first is to attribute a long history or genealogy to a distinctive theory of international relations. Realism is cast here as theoretically coherent and markedly different from its principal rivals: liberalism, Marxism, constructivism, poststructuralism, etc. The idea that it constitutes a tradition is partly about bolstering its authority over other, newer theories and partly about reading its history selectively to sanction particular interpretations of what realism is. An excellent example is Jeffery Legro and Andrew Moravcsik's article 'Is Anybody Still a Realist?', which seeks to define realism as a coherent and distinctive theoretical paradigm, in part by tracing the recurrence of key ideas in the writings of great historical thinkers, in their case Thucydides, Machiavelli, Hobbes, E. H. Carr, Hans Morgenthau, and Kenneth Waltz.[3] The second use of tradition also gives realism a venerable history. The purpose, though, is not to cast it as a distinctive theory or paradigm; quite the opposite. 'Tradition' is used here to characterize a rich, complex, and at times contradictory body of thought, one betraying certain predispositions and commitments, but one that defies reduction to a coherent or single theory of international relations. With notable exceptions,[4] those who read realism in this way often identify similar

---

[3] Jeffrey W. Legro and Andrew Moravcsik, 'Is Anybody Still a Realist?', *International Security*, 24.2 (1999), 5–55.

[4] Michael Williams's reading of the tradition is just such an exception, presenting an understanding of realism radically at odds with conventional readings, one that blurs the boundaries between realism, liberalism, and constructivism.

characteristics of the tradition, but all deny that these amount to one clearly delineated theory, easily amenable to testing against other theories.

In what follows I too characterise realism as a tradition of thought, but in the second sense of a diverse if identifiable and interconnected body of ideas with a complex genealogy. The alternative, that it can be reduced to a distinct paradigm, not only denies the richness and complexity of realist thought but also encourages simplistic defences and misdirected critiques. As Wohlforth observes, '[t]he notion that realism – this centuries-old foundational school of thought – can be and has to be reduced to a single, internally consistent, and logically coherent theory is the taproot of the greatest misunderstanding'.[5] A better characterization, Wohlforth argues, is C. A. J. Coady's analogy with religion, in which realism appears as 'a combination of an often loosely related set of beliefs, a way of thinking and responding, a sometimes desperate desire to preach to the uncomprehending heathen, and a pantheon of canonical exemplars or saints whose very diverse intellectual and practical lives are seen to embody the virtues of the religion'.[6] My own position is close that of Jack Donnelly, who sees realism as 'an approach to international relations that has emerged gradually through the work of a series of analysts who have situated themselves within, and thus delimited, a distinctive but still diverse style or tradition of analysis'.[7]

Describing realism as a rich and varied tradition of thought does not mean that it lacks distinctive characteristics. If this were the case, nothing would distinguish it from other traditions, and nothing would define it as a field of debate, however complex and contradictory. The beauty of the concept of tradition is that it admits both complexity and commonality. Indeed, for Martin Wight this was what distinguished a 'tradition' from a 'pattern' of thought. The idea of a pattern focuses attention on 'the logical coherence of the complex of thought and how acceptance of any one unit-idea is likely to entail most of the others, so

---

See *The Realist Tradition and the Limits of International Relations* (Cambridge: Cambridge University Press, 2005).

[5] Wohlforth, 'Realism', p. 131.

[6] C. A. J. Coady, 'The Moral Reality in Realism', *Journal of Applied Philosophy*, 22.2 (2005), 122.

[7] Jack Donnelly, *Realism and International Relations* (Cambridge: Cambridge University Press, 2000), p. 6.

that the whole is capable of being a system of political philosophy'.[8]
The idea of a tradition, by contrast, presupposes recurrent or even
common ideas, but also accommodates the 'illogicalities and discontinuities' that necessarily condition ideas over time.[9]

Most accounts of realism as a tradition thus go beyond cataloguing
its diverse manifestations and expressions to identify key ideas characteristic of the tradition. Read from one angle, the ideas identified vary
dramatically. Michael Williams's revisionist reading, for example,
identifies 'scepticism', 'relationality', and 'power politics' as core
ideas.[10] By contrast, Legro and Moravcsik stress 'rational unitary
actors', 'fixed and uniformly conflictual goals', and 'the primacy of
material capabilities'.[11] Important as these two interpretations are,
they are outliers in the broader field of interpretation, with most
accounts evincing far greater convergence. For example, after distilling
key propositions from canonical realist writings, Donnelly sees realists
emphasizing the constraints on politics posed by human nature and/
or international anarchy, and the way these encourage struggles for
power and the pursuit of egoistic interests.[12] In a similar vein, Wohlforth identifies groupism, egoisim, anarchy, and power politics as
trademark realist ideas.[13] For both scholars, it is egoistic human
nature, international anarchy, and power politics that come to the
fore. And even groupism, which Donnelly leaves off his final selection, features prominently in the ideas he distils from great realist
works, with the centrality of states or 'conflict groups' appearing time
and again.[14]

Default Materialism

Behind many of these features of the realist tradition lies a persistent
starting assumption: the primacy of the material. When aggressive,
domineering human nature is stressed, it appears as an innate material
condition. When, more modestly, states are seen as atomistic, self-
interested actors – 'egoists' – their primary interests are presented as

---

[8] Martin Wight, 'An Anatomy of International Thought', *Review of International Studies*, 13.3 (1987), 226.

[9] Ibid.   [10] Williams, *The Realist Tradition*, pp. 5–6.

[11] Legro and Moravcsik, 'Is Anybody Still a Realist?', pp. 13–17.

[12] Donnelly, *Realism*, p. 9.   [13] Wohlforth, 'Realism', p. 133.

[14] Donnelly, *Realism*, pp. 7–8.

material: physical security to material might, all dependent on guns and money. When the structure of the international system is emphasized, its most important features are the absence of a central authority – 'anarchy' – and the distribution of capabilities, understood as material resources. And when realists stress the ubiquity of power politics, power is understood in terms of such capabilities, assumed to translate unproblematically into political influence.

Many commentators highlight this default materialism as a distinctive feature of realist thought. As we have seen, Legro and Moravcsik see 'the primacy of material capabilities' as a core realist assumption. For realists, they argue, 'interstate bargaining outcomes reflect the relative costs of threats and inducements, which is directly proportional to the distribution of material resources'.[15] Stefano Guzzini, although critical of Legro and Moravcsik's efforts to reformulate realism as a coherent and distinctive theory, acknowledges that '[r]ealism's theory of action is based on self-interest which is defined in a predominantly materialist way in order to distinguish it from idealism'.[16] Shifting the focus from self-interest to understandings of power, David Baldwin argues that '[r]ealists ever since the 1930s have tended to attribute more utility to military force as an instrument of statecraft than other approaches. Thus, it is not just power that lies at the heart of realist theories, but a particular kind of power'.[17]

Stark characterizations of realism as inherently materialist – radically different from idealist constructivism – have rightly suffered sustained critique.[18] Conceptually, the boundary between the material and the ideational is difficult to sustain; even the most materialist of realists acknowledge non-material state interests and sources of national power, and all but the most extreme constructivists admit the constraints and opportunities of the material world.

---

[15] Legro and Moravcsik, 'Is Anybody Still a Realist?', p. 17.

[16] Stefano Guzzini, 'The Enduring Dilemmas of Realism in International Relations', *European Journal of International Relations*, 10.4 (2004), 536.

[17] David A. Baldwin, *Power and International Relations: A Conceptual Approach* (Princeton, NJ: Princeton University Press, 2016), p. 125.

[18] For a particular sustained and penetrating critique, see Samuel Barkin, *Realist Constructivism* (Cambridge: Cambridge University Press, 2010), chapter 3. An insightful discussion of Barkin's earlier article on the topic can be found in the following forum: Patrick Thaddeus Jackson (ed.), 'Bridging the Gap: Toward a Realist-Constructivist Dialogue', *International Studies Review*, 6.2 (2004), 337–352.

My argument about realism's default materialism assumes no stark distinction between the material and the ideational; in fact, much of this chapter details just how dependent realism is on the latter. My claim is not that realism is materialist through and through, but that in much, if not all, realist thought the material is 'primitive'. I borrow this term from Wendt's discussion of the agent–structure problem, where he argues that conventional answers to the question of how agents and structure relate invariably treat one or other as ontologically primitive, as more fundamental and causally primary.[19] In Wendt's broader work, he introduces a second axis of ontological variation in international relations theories: the extent to which the material or the ideational are privileged.[20] Wendt does not use the language of 'primitive' to describe those that are privileged, but the term is usefully extended. Materialists don't just focus on material factors; they see them as fundamental, with ideas playing a secondary role. The reverse is true of idealists: intersubjective meanings are fundamental, and 'material forces are secondary, significant only insofar as they are constituted with particular meanings for actors'.[21]

When thinking about the characteristic features of the realist tradition, treating the material as ontologically primitive is compelling. Two things should be noted, however. First, saying that realists treat the material as primitive does not mean they ignore ideational phenomena or deny them any causal significance. All it means is that they focus more readily on material factors, and that their first cut in any analysis will be the material. In this respect, their position on the material is similar to Kenneth Waltz's on the priority of structural analysis: it doesn't explain everything, but it highlights the field of fundamental forces bearing on state action, and should thus be the first cut in any analysis.[22] Second, it does not mean that the things realists treat as material are actually material. When Waltz argues that a system's structure is defined in part by its distribution of capabilities, he wants capabilities to be measurable, so he focuses principally on material factors. Yet the very notion of 'capabilities' infuses many of

---

[19] Alexander Wendt, 'The Agent–Structure Problem in International Relations Theory', *International Organization*, 41.3 (1987), 339.

[20] Wendt, *Social Theory*, pp. 22–33.   [21] Ibid., p. 24.

[22] Kenneth N. Waltz, *Man, the State, and War: A Theoretical Analysis* (New York: Columbia University Press, 1959), Conclusion.

these with implied social capacity: a good example being 'economic capability'.[23] What matters for the present argument, however, is that realists routinely appeal to factors they think are material, allowing them to contrast their theories with rivals that pay unwarranted attention to ideas.

The tendency to treat material factors as primitive is most apparent in realist discussions of power. A central concern with power politics is a defining characteristic of the realist tradition, highlighted by a broad spectrum of commentators. Elsewhere I have distinguished between possessive and relational conceptions of power, the first seeing power as attribute of an individual actor, the second as a quality of a relationship between actors.[24] Both conceptions are found in realist thought, even if the former predominates (especially since the 1970s). What is striking, however, is that regardless which conception is held, realists feel compelled to enumerate the 'elements of national power' or 'count poles'. It is here that the default materialism in realist thought is most pronounced, but it is also where scholars vary in the degree of their materialism. Both this commonality and variation are evident in the writings of Mearsheimer, Waltz, and Morgenthau.

Mearsheimer is the starkest materialist, stripping power to its most basic – supposedly measurable – material elements. 'For all realists', he writes, 'calculations of power lie at the heart of how states think about the world around them. Power is the currency of great-power politics, and states compete for it among themselves. What money is to economics, power is to international relations'.[25] He is critical, however, of the expansive and imprecise ways realists and others have understood power, and one of his first moves is to define it more narrowly, seeking to enhance its analytical utility. Explicitly rejecting arguments that power should be understood as relational, and that control over outcomes is the true measure of power, he reduces it to the material capabilities of states. Power, he argues, 'is based on the particular

---

[23] Kenneth N. Waltz, *Theory of International Politics* (New York: Random House, 1979), p. 131.

[24] Christian Reus-Smit, *American Power and World Order* (Cambridge: Polity Press, 2004), pp. 41–45. David Baldwin draws a similar distinction between 'relational' and 'property' conceptions. See his *Power and International Relations*, p. 50.

[25] John J. Mearsheimer, *The Tragedy of Great Power Politics* (New York: Norton, 2001), p. 12.

material capabilities that a state possesses. The balance of power, therefore, is a function of tangible assets – such as armoured divisions and nuclear weapons – that each great power controls.'[26] Refining this claim further, he distinguishes between two kinds of power: 'latent power' and 'military power'. Although he defines the former as 'the socio-economic ingredients that go into building military power', there is little social about them. Latent power, he writes, 'is largely based on a state's wealth and the overall size of its population. Great powers need money, technology, and personnel to build military forces and to fight wars, and a state's latent power refers to the raw potential it can draw on when competing with rival states.'[27] Military power is a product of this latent power, and 'is based largely on the size and strength of a state's army and its supporting air and naval forces'.[28] This privileging of military capabilities is justified, he argues, because 'a state's effective power is ultimately a function of its military forces and how they compare with the military forces of rival states'.[29]

This unabashed materialism does not mean Mearsheimer ignores ideational factors altogether, but how he deals with them reaffirms the primacy of the material. As we shall see, other prominent realists integrate non-material factors within their conception of power, however marginal this inclusion might be. Mearsheimer, by contrast, admits the importance of non-material factors, such as strategy and intelligence, in shaping outcomes, but sees them as intervening variables, mediating between power and outcomes. This is why the balance of power is an insufficient predictor of military outcomes, and why Mearsheimer rejects definitions of power that emphasize control over outcomes. Focusing on outcomes, he claims, not only leads to the unsatisfying conclusion that a state has no power if it fails to produce results but makes it impossible to measure power until after outcomes are settled. The imperative to quantify – to count power – thus drives the conceptual privileging of the material.

When elaborating his structural theory of international politics, Waltz famously identifies three elements of political structures: their organizing principle, the functional differentiation of the constituent units, and the distribution of capabilities. The international system as a political structure has the organizing principle of anarchy, states are functionally undifferentiated (they are 'like units'), and the

---

[26] Ibid., p. 55.   [27] Ibid.   [28] Ibid., p. 56.   [29] Ibid., p. 55.

distribution of capabilities varies. It is in the last of these elements
that his default materialism is most readily apparent. The distribution
of capabilities, he argues, is a property of a system's structure, not
its units. Yet estimating this distribution involves comparing the
capabilities of those individual units, in effect, 'counting poles and
measuring power'.[30] Five capabilities are identified as especially
important: 'size of population and territory, resource endowment,
economic capability, military strength, [and] political stability and
competence'.[31] Rejecting arguments that seek to disaggregate these,
ranking states differently according to different capabilities, Waltz
insists that where states stand, and how many poles this produces in a
system, is determined by how they score when all of their capabilities
are combined.[32]

As will be apparent, Waltz identifies a broader range of capabilities
than Mearsheimer. Some of these are reasonably cast as material: size
of population and territory and resource endowment, for example.
Others are more problematic, however. Economic capability, military
strength, and political stability and competence all imply a constitutive
social element. Yet how Waltz deals with these reinforces his default
materialism. The last is easily dispensed with, as it never reappears in
any of his subsequent characterizations of different states' capabilities,
discussions of different forms of polarity, or shifts in polarity. (His
failure to see the fragility of the Soviet Union is evidence of this.)
Economic capability and military strength are more interesting,
though. Both depend, he argues, on technology and underlying scientific knowledge, the social dimensions of which are well established.
Two things should be noted, however. First, while technology and
scientific knowledge are essential to economic and military capability,
neither appears in Waltz's schema as a primary state capability; they
are enabling factors. Second, when estimating primary capabilities
Waltz relies on material indices: national GDP for economic capability,
and size of military forces and quality of weaponry for military capability. Not only is the material primary, therefore; it is a proxy for
whatever social inputs are acknowledged.

Like Mearsheimer, Waltz rejects relational conceptions of power,
where power is defined as the ability of A to get B to do what A wants.
Such conceptions equate power with control over outcomes. Yet even

---

[30] Waltz, *Theory*, p. 129.   [31] Ibid., p. 131.   [32] Ibid.

for those with the greatest relative capabilities, control over outcomes can be partial and attenuated. 'Whether A, in applying its capabilities, gains the wanted compliance of B depends on A's capabilities and strategy, on B's capabilities and strategy, and on all of these factors as they are affected by the situation on hand.'[33] If outcomes were the measure of power, power would be measurable only after the fact. And if this were the case, calculations of polarity, as mappings of relative power, would be impossible (and largely irrelevant). Many scholars, including myself, advance relational conceptions of power not just because they stress control over outcomes, but because some sources of power, like authority and legitimacy, are inherently social, in the sense that they depend on perceptions and judgements of others.[34] To the extent that Waltz considers such things, however, he treats them as epiphenomenal, as expressions of underlying capabilities. 'Whatever elements of authority emerge internationally', he writes, 'are barely once removed from the capability that provides the foundation for the appearance of those elements. Authority quickly reduces to a particular expression of capability.'[35]

A distinction is commonly drawn between classical and structural realisms, the former typified by Morgenthau's writings, the latter by the work of Waltz and Mearsheimer. A veritable industry exists probing the complexities of these strands of realist thought, mapping their principal differences and identifying their commonalities. Engaging this literature is beyond the scope of this chapter. It is sufficient to note, however, that two differences are widely highlighted. The first concerns the cause of power politics, with Morgenthau emphasizing human nature and Waltz and Mearsheimer stressing the logic of anarchy. The second concerns their contrasting scientific pretensions, with classicists interpreted as more humanistic and structuralists as more positivistic. Both differences are relevant to understanding the distinctive nature of Morgenthau's materialism.

Morgenthau defines politics as a discrete realm of human activity, differentiated from economics, law, morality, and religion. Its distinguishing feature is the will to power: 'International politics, like all

[33] Ibid., p. 191.
[34] See Christian Reus-Smit, 'International Crises of Legitimacy', *International Politics* 44.2/3 (2007), 157–174.
[35] Waltz, *Theory*, p. 88.

politics', he wrote, 'is a struggle for power'.[36] He readily acknowledges that humans (and states) pursue a rich variety of ends, but power is the essential, and thus recurrent, means. Morgenthau's goal is to develop a rational theory of international politics, based on 'objective laws that have their roots in human nature'.[37] His key move, therefore, is to attribute the will to power, which defines politics as a distinct realm, to the essential nature of humans. In contrast to Waltz and Mearsheimer, he defines power in relational terms: it 'is a psychological relation between those who exercise it and those over whom it is exercised. It gives the former control over certain actions of the latter through the impact which the former exert on the latter's minds'.[38] The will to exercise such control is inherent to human nature: 'The tendency to dominate', he argues, 'is an element of all human associations, from the family through fraternal and professional associations and local political organizations, to the state'.[39] By attributing the struggle for power to such human nature, Morgenthau asserts a quasi-material substratum to international politics.[40] The impulse to power is presented as fixed and timeless, and thus an appropriate basis on which to derive objective laws.[41] He insists, it should be noted, that human nature is pluralist, that it consists not only of the will to power: 'Real man is a composite of "economic man", "political man", "moral man", "religious man", etc.'[42] The anarchic structure of the international system brings the struggle for power to the fore, however. In domestic political orders, formal political hierarchy fosters social cohesion and constrains the exercise of violence, but it is the absence of such hierarchy that defines the international realm.[43]

Both Morgenthau and Waltz seek a rational theory of international politics; both claim to uncover objective 'laws' animating such politics; and both clothe their theories in the mantle of 'science'. Yet as many

---

[36] Hans J. Morgenthau, *Politics among Nations: The Struggle for Power and Peace*, 6th edn. (New York: McGraw Hill, 1985), p. 31.
[37] Ibid., p. 4.   [38] Ibid., p. 32.   [39] Ibid., p. 39.
[40] I term this emphasis on human nature 'quasi-material' because although Morgenthau's claims are often interpreted as 'biological' (see Donnelly, *Realism*, for example), there are unresolved debates about whether psychological impulses, however recurrent among humans, should be understood as material, in any strict sense of the word.
[41] '[T]he struggle for power', he writes, 'is universal in time and space and is an undeniable fact of experience'. Ibid., p. 38.
[42] Ibid., p. 16.   [43] Ibid., p. 52.

scholars observe, how they understand science, and what this means for the nature of their theories, is very different. Most importantly for our purposes, these differences affect the nature of Morgenthau's materialism. For Morgenthau, a rational, scientific theory should 'detect and understand the forces that determine relations among nations', a task greatly complicated by the diversity and ambiguity of international actions and events.[44] To bring order to this complexity, and bring underlying forces into focus, he introduces the concept of 'interest defined as power', which simultaneously grounds the struggle for power in human nature and enables the differentiation of political from non-political facts.[45] This ordering move is the limit of Morgenthau's 'science', though: the rest of his account of international politics is a conceptually informed description. This reflects two features of his thinking. First, as many scholars have observed, he rejected the scientism that would become ascendant with theorists such as Waltz, where the aim of theory was the generation of testable hypotheses between measurable causal variables. Second, as Williams explains, Morgenthau did stress interest defined as power, but understood power expansively, in ways not amenable to quantification.[46] 'Power', he writes, 'may comprise anything that establishes and maintains the power of man over man. Thus power covers all social relationships which serve that end, from physical violence to the most subtle psychological ties by which one mind controls another.'[47]

Like Waltz, Morgenthau seeks to identify the 'elements of national power'. Yet the limits of his scientific pretentions and his broad conception of power affect how he does this. In Waltz's schema the need to formulate a sparse conception of international structure, and to reduce variations in structure to shifts in the distribution of capabilities, led him to define capabilities in largely material terms, a tendency even more pronounced in Mearsheimer's writings. Morgenthau is free of such impulses, however, allowing him to identify both quantifiable and non-quantifiable elements of national power. The former, which include geography, natural resources, industrial capacity, population, and military preparedness, are joined by national character and morale (to which we return below), and the quality of diplomacy and

---

[44] Ibid., p. 20.   [45] Ibid., p. 5.
[46] Williams, *The Realist Tradition*, pp. 107–109.
[47] Morgenthau, *Politics among Nations*, p. 11.

government.[48] A key feature of Morgenthau's understanding of power is the stress he places on non-material sources. For example, '[t]he quality of a nation's diplomacy combines those different factors (elements of power) into an integrated whole, gives them direction and weight, and awakens them from their slumbering potentialities by giving them the breath of actual power'.[49] This does not mean, however, that material elements lack importance; to the contrary. As with all realists, Morgenthau highlights the importance of military preparedness to national power, and such preparedness is undergirded principally by geography, natural resources, and industrial capacity.[50] Added to this, Morgenthau distinguishes between sources of power that are relatively stable and those that fluctuate over time. Again, it is the material elements of power that he considers most robust, providing a stable foundation for national power.[51]

Cultural Dependencies

As this discussion shows, realists vary in the degree of their materialism – it becoming more pronounced and categorical with the structural and positivist turn – but the tendency to treat the material as primitive is a persistent if varied feature of realist thought. Yet this default materialism is routinely compromised, both implicitly and explicitly. One of the first lines of constructivist critique was to show how key realist propositions hold only in particular cultural contexts – contexts either unrecognized or unacknowledged. In addition to this, however, realists also invoke culture explicitly when seeking to address key questions, not the least being the foundations of international order. I am concerned principally with the nature of these explicit invocations, but a brief discussion of the earlier constructivist critique is merited first.

As Wendt explains, and we have already seen, materialist assumptions are especially pronounced in Waltz's theory. There is a crucial element of this theory that Wendt neglects, however: one that sets the context for the things he does address. The first feature of any political structure is its organizing principle, which determines 'the arrangement of the parts of a system'. In an international political structure', Waltz

---

[48] Ibid., pp. 127–169.   [49] Ibid., pp. 158–159.   [50] Ibid., p. 139.
[51] Ibid., p. 172.

argues, 'each [state] is the equal of all others. None is entitled to command: none is required to obey.'[52] The language Waltz uses here is instructive. He is referring to an organizing *principle* under which states are *equal* and none is *entitled* to command. Since he insists that states have unequal capabilities, he must be referring to their formal, legal equality. And since well-endowed states may actually be able to command weaker states, his denial that they are 'entitled' to do so must refer to a lack of 'right'. All of this suggests that the international structure rests on intersubjective meanings, that anarchy is an organizing *principle* in the true sense of the word.

This is the last thing Waltz wants to admit, though. His goal is to show how international structures condition relations between states, and he has little to say about how these structures arise. He is clear, however, that they are not products of design, that they, like economic markets, 'are individualist in origin, spontaneously generated, and unintended'.[53] None of this means, of course, that international structures don't rest on intersubjective meanings. As practice theorists explain, norms often emerge through doing, not design.[54] Waltz resists this as well, though. The structure of anarchy is sustained not by norms but by the socializing effects of competition among egoistic, security-seeking states. It is not at all clear, however, how such 'socialization' can generate a structure of sovereign equality and limited entitlements to command. In building his theory Waltz draws constant analogies with micro-economic theory: international structures are like markets, emerging as unintended consequences of co-acting units. We know, however, that markets are not self-sustaining. Among other things, without regulatory constraints they tend toward monopoly. As Waltz himself admits, markets are 'hedged about' by 'governmentally contrived limits': 'pure food-and-drug standards, antitrust laws, securities and exchange regulations, laws against shooting a competitor, and rules forbidding false claims in advertising'.[55] Waltz denies that international structures have such features: 'International politics is more nearly a realm in which anything goes.'[56] Yet this contradicts his definition of anarchy as a realm of equal states with no right to command one another. However imperfect, this is clearly not a

---

[52] Waltz, *Theory*, p. 88.   [53] Ibid., p. 91.
[54] See Emanuel Adler and Vincent Pouliot, 'International Practices', *International Theory*, 3.1 (2011), 1–36.
[55] Waltz, *Theory*, p. 91.   [56] Ibid.

structure in which anything goes, and it is a structure that can be sustained only by intersubjective understandings – an *organizing principle*.[57]

Wendt criticizes the materialism of IR theories from two directions: he argues that Waltz's claims about the logic of anarchy rest on unacknowledged cultural assumptions, and that rationalists misunderstand the relationship between ideas and interests. Ideas aren't just intervening variables between material interests and political outcomes; they constitute interests. Because this chapter focuses on realist materialism and the subterranean place of culture, I am concerned principally with the first of these arguments.

For Waltz, international anarchy has a logic. The absence of a central authority makes survival a primary state interest, places a premium on self-help, and drives security-seeking states to maximize their relative power, fuelling incessant struggles for power. As Wendt explains, though, Waltz's argument assumes a particular distribution of interests and configuration of knowledge. Waltz assumes that because states want to survive they are necessarily security seekers, that they want to preserve what they have, not conquer more. The survival motive makes states status quo powers, therefore.[58] But as other realists have observed, not only is it contestable that states merely want to survive;[59] even if they do, it does not mean that they are necessarily status quo security seekers. Sometimes states can survive and conquer, and sometimes conquering is considered the only way to survive. The survival motive and revisionism are quite compatible.[60] Even if the survival motive is an inevitable product of anarchy, therefore, the step from survival to security seeking requires an assumption

---

[57] It was changes in this 'principle' that John Ruggie referred to when describing the shift from medieval heteronomy to the European sovereign order. See John Gerard Ruggie, 'Continuity and Transformation in the World Polity: Toward a Neorealist Synthesis', *World Politics*, 35.2 (1983), 261–285, and 'Territoriality and Beyond: Problematizing Modernity in International Relations', *International Organization*, 47.1 (1993), 139–174.

[58] Alexander Wendt, *Social Theory of International Politics* (Cambridge: Cambridge University Press, 1999), p. 104.

[59] Mearsheimer's distinction between 'offensive' and 'defensive' realism, and his case for the former, is based very much on this uncertainty. See his *Tragedy of Great Power Politics*, p. 21.

[60] Randall Schweller examines this detail. See *Deadly Imbalances: Tripolarity and Hitler's Strategy of World Conquest* (New York: Columbia University Press, 1998).

about the distribution of interests. Furthermore, it is an assumption
of some consequence, as a world of security-seeking status quo powers
can be expected to be more peaceful and stable than a world of
revisionist powers.[61]

Wendt's point here is that the logic of anarchy is indeterminate, that
the effects of anarchy depend on the prevailing distribution of interests,
that interests are informed by actors' identities, and that identities are
shaped by intersubjective meanings: by a 'culture of anarchy'. Self-help
is not an inevitable product of anarchy; it is but 'one of various
structures of identity and interest that may exist under anarchy'.[62]
When there is no central authority, Wendt argues, identity formation
is centrally concerned with the security of the self, but understandings
of security 'differ in the extent to which and the manner in which the
self is identified cognitively with the other'.[63] The key thing is that the
nature of such identification is determined by intersubjective meanings.
Some cultures of anarchy constitute state selves that identify negatively
with each other, producing the competitive self-help system Waltz
theorizes. But other cultures of anarchy, which constitute selves that
identify positively with one another, and where 'the security of each is
perceived as the responsibility of all', don't produce self-help systems at
all.[64] One of Waltz's key theoretical propositions – that the logic of
anarchy drives self-help behaviour –stands, therefore, only where a
Hobbesian culture of anarchy prevails. Vary this culture, Wendt holds,
and states will behave differently under anarchy.

Cultural Propositions

In addition to cultural assumptions undergirding key realist claims,
and certain realist propositions standing only in particular cultural
contexts, culture also appears more explicitly in realist accounts. There
are several issues that realists struggle to avoid – or can't resist – and
in addressing these issues cultural propositions come to the fore.
Three issues stand out in this regard: the assumption of groupism,
the question of strategic choice, and the foundations of international
order. In each of these areas, realists reach for culture. What matters

[61] Wendt, *Social Theory*, p. 105.
[62] Alexander Wendt, 'Anarchy Is What States Make of It: The Social Construction
of Power Politics', *International Organization*, 46.2 (1992), 399.
[63] Ibid.   [64] Ibid., p. 400.

here, though, is that time and again culture is understood in a particular way, as a coherent system of meaning and practice: a clearly bounded, tightly integrated, and powerfully constitutive whole. On key issues, therefore, a tradition of thought known for privileging the material ends up appealing to the default conception of culture discussed in Chapter 1.

Groupism

As we saw earlier, groupism is commonly identified as a key feature of realist thought. It is assumed, Wohlforth argues, that '[p]olitics takes place within and between groups. Group solidarity is essential to domestic politics and conflict and cooperation between polities is the essence of international politics.'[65] All but one of the ten 'representative definitions of realism' summarized by Donnelly express some version of this groupism. Either states are treated as the primary unit of analysis or international relations is seen as a realm of competing 'conflict groups'.[66]

That realism is state-centric hardly needs repeating. How realists understand the state is more interesting, though. It is useful here to distinguish between two different conceptions of the state. The first treats the state as a particular kind of administrative, bureaucratic entity: one in which political authority is centralized, hierarchical, territorially bounded, and sovereign. On this view, the state is an institution not an actor: 'States do not act – governments do', as Peter Katzenstein puts it.[67] The second conception admits the institutional features of the state, but treats it as more than this, as a social or communal entity. The state remains territorially bounded and sovereign, and authority within the state may be centralized and hierarchical, but the state is in essence a people, a 'nation' in common parlance. The institutions of the state may govern society, but ultimately they are an expression of that society, the locus of sovereign authority. These contrasting understandings of the state are reflected in the definitions provided by the *Oxford Dictionary of English*, one defining it as 'a nation or territory considered as an

---

[65] Wohlforth, 'Realism', p. 133.   [66] Donnelly, *Realism*, pp. 7–8.
[67] Peter J. Katzenstein, 'International Relations Theory and the Analysis of Change', in Ernst-Otto Czempiel and James N. Rosenau (eds.), *Global Changes and Theoretical Challenges* (Lexington, MA: Lexington Books, 1989), p. 297.

organized political community under one government', the other as 'the civil government of a country'.[68]

The further one moves from the first conception of the state toward the second – from the state as an institution to a collectivity – the greater the inclination to groupism. A committed structuralist might argue that the first conception is sufficient, that state behaviour is explicable without assuming that states are social or communal groups. In a structural theory, states can be conceived minimally, and their primary interests and tendencies derived from the logic of anarchy. Yet few realists hold this line, with most advancing views of the state much closer to the second conception. This is because of the convergence of two imperatives. The first relates to the concept of the national interest, a concept ubiquitous in realist thought. While Waltz attributes a bare survival motive to states, other realists prefer the more expansive idea of the national interest: an interest that is both primary and notoriously difficult to define. Appealing to such an interest draws theorists toward the second, collectivist understanding of the state, as national interests, such as physical security and economic well-being, are more plausibly attributed to groups than institutions. The second imperative is the need to cast the national interest as singular. A state may not have one national interest, but it has one hierarchy of interests, and rational state action is the prudent pursuit of these interests. If states were imagined as fragmented social realms with multiple, conflicting conceptions of social interest, the coherence of realist theory – as a theory of interstate relations – would dissipate. Taken together, if the first imperative encourages a view of the state as a social or communal entity, the second requires this entity to be sufficiently coherent that it can express and pursue a hierarchy of national interests.

In response to these imperatives, two forms of groupism have emerged in realist thought: one societal, the other communal. The first is succinctly expressed in Robert Gilpin's classic work *War and Change in World Politics*. Gilpin adopts the first of our two conceptions of the state, defining it as an organization that provides public goods (security and welfare) in return for taxes.[69] While

---

[68] *Oxford Dictionary of English*, 3rd edn. (Oxford: Oxford University Press, 2010), p. 1741.

[69] Robert Gilpin, *War and Change in World Politics* (Cambridge: Cambridge University Press, 1981), pp. 15–16.

distinguishing conceptually between the state and society, Gilpin embeds the state deeply in social formations, processes, and cleavages. This interconnection comes to the fore when he seeks to define and explain national interests. 'Strictly speaking', he argues, 'states, as such, have no interests ... Only individuals and individuals joined together into various types of coalitions can be said to have interests.'[70] It follows that the national interest is really the interest of dominant actors within the state, actors who have emerged victorious from struggles with other social actors. 'From this perspective', Gilpin writes, 'the state may be conceived as a coalition of coalitions whose objectives and interests result from the powers and bargaining among the several coalitions composing the larger society and political elite'.[71] While agreeing that states have a hierarchy of interests, and that they seek to maximize these, Gilpin rejects the notion that there is a universal hierarchy of state interests, that national security always trumps economic welfare, for example. In reality, he argues, states seek to maximize a bundle of interests, and the nature of this bundle and how interests are optimized depends on the interests of dominant coalitions and the nature of the international environment. 'Thus it is impossible in general terms to determine what bundles of security, economic, or other objectives will satisfy states.'[72] What we see here is a societal form of groupism, in which the 'conflict group' is a collectivity of competing coalitions, and a singular national interest emerges through the rationalizing processes of competition and satisficing.

This first form of groupism evinces little cultural content – the group is a society of competing coalitions, constituted and animated little by intersubjective meanings. By contrast, the second form of groupism is culturally thick, and finds clear expression in Morgenthau's *Politics among Nations*. Unlike Gilpin, Morgenthau conceives the state as a communal entity, not just an institution. Indeed, nowhere does he define the state as a distinct concept, referring instead to the 'nation'. This is not a matter of linguistic slippage, but reflects Morgenthau's decision to cast the state as a cultural unit. Recall here how he defines the 'elements of national power'. First, he is clearly referring to the sovereign political units others call states. More importantly, unlike a more thoroughgoing materialist such as Mearsheimer, he includes among the elements of national power qualities of nations as cultural

---

[70] Ibid., p. 18.   [71] Ibid., p. 19.   [72] Ibid., p. 21.

entities, most notably, 'national character' and 'national morale'. Nations, Morgenthau argues, have distinct characters: 'certain qualities of intellect and character occur more frequently and are more highly valued in one nation than in another ... These qualities set one nation apart from others, and they show a high degree of resiliency to change.'[73] Furthermore, a nation's character has a profound effect on how it exercises power: 'for those who act for the nation in peace and war, formulate, execute, and support its policies, elect and are elected, mold public opinion, produce and consume – all bear to a greater or lesser degree the imprint of those intellectual and moral qualities that make up the national character'.[74]

Claims such as these locate Morgenthau in the milieu of cultural thinking that spanned the 1930s–1950s (not surprisingly given when he first penned *Politics among Nations*). He invokes explicitly Benedict's idea of a 'cultural pattern',[75] and his comments echo her claim (quoted in Chapter 1) that a 'culture, like an individual, is a more or less consistent pattern of thought and action. Within each culture there come into being characteristic purposes not necessarily shared by other types of society.'[76] To give such views a long pedigree, he reaches back to the middle of the nineteenth century, quoting Taylor Coleridge's thesis that 'there is an invisible spirit that breaths through a whole people, and is participated by all, though not by all alike; a spirit which gives color and character to both their virtues and vices'.[77]

We should resist the temptation, however, to see this form of groupism, any more than Gilpin's, as a thing of the past, no longer present in realist thought. To be sure, with the growing influence of rational choice theory, prominent strands of contemporary realism treat the state as a unitary actor by assumption, acknowledging internal division and contestation, but arguing that theory can proceed *as if* the state were a coherent entity with a set hierarchy of preferences.[78] Yet Gilpin's societal form of groupism lives on in the neoclassical realist scholarship that has proliferated in recent years. An excellent example is Wohlforth's argument about the end of the Cold War, in which the

---

[73] Morgenthau, *Politics among Nations*, p. 147.   [74] Ibid., p. 151.
[75] Ibid., p. 147.   [76] Benedict, *Patterns of Culture*, p. 46.
[77] Quoted in Morgenthau, *Politics among Nations*, p. 147.
[78] An excellent example is Charles Glaser's *Rational Theory of International Politics* (Princeton, NJ: Princeton University Press, 2010).

relative decline of Soviet power vis-à-vis the United States accentuates factional divisions with the Soviet Union, enabling revised understandings of the Soviet national interest.[79]

The communal form of groupism articulated by Morgenthau also finds contemporary expression, but the nature of the 'conflict group' varies. While groupism is a feature of realism, Wohlforth is clear that realism is agnostic about the nature or level of the group. [80] Historically, the group most commonly assumed by realists has been the nation-state, and this remains a key contemporary focus. But where Morgenthau treated the nation as the animating cultural substratum of the state,[81] more recent work sees the construction of coherent national identities as an international exigency. In a now classic article, Barry Posen argues that the ability of states to mobilize mass armies depends on their success in cultivating nationalism, on their ability to forge a common culture and fuel beliefs that the nation, as a cultural community, needs a militarily strong state.[82] More recently, Sambanis, Skaperdas, and Wohlforth have linked state capacity, national identification, and war fighting. The strength of the state as an institution, they argue, 'is partly endogenous to a pre-existing reservoir of commonalities among social groups in a given territory'.[83] Victory in war is a particularly potent way to build such commonalities, enabling state builders to 'fill that reservoir to induce cooperation among groups that might otherwise be in conflict, not seeing themselves as part of the

[79] William C. Wohlforth, 'Realism and the End of the Cold War', *International Security*, 19.3 (1994–1995), 112. Other examples are Thomas J. Christensen, *Useful Adversaries: Grand Strategy, Domestic Mobilization, and Sino-American Conflict, 1947–1958* (Princeton, NJ: Princeton University Press, 1996); Fareed Zakaria, *From Wealth to Power: The Unusual Origins of American's World Role* (Princeton, NJ: Princeton University Press, 1998); and Jack Snyder, *Myths of Empire: Domestic Politics and International Ambition* (Ithaca, NY: Cornell University Press, 1991).

[80] Wohlforth, 'Realism', p. 133.

[81] Although Morgenthau focused on the nation-state, he held that 'the contemporary connection between interest and the nation state is a product of history, and is therefore bound to disappear in the course of history'. Morgenthau, *Politics among Nations*, p. 12.

[82] Barry R. Posen, 'Nationalism, the Mass Army, and Military Power', *International Security*, 18.2 (1993), 85.

[83] Nicholas Sambanis, Stergios Skaperdas, and William C. Wohlforth, 'Nation-Building through War', *American Political Science Review*, 109.2 (2015), 280.

same nation'.[84] While this is presented as a rationalist augmentation of realist theory, connecting as it does individual social identification dynamics with state building and the impulse to war, it relies nonetheless on thick conceptions of cultural community. To begin with, behind their model lies an assumed distinction between states with high and low levels of national identification, and they define the latter as fragmented into contending ethnic groups. We can only assume from this that states with robust national identification are states with a degree of cultural homogeneity. Second, although Sambanis, Skarperdas, and Wohlforth hold that the national identification generated by victory in war need not be culturally thick – indeed, it needs to be 'open to any group in the country'[85] – they argue that it will be vulnerable to prior, culturally rooted identifications if it is not based on nation-wide cultural bonds.[86]

While the nation-state has been the group garnering most realist attention, civilizations have also been identified as key conflict groups. Samuel Huntington's *Clash of Civilizations* is, of course, the archetypal example. After the end of the Cold War, he argues, civilizations replaced nation-states as the primary conflict groups, with these groups imagined as coherent, deeply constitutive cultural wholes. Civilizations, in Huntington's view, 'are differentiated from each other by history, language, culture, tradition and, most important, religion. The people of different civilizations have different views on the relations between God and man, the individual and the group, the citizen and the state, parents and children, husband and wife, as well as differing views of the relative importance of rights and responsibilities, liberty and authority, and equality and hierarchy.'[87] As we shall see below, civilizations also appear in realist thought as foundations of legitimate international orders.

---

[84] Ibid., p. 280.   [85] Ibid., p. 284.

[86] In their case of the national identification generated by Prussian victory in the Franco-Prussian War, they write that 'the social identity shift produced by the war might not have been long-lived had it not been for the underlying cultural bonds tying Germans together, which in turn explained their investments in state capacity in the aftermath of victory'. Ibid., p. 292.

[87] Samuel Huntington, 'The Clash of Civilizations?', *Foreign Affairs*, 72.3 (1993), 25.

Strategic Choice

A common critique of structural realism is that it is indeterminate, that it may explain broad tendencies in international relations – the recurrence of conflict, the difficulty of cooperation, and the relative stability of different distributions of power – but it struggles to explain the rich variety of state behaviour. Waltz himself stressed this point: his was a theory of international politics, not foreign policy. Many attempts have been made to overcome this limitation. The aforementioned arguments about coalitional struggles in the definition of national interests are examples, as are attempts to draw finer grained distinctions between types of status quo and revisionist states.[88] I am interested here, however, in one particular solution: the attempt to explain variations in security behaviour with reference to differences in strategic culture.

For structural realists, security behaviour is explained by three things: the security preferences of states, their relative capabilities, and the incentives and constraints presented by the anarchic international system. One axis of variation lies in states' preferences (whether they are status quo or revisionist, for example), another in their relative capabilities (whether they are weak or powerful), and yet another in the international distribution of capabilities or spectrum of threats (depending on who you read). Within this limited range of variation, security behaviour is seen as the product of utility-maximizing choices, pursued with available sources, under prevailing environmental constraints.[89] The starting expectation of such a perspective is that states operating under similar structural constraints and opportunities will evince similar security behaviour. Variation is explained principally by where states fall on the status quo–revisionist spectrum or, failing that, with reference to compromised rationality, induced by misperceptions or organizational failure.[90]

The indeterminacy of this perspective has been widely noted, with scholars pointing to a host of inconsistent cases, including states behaving differently, and often pathologically, in the face of similar environmental challenges. For the past four decades an evolving body

---

[88] A good example is Schweller, *Deadly Imbalances*.
[89] See, for example, Bruce Bueno de Mesquita's classic work *The War Trap* (New Haven, CT: Yale University Press, 1981).
[90] Robert Jervis, *Perception and Misperception in International Politics* (Princeton, NJ: Princeton University Press, 1976).

of largely realist scholarship has employed the concept of 'strategic culture' to account for such variations. States, according to this literature, exhibit different security behaviour because they have different strategic cultures. The deep-seated norms, ingrained beliefs, routinized forms of reasoning, and established modes of decision making that characterize these cultures engender distinctive ways of thinking strategically, which in turn inform and license particular forms of strategic behaviour. This literature has evolved through several generations, and has been subject to considerable internal debate. Central to these debates has been how culture should be understood, with some scholars drawing it narrowly, others more broadly. What interests me, though, is that basic assumptions about what culture *is* are remarkably consistent across these debates: culture is a coherent system of meaning, constitutive of thought and action.

It is beyond the scope of this chapter to offer a comprehensive survey of the strategic culture literature, a literature riddled with internal debate and extending well beyond the bounds of realism.[91] The recurrence within this literature of a distinctive conception of culture is usefully illustrated, however, by the debate between Colin Gray and Iain Johnston: the work of the first fitting within the broad realist tradition, the work of the second straddling realism and constructivism.

Gray's work is emblematic of what Johnston identifies as 'first-generation' scholarship on strategic culture. In the early 1980s, as the Cold War intensified, Gray published a series of influential articles that sought to explain differences in how the United States and Soviet

---

[91] This varied literature includes among its key works Jack Snyder, *The Soviet Strategic Culture* (Santa Monica, CA: Rand Corporation, 1977); Ken Booth, *Strategy and Ethnocentrism* (New York: Holmes and Meier, 1979); Colin Gray, 'National Styles in Strategy: The American Example', *International Security*, 6.2 (1981), 21–47; Colin S. Gray, *Nuclear Strategy and National Style* (Lanham, MD: Hamilton Press,1986); Reginald C. Stuart and Dan P. Silverman, *War and American Thought* (Kent, OH: Kent State University Press, 1982); Bradley Klein, 'Hegemony and Strategic Culture: American Power Projection and Alliance Defence Politics', *Review of International Studies*, 14.2 (1988), 133–148; Elizabeth Keir, *Imagining War: French and British Military Doctrine between the* Wars (Princeton, NJ: Princeton University Press, 1999); Jeffrey Legro, *Cooperation under Fire: Anglo-German Restraint during World War II* (Ithaca, NY: Cornell University Press, 1995); and Alastair Iain Johnston, *Cultural Realism: Strategic Culture and Grand Strategy in Chinese History* (Princeton, NJ: Princeton University Press, 1995).

Union understood the strategic utility of nuclear weapons, attributing these differences to fundamentally different strategic cultures. An outspoken advocate of deterrence through nuclear war fighting doctrines, Gray bemoaned what he saw as the American inability to think beyond deterrence, to reason strategically about the use of nuclear weapons in war (a quality he saw in the Soviets). This inability, he argued, stemmed from a strategic culture rooted in American history and self-identity. He wrote:

It is hypothesized here that there is a discernible American *strategic* 'culture': that culture referring to modes of thought and action with respect to force, derives from perception of the national historical experience, aspiration for self-characterization (e.g., as an American, what am I? how should I feel, think, and behave?), and from all of the many distinctively American experiences (of geography, political philosophy, of civil culture, and 'way of life') that characterize an American citizen. The idea of American national style is derivative from the idea of American strategic culture, suggesting that there is a distinctively American way in strategic matters.[92]

Somewhat paradoxically, the peculiarities of American strategic culture produced, in Gray's view, a decidedly unstrategic strategic practice. Deep-seated American beliefs that good always triumphs, that Americans can do anything, that they're always victorious in war, and that their knowledge, management, and technology give them an unassailable edge, coupled with their long experience of continental security, provided few incentives for systematic strategic thought.[93] To the contrary, between 1960 and 1981 American strategic culture led the United States to forfeit its nuclear strategic advantage over the Soviet Union. Gray lamented that 'the defense community, at the high policymaking level, came to be profoundly disinterested in nuclear (operational) strategy. Nuclear weapons had "Utility [only] in Nonuse".'[94]

Johnston criticizes first-generation scholarship like Gray's for being unfalsifiable. A common tendency of such scholarship is to include within the definition of culture both thought and behaviour: note Gray's inclusion of both 'modes of thought and action with respect to force'.[95] This leads, Johnston argues, to very simplistic claims about the effects of strategic culture, where culture has to shape behaviour

[92] Gray, 'National Styles', p. 22.   [93] Ibid., pp. 26–30.   [94] Ibid., p. 37.
[95] Ibid., p. 22.

because behaviour is integral to culture. 'How', Johnston asks, 'does one evaluate a strategic culture where thought and action seem inconsistent? Alternatively, is it always the case that one type of behaviour reveals one set of distinctive patterns of strategic thinking?'[96] Gray's response to this critique is interesting. While applauding Johnston's calls for more rigorous conceptions of strategic culture, he rejects outright attempts to isolate behaviour from culture. His inclusion of action within the definition of culture was not sloppy thinking; it reflected a deeper view about causality, a view that is the real divide between he and Johnston. Where the latter treats culture as something external to behaviour, leaving open the relationship between the two, Gray wants to see culture as constituted significantly by behaviour. More specifically, strategic culture, he holds, is 'in good measure socially constructed by both people and institutions, which proceed to behave to some degree culturally'.[97] Where Johnston wants to separate culture and behaviour as independent and dependent variables, therefore, Gray denies this very possibility: 'The problem is that we cannot understand strategic behaviour by that method, be it ever so rigorous. Strategic culture is not only "out there", also it is within us; we, our institutions, and our behaviour, are the context.'[98]

The relative merits of these views are not my principal concern here. What interests me is that despite these differences, Gray's and Johnston's conceptions of culture bear fundamental similarities. Putting aside the question of whether behaviour should be included in the definition, both authors see culture as a coherent system of meaning: a bounded, integrated whole. In his reply to Johnston, Gray provides this elaboration of how he understands culture: 'Culture or cultures comprises the persisting (though not eternal) socially transmitted ideas, attitudes, traditions, habits of mind, and preferred methods of operation that are more or less specific to a particular geographically based security community that has had a necessarily unique historical experience.'[99] In a very similar vein, Johnston says that 'culture consists of shared decision rules, recipes, standard operating procedures, and decision routines that impose a degree of order on individual and group conceptions of their relationship to their environment, be it

---

[96] Johnston, *Cultural Realism*, p. 8.
[97] Colin S. Gray, 'Strategic Culture as Context: The First Generation Strikes Back', *Review of International Studies*, 25.1 (1999), 50.
[98] Ibid., p. 53.   [99] Ibid., p. 51.

social, organizational, or political'.[100] And when defining strategic culture, more specifically, he borrows directly from Geertz's conception of religion as a social system (discussed in Chapter 1). Strategic culture, he argues, 'is an integrated system of symbols ... that acts to establish pervasive and long-lasting grand strategic preferences by formulating concepts of the role and efficacy of military force in interstate political affairs, and by clothing these conceptions with such an aura of factuality that the strategic preferences seem uniquely realistic and efficacious'.[101]

Both work, therefore, with very similar conceptions of culture: the default conception to which IR scholars routinely return. Even their differences over how culture and behaviour should be conceived may amount to less than first appears. Gray insists that behaviour is cultural, and thus the two cannot be isolated as distinct variables. Johnston demands that culture and behaviour be separated; otherwise, it is impossible to determine when culture is, or is not, affecting behaviour. In reality, though, both assume that culture strongly influences behaviour, regardless of whether the two are separated conceptually and analytically. As we have seen, Gray holds that strategic culture produces a distinctive national 'way in strategic matters'.[102] Johnston specifies more clearly the connections between culture and behaviour, but the connections remain strong. The values inherent to strategic culture do two things, he argues: they 'provide a limited set of strategic options, but then rank these as well'.[103] The assumption is that although culture and behaviour are distinct, by placing cognitive limits on strategic choice, the former has powerful effects over the latter. Despite their methodological differences, therefore, Gray and Johnston both express two key elements of the default conception of culture: that it is a coherent system of meaning, and that it is powerfully constitutive.

International Order

As we shall see in Chapter 6, IR scholars use the term 'international order' in two ways: as a synonym for stability and to describe a particular arrangement of interstate relations (the early modern

---

[100] Johnston, *Cultural Realism*, p. 35.   [101] Ibid., p. 36.
[102] Gray, 'National Styles', p. 22.   [103] Johnston, *Cultural Realism*, p. 36.

European international order, for example). When used in the latter sense, some scholars see international order as an unintended consequence of competition, while others treat it as an institution, as an arrangement that serves certain ends, upheld by rules, norms, and practices.[104] Not surprisingly, realists often hold the first of these views. Mearsheimer, for example, denies emphatically that orders emerge from purposeful cooperation among states, and insists that they always reflect the interests of the dominant, rising or falling with shifts in the balance of power. Yet whenever he refers to international order, it is as a particular configuration of interstate relations, not a synonym for stability. He talks about more or less stable orders, and about how states seek to preserve or undermine existing orders.[105] Not all realists accept such a spare conception of international order, however. Gilpin prefers the term 'international system', but is referring to the essentially the same thing. A system consists, he writes, of 'diverse entities', engaged in 'regular interaction', where there 'is some "form of control" that regulates behaviour and may range from informal rules of the system to formal institutions'.[106]

My claim here is that when realists conceive international order as an institution, they venture onto the cultural terrain, a tendency they share with constructivists and liberals. Recent writings by Henry Kissinger and Charles Kupchan on the future of the modern international order illustrate this. Kissinger's *World Order* renews arguments from his classic study of the post-Napoleonic European Order, *A World Restored*. A stable international order, he argued there, rests on two things: 'a generally accepted legitimacy' and an equilibrium of power. Both were crucial. Equilibrium was needed to sustain order when norms of legitimacy lost purchase, and strong norms were needed, as states that identified their security with revolutionary change would seek to overturn the prevailing balance of power.[107] Written more than half a century later, and concerned primarily with contemporary

---

[104] This latter view is articulated most famously by Hedley Bull, but as explained in Chapter 6, is now accepted by scholars from diverse theoretical perspectives. See Hedley Bull, *The Anarchical Society: A Study of Order in World Politics* (New York: Columbia University Press, 1977).

[105] Mearsheimer, *Tragedy of Great Power Politics*, pp. 48–51.

[106] Gilpin, *War and Change*, p. 26.

[107] Henry Kissinger, *A World Restored: Metternich, Castlereagh and the Problems of Peace, 1812–1822* (Boston: Houghton Mifflin, 1057), pp. 1–6, 144–147, 172–173.

challenges, *World Order* identifies the same two factors. International order, Kissinger writes, depends on 'a set of commonly accepted rules that define the limits of permissible action and a balance of power that enforces restraint when the rules break down, preventing one unit from subjugating all others'.[108]

The cultural aspects of Kissinger's thought come to the fore when we ask what enables the emergence and maintenance of 'a generally accepted legitimacy'. *A World Restored* focused on the minutiae of the diplomatic negotiations that surrounded the Congress of Vienna, as Kissinger took the broader European cultural context as given. In *World Order*, by contrast, culture takes centre stage. The modern international order that came to encompass the globe is a product of Western power and culture, Kissinger holds. Weaving a history now widely discredited outside IR, he argues that Westphalian negotiators, exhausted by the religious and political turmoil of the Thirty Years' War (1618–1648), constructed an order of sovereign states that 'shaped and prefigured the modern sensibility: it reserved judgement on the absolute in favour of the practical and ecumenical: it sought to distill order from multiplicity and restraint'.[109] Between the seventeenth and twentieth centuries this 'system spread around the world as the framework for a state-based international order spanning multiple civilizations and regions because, as European nations expanded, they carried the blueprint of their international order with them'.[110] Western power was critical in this process, but it was also a distinctly Western cultural process. The 'Westphalian peace represented a judgement of reality ... as the temporal ordering concept over the demands of religion'.[111] Other civilizations could not have reached this solution, Kissinger believes. Not only were the challenges of the Reformation unique, other civilizations understood reality differently: they 'conceived it as internal to observer, defined by psychological, philosophical, and religious convictions'.[112] The pragmatism of Westphalia was thus culturally contingent, dependent on a prior set of civilizational understandings about the nature and malleability of reality.

This understanding of the politico-cultural roots of the modern international order informs Kissinger's deeply pessimistic conclusions

---

[108] Henry Kissinger, *World Order: Reflections on the Character of Nations and the Course of History* (London: Allen Lane, 2014), p. 9.
[109] Ibid, pp. 3–4.　　[110] Ibid., p. 6.　　[111] Ibid., p. 363.　　[112] Ibid., p. 363.

about the contemporary predicament. 'A reconstruction of the international order is the ultimate challenge to statesmanship in our time',
he writes, as '[o]ur time, facing even graver prospects [than at West-
phalia], needs to act on its necessities before it is engulfed by them'.[113]
Why, though, are the prospects 'graver' than at Westphalia? The
answer lies in the erosion of both pillars of international order: an
equilibrium of power and an accepted principle of legitimacy. Legitimacy is easier to construct, he argues, 'the smaller the geographic area
to which it applies and the more coherent the cultural convictions
within it'.[114] But how, in today's global system, '[c]an regions with
such diverse cultures, histories, and traditional theories of order vindi-
cate the legitimacy of any common system?'[115] The implications of
this cultural fragmentation are accentuated by the diffusion of power
away from the West. Western power promoted and upheld the order's
core principles, Kissinger holds, but the rise of non-Western centres of
power is likely to fuel disorder. 'An array of entities unrelated to each
other by history or values (except at arm's length), and defining themselves essentially by the limit of their capabilities, is likely to generate
conflict, not order.'[116]

Although written from an avowedly 'liberal realist' position, Kupchan's argument in *No One's World* bears much in common with
Kissinger's. The modern international order is again presented as an
accomplishment of Western power and values. Like Kissinger, Kupchan treats the Reformation and the Thirty Years' War as a politico-
cultural trial by fire, which produced, through the Westphalian settlement, a European order of sovereign states characterized by religious
tolerance and political pluralism.[117] The resulting decentralized order,
combined with the relative weakening of established institutions,
fostered an economic dynamism that gave Europeans the edge over
other civilizations, fuelling, among other things, successive ways of
imperial expansion.[118] After the Second World War, with Europe's
imperial powers exhausted, the United States took up leadership of the
globalizing Western order. Single-handedly, in Kupchan's account,
the United States transformed the world of empires into a global
system of sovereign states: 'Washington insisted on the dismantlement

[113] Ibid., pp. 371, 373.   [114] Ibid., 9.   [115] Ibid., 8.   [116] Ibid., pp. 9–10.
[117] Charles A. Kupchan, *No One's World: The West, the Rising Rest, and the
Coming Global Turn* (New York: Oxford University Press, 2012), p. 32.
[118] Ibid., pp. 46–73.

of empire', he writes, 'and Europe's great powers were in no position to resist'.[119] The United States also promoted the ever-denser institutionalization of the order, embedding Western economic and political interests in a complex architecture of multilateral institutions. And to sustain this order, Washington sought to reconstitute domestic political orders, promoting the spread of democracy, most notably in its former enemies, Japan and Germany.[120] In sum, the 'concurrent ascent of the Atlantic democracies ... gave rise to a distinctive Western approach to managing global affairs. The West sought to universalize the values and institutions that its constituent members embrace at home; for reasons of both interest and principle, Europe and North America worked hard to export democracy, secular nationalism, and capitalism. The global spread of the West's founding ideas marked the first time that a single conception of order took hold in most quarters of the world.'[121]

This order now faces profound challenges, Kupchan argues. Again, shifts in the balance of power are linked to cultural and ideological fragmentation. 'The spread of this order has in large part been a product of the West's material dominance, not the universal appeal of its ideas ... But now the West's material primacy is waning, its ideological dominance is very much in question.'[122] Liberal commentators and policymakers wrongly assume, Kupchan contends, that as the West declines the rest of the world will Westernize, taking on liberal democracy, industrial capitalism, and secular nationalism. Domestic convergence will thus save the modern international order. Yet this is not what is happening, Kupchan argues. '[M]ost rising powers – China, India, Turkey, and Brazil among them – are not tracking the development path followed by the West. They have different cultural and socioeconomic foundations, which give rise to their own domestic orders and ideological orientations.'[123] What we are seeing is an emerging world of multiple modernities, in which fundamental differences greatly complicate the maintenance of order. 'The bottom line', Kupchan holds, 'is that states around the world are on very different political trajectories. The divergence is a function of profound variation on many dimensions, including political culture, path of socioeconomic development, and religion. Even among states

---

[119] Ibid., p. 71.   [120] Ibid., pp. 71–72.   [121] Ibid., pp. 6–7.   [122] Ibid., p. 7.
[123] Ibid., p. 7.

that share a commitment to liberal democracy, competing interests
and jockeying for position and status will stand in the way of international consensus.'[124]

Conclusion

Wendt notes correctly that the proposition that power relations characterize international relations 'cannot be a *uniquely* realist claim', as
many theories of IR talk about power: 'Neoliberals think power is
important, Marxists think power is important, postmodernists even
think it is everywhere.'[125] The same can be said for culture. Constructivists, postcolonial scholars, and poststructuralists all claim special
insights into culture, but as this chapter shows, even realists venture
onto the cultural terrain. This is despite the default materialism that
characterizes the realist tradition. When pushed on what drives international relations, realists generally reach (metaphorically) for guns or
money, asking about other factors only later. The material is primitive
in realist thought, evident most readily in attempts to define the elements of national power or count poles. This does not mean, however,
that realist thought is purely materialist: non-material factors appear as
intervening variables between power and outcomes, and in less positivistic accounts, as elements of power. The central argument of this
chapter, however, is that culture, very specifically, plays an important
role in realist arguments. Implicitly, key realist claims depend on
unrecognized or unacknowledged cultural foundations, like Waltz's
claim that the organizing principle of anarchy holds that states are
equal with none entitled to command. More importantly for our
purposes, realists rely on explicit cultural propositions when addressing certain questions, such as the nature of groups, strategic choice,
and the foundations of international order.

   As noted above, my purpose has not been to criticize realists for
making cultural assumptions. Rather, I have sought to excavate the
understanding of culture at work when they do. Chapter 1 argued that
when IR scholars refer to culture, one understanding recurs time and
again. In this default conception, cultures are treated as coherent
entities, deeply constitutive in effect, a conception rooted in 1930s to
1950s anthropology and sociology. Curiously, it is this conception we

---

[124] Ibid., p. 145.   [125] Wendt, *Social Theory*, p. 97.

have seen in realist discussions of nations, strategic cultures, and civilizations. A supposed trademark of realist thought is sensitivity to the hidden workings of politics, but this sensitivity is dulled when realists turn to culture. Politics is something that occurs between cultural units, be they ethnic groups, nations, or civilizations. The vigorous cultural politics needed to construct and sustain such units gets little attention. And when it is addressed, in arguments about nation building and war, states with strong national identification have robust, preexisting cultural bonds, and states with weak identification are fragmented by competing ethnic groups. A distinguishing feature of realism, Morgenthau argued, is the ability to distinguish truth from idolatry: to know when nations seek 'to clothe their own particular aspirations and actions in the moral purposes of the universe'.[126] Yet this critical sensibility is missing when he came to understand nations themselves, treating them as unproblematic cultural wholes with distinctive characters, a tendency also apparent in the realist literature on strategic culture and the relationship between Western civilization and the modern international order.

---

[126] Morgenthau, *Politics among Nations*, p. 13.

3 | The Culture of International Society

Nowhere does the relationship between culture and international order receive more sustained attention than in the writings of the English School. Indeed, fathoming this relationship constitutes a core, structuring theme in the School's evolving contributions to international theory and history. That this should be the case is hardly surprising, as the English School, in its foundational era, was a child of the end of Empire. Martin Wight's formative work was on colonial constitutions, Adam Watson served a term as head of the African Department of the British Foreign Office, and in the 1970s Hedley Bull took a road to Damascus-like sabbatical in India, deeply influencing his thoughts on 'the revolt against the West'. For each of these scholars, the fate of international society in a postcolonial, multicultural world was more than an academic curiosity; it was among the most important questions facing contemporary world politics.

Yet English School writings on culture and international order are Janus-faced, evincing two distinct positions. The first, which I term 'culturalist', is most pronounced in Wight's writings. In a view emblematic of the default conception of culture discussed in Chapter 1, Wight held that international societies emerge only where there is 'a degree of cultural unity',[1] and feared that cultural diversity undermined order. The second position, commonly termed 'pluralist', conceives international society as a practical association, the cardinal norms of which enable states with different purposes and cultural complexions to coexist and cooperate. From this standpoint, functional imperatives sustain international society and diversity is the norm. The most categorical proponent of this position is Robert Jackson, a belated convert to the English School. Both the culturalist and pluralist positions find expression in Bull's writings, reflecting his

---

[1] Martin Wight, *Systems of States* (Leicester: University of Leicester Press, 1977), p. 33.

complex intellectual debts, most famously to Wight but also to the legal positivist H. L. A. Hart and realist philosopher John Anderson.

These contrasting positions on culture and order, and the internal debate they fuel, are not just another of the School's distinguishing features, sitting side by side with the concept of international society, meditations on order and justice, and a classical approach to the study of international relations. Rather, these positions undergird how the English School understands and debates some of its trademark problematics. They affect how different thinkers understand the relationship between international systems and societies, for example, as well as the tension between order and justice. They have also had a profound effect on how the English School has narrated the history of modern international society, resulting in two distinct, even contradictory, narratives. The culturalist position informs a deeply pessimistic narrative of decline; the pluralist, a more optimistic tale of sovereign equality and the accommodation of difference.

Leaving aside the question of how productive these contrasting positions have been in conditioning English School thought and debate, on their own terms, as understandings of culture and international order, both are deeply problematic. Wight's argument about the civilizational foundations of the modern international order, and his resulting anxiety about a postcolonial order that had 'outrun cultural and moral community',[2] is a quintessential example of the now discredited default conception of culture. Moreover, his assertion that orders emerge only in unified cultural contexts is belied by the mounting body of historical research that shows precisely the opposite: international orders have usually emerged in heterogeneous contexts, and governing diversity has been key imperative of order building. The pluralist position lacks Wight's anxieties about culture, but ultimately fares no better. Theoretically, it falsely assumes that international society as a practical association can be sustained by functional imperatives alone, ignoring the politics of recognition that attends any membership grouping, a politics inextricably connected with issues of culture. Historically, it presents pre-Westphalian Europe as riven by religious conflict, and international society after Westphalia as liberated from cultural politics by the ingenious institution of sovereignty. Yet this seriously misrepresents the history of globalizing international

---

[2] Ibid., p. 34.

society over the past three centuries. What was the notorious nineteenth-century standard of civilization if not cultural politics – politics that sought to define the very boundaries of international society?

This chapter details the English School's perspective(s) on culture and international order. I begin by clarifying three key concepts that recur in English School writings, and that will feature prominently as the chapter unfolds: international society, international system, and international order. I then, in the second section, unpack the culturalist and pluralist positions, arguing that these emerge as contrasting answers to two sets of questions: What are the foundations of international society, and what sustains it over time? How far does international society extend, and how does it relate the underlying international system? In the third section, I explore the contrasting historical narratives that accompany the culturalist and pluralist positions, highlighting tensions between these narratives and the School's much-mooted historical sensibility. The fourth section examines recent efforts to extend the boundaries of English School thinking, especially on questions of culture and order. The conclusion reflects, somewhat sceptically, on claims that the English School evinces a critical, interpretive approach to the study of culture in world politics.

Three Concepts

The contours of the English School have been surveyed many times, and I make no attempt to cover this terrain again.[3] There are, however, three concepts that reappear in the following discussion, and thus merit clarification. The first is that of an *international system*. Wight moved back and forth between several different terms, including 'states system', 'international society', and 'international community', sometimes referring to the same thing, at other times to something different.

---

[3] The most important book-length treatments are Barry Buzan, *An Introduction to the English School of International Relations: The Societal Approach* (Cambridge: Polity Press, 2014); Barry Buzan, *From International to World Society: English School Theory and the Social Structure of Globalisation* (Cambridge: Cambridge University Press, 2004); Tim Dunne, *Inventing International Society: A History of the English School* (Basingstoke: Macmillan, 1998); and Andrew Linklater and Hidemi Suganami, *The English School of International Relations* (Cambridge: Cambridge University Press, 2006).

It was Bull who gave the concept a distinctive and settled meaning for the English School, influenced very much by systems theorizing in the United States, especially the work of Morton Kaplan.[4] An international system, Bull argues, 'is formed when two or more states have sufficient contact between them, and have sufficient impact on one another's decisions, to cause them to behave – at least in some measure – as parts of a whole'.[5] The key feature of this conception is its unsocial character. International systems are imagined as interactional realms, lacking any appreciable social content. As Barry Buzan observes, '[s]ystem here represents the physical mode of interaction typical of the mechanistic, realist-style analyses of the balance of power as an automatic process rooted in the relative material capabilities of states'.[6]

It is against this idea of an international system that the signature English School concept of *international society* is cast. As the term suggests, this conception of the international is distinguished by its social content. In his early writings Wight used the term 'states system', only later adopting 'international society'. His conception of a states system, however, includes most of the ingredients that Bull and others wove subsequently into the concept of international society. A states system is not just a group of interacting states, but one characterized by common interests and various 'kinds of communication or intercourse'.[7] Moreover, and we discuss below, Wight stressed the civilizational ties binding a system together, quoting approvingly A. H. L. Heeren's characterization of the European states system as a 'union of several contiguous states, resembling each other in manners, religion, and degree of social improvement'.[8] Again, it was Bull who sifted these and other ideas, refining them into the definition of international society most commonly associated with the English School. An international society, he writes, 'exists when a group of states, conscious of certain common interests and common values, form a society in the sense that they conceive themselves to be bound by a common set of rules in their relations with one another, and share in the working of common institutions'.[9] Unlike Wight, Bull stressed the functional

---

[4] Morton Kaplan, *System and Process in International Politics* (New York: Wiley, 1957).
[5] Bull, *Anarchical Society*, p. 10.
[6] Buzan, *From International to World Society*, p. 99.
[7] Wight, *Systems of States*, p. 22.   [8] Ibid.   [9] Bull, *Anarchical Society*, p. 13.

imperatives driving the development of society among states, but as
we shall see, he too stressed the importance of common culture (also
quoting Heeren with approval).

We saw in Chapter 2 how IR scholars use the term *international
order* in two ways: as a synonym for stability and in referring to a
pattern of interstate relations. It is Bull who provides the classic definition of the latter. 'By international order', he writes, 'I mean a pattern
of activity that sustains the elementary or primary goals of the society
of states, or international society'.[10] Two things should be noted about
this definition. First, it refers to a purposive pattern: an arrangement
that serves certain ends. Like the order of books on a library shelf,
international order is reasoned, not random. Second, international
order and international society are mutually dependent. On the one
hand, Bull's definition of order presupposes the existence of society: the
former serves the goals of the latter. On the other hand, Bull is clear
that the rules and institutions of international society are what produce
and maintain international order. While acknowledging that there are
'contingent facts' (such as power balancing) that can contribute to
order even in an international system, he holds that in an international
society 'order is the consequence not merely of contingent facts such as
this, but of a sense of common interests in the elementary goals of
social life; rules prescribing behaviour that sustains these goals; and
institutions that help to make these rules effective'.[11]

Before proceeding, it is important to note that in Bull's writings, and
much of the English School theorizing that has followed, these three
concepts sit within a series of dichotomies. International system is
contrasted with the concept of a 'world political system'. If the former
is the interactional realm between sovereign states, the latter is 'the
world-wide network of interaction that embraces not only states but
also other political actors, both "above" and "below" it'.[12] Similarly,
Bull contrasts international society with the concept of 'world society'.
Where the first adds sociality to the idea of an international system, the
second does so with the world political system. 'By world society', he
writes, 'we understand not merely a degree of interaction linking all
parts of the human community to one another, but a sense of common
interest and common values, on the basis of which common rules
and institutions may be built. The concept of world society, in this

---

[10] Ibid., p. 8.   [11] Ibid., p. 65.   [12] Ibid., p. 276.

sense, stands to the totality of global social interaction as our concept of international society stands to the concept of the international system.'[13] Last, Bull contrasts the concept of international order with that of world order, by which he means 'those patterns or dispositions that sustain the elementary or primary goals of social life among mankind as a whole'.[14] The underlying realism in Bull's thought is evident in his consistent privileging in each of these dichotomies of the 'international' over the 'world'. While he readily acknowledges that the 'states system has always been part of a wider system of interaction',[15] he assumes that international society constitutes the political architecture of this world political system. This reflects his deep scepticism about the possibility of world society.

The Culturalist and Pluralist Positions

It is possible to give an account of English School theory without ever mentioning culture; indeed, this is the account most undergraduates get. States can form more than systems; they can form societies. Sharing certain common interests (the 'elementary goals of social life'), states agree on a set of basic rules that enable them to coexist and cooperate (sovereign equality, non-intervention, self-determination, etc.), and they maintain a framework of basic institutions to uphold these rules (diplomacy, international law, management by the great powers, the balance of power, and, more controversially, war). Questions of culture surface, however, whenever English School theorists address two sets of questions. The first concern the foundations of international society, and what sustains it over time. The second concern its extension: Does international society extend as far as the international system? The world's states might be connected through complex webs of interaction, but does international society encompass all of humanity?[16]

As noted in the introduction to this chapter, the English School has no single answer to these questions. Rather, it constitutes a bounded field of debate, circling around two distinct positions. For culturalists, international society depends on an underlying common culture, and

---

[13] Ibid., p. 279.   [14] Ibid., p. 20.   [15] Ibid., p. 278.
[16] On the centrality of these questions to the English School, see Hurrell, *On Global Order*, p. 40.

extends only so far as the values and practices of that culture. For pluralists, international society is driven by functional imperatives and sustained by practical institutions. It includes all states animated by these imperatives and committed to these institutions, regardless of their cultural complexion. In the following discussion, I treat Wight as emblematic of the culturalist position, Jackson of the pluralist, and Bull as expressing elements of both. Two things should be noted, though. First, the two positions are ideal types, and their expressions in the writings of particular authors are complex and variegated. Second, while Wight and Jackson are indicative of the two positions, with Bull pulled in both directions, this is not how their thinking emerged historically. Wight's writings were catalytic, inspiring much of Bull's thought. Bull had other intellectual inspirations, though, and these seeded the pluralist dimensions of his work. Jackson is a relative latecomer to these debates, distilling elements of earlier thought into a more categorical pluralism. The following discussion reflects this evolution, addressing, in turn, Wight, Bull, and then Jackson.

Martin Wight

Elsewhere I argue that Wight's oft-cited claim that 'a states-system will not come into being without a degree of cultural unity among its members'[17] and his related fear that modern international society had 'outrun cultural and moral community'[18] provide a classic statement of a culturalist perspective on international order: order emerges in unitary cultural contexts, and diversity is corrosive of order.[19] This poses a series of questions, though. What did Wight mean by culture? What degree of cultural unity was necessary to sustain international society? What, precisely, were the cultural foundations of European international society? And how were these eroding in the second half of the twentieth century?

The cultural unit of importance for Wight was civilization (not the nation, as was the case for Morgenthau). Immediately after asserting that states systems emerge only in unitary cultural contexts, he singled out three paradigmatic cases (the Greek, the Western, and the Chinese),

[17] Wight, *Systems of States*, p. 33.   [18] Ibid.
[19] Christian Reus-Smit, 'Cultural Diversity and International Order', *International Organization*, 71.4 (2017), 851–885.

claiming that 'each arose in a single culture', by which he means civilization.[20] The key to understanding this connection between states systems and civilizations is Wight's view on society beyond the state. As Ian Hall explains in his definitive study, Wight thought society was at its thickest within the state, but also saw social bonds extending to the limits of civilization. Importantly, in the European case, Wight thought that the society of Western Christendom preceded the emergence of sovereign states, thus providing the cultural foundations for the development of the European states system, or international society.[21] This is clearly apparent in his characterization of modern international society as 'the habitual intercourse of independent communities, beginning in the Christendom of Western Europe and gradually extending throughout the world'.[22] As we shall see, Wight lamented that as the states system expanded and secularized, becoming doubly dislocated from its roots in Western Christendom, it became ever more fragile.

If civilization provides the necessary cultural conditions for international society to emerge, what degree of cultural unity is required?[23] Does it entail, Wight himself asked, 'a common morality and a common code, leading to agreed rules about warfare, hostages, diplomatic immunity, the right of asylum, and so on', or does it need deeper religious or ideological beliefs?[24] Wight was decidedly unclear about this, but his writings suggest some combination. The cultural foundations provided by a civilization have to be sufficiently thick, it seems, to do three things. First, they have to engender a strong sense of shared identification: a feeling of we-ness. All states systems, Wight argued, have displayed insider/outsider mentalities: 'hence the designation of those outside the states system as "barbarians".'[25] Second, the culture underlying a states system has to generate shared understandings of

---

[20] Wight, *Systems of States*, p. 33.
[21] Ian Hall, *The International Thought of Martin Wight* (Basingstoke: Palgrave, 2006), p. 113.
[22] Martin Wight, 'Western Values in International Relations', in Herbert Butterfield and Martin Wight (eds.), *Diplomatic Investigations: Essays in the Theory of International Politics* (London: George Allen and Unwin, 1966), p. 96.
[23] The discussion here draws on interpretations rehearsed in Christian Reus-Smit, 'International Law and the Mediation of Culture', *Ethics and International Affairs*, 28.1 (2014), 65–82.
[24] Wight, *Systems of States*, p. 34.   [25] Ibid.

political legitimacy. In the European case, for example, dynastic rule was once the norm, but was later replaced by the concept of popular sovereignty. For Wight, such understandings 'mark the region of approximation between international and domestic politics. They are the principles that prevail (or are at least proclaimed) *within* the majority of states that form international society, as well as in the relations between them.'[26] Finally, the civilizational culture undergirding a states system has to express a distinctive kind of institutional rationality: a set of intersubjective understandings about appropriate institutional forms, especially law. This belief that interstate institutions express underlying cultural beliefs is evident in Wight's account of why the ancient Greeks never developed the institution of international law: '[T]hey did not have the enormous inheritance of legal codes, legal thinking, and legal practice which modern Europe derived from the Civilians and the Canonists, out of which the rules of nascent international society were educed'.[27]

Wight's discussion of the specific effects of Western civilization on European international society focuses on two different levels. He identified, first, a distinctive set of 'Western values' that shaped how Europeans approached international relations. He readily admitted that 'Western men are perhaps more various in their range of beliefs than the men of any other culture', and that '[a]t best, Western values are the highest common factor of the range of beliefs by which Western men live'.[28] He insisted, however, that there was 'a certain coherent pattern of ideas' that informed, structured, and licensed European practices.[29] The defining feature of these ideas, Wight argued, was their moderate and prudential quality, their status as a '*via media*' or '*juste milieu* between definable extremes'.[30] This value orientation engendered a particular approach toward international society, one that denies realist scepticism as much as revolutionist idealism. It 'does not see international society as ready to supersede domestic society; but it notes that international society actually exercises restraints upon its members'.[31] International society, on this view, 'exists and survives by virtue of some core common standards and common custom', depends on the judicious maintenance of a balance of power, and has, as a distinctive kind of society, a 'right of self-defence'.[32] This orientation

---

[26] Ibid., p. 153.   [27] Ibid., pp. 51–52.   [28] Wight, 'Western Values', p. 89.
[29] Ibid., p. 90.   [30] Ibid., p. 91.   [31] Ibid., p. 95.   [32] Ibid., p. 103.

toward international society, Wight held, was an expression of Western values rooted in a distinctive civilization. 'The golden mean', he wrote, 'can be an overcautious and ignoble principle as a guide to action, but it may also be an index to the accumulated experience of a civilization which has valued disciplined scepticism and canonized prudence as a political virtue'.[33]

In addition to these Western values, Wight addressed a second, arguably deeper, level of civilizational influence: the role of natural law in the constitution of international society. 'The most essential evidence for the existence of international society', he argued, 'is the existence of international law. Every society has law, which is the system of rules laying down the rights and duties of its members.'[34] It is common today to see international law as a product of international society, to imagine states with common interests existing prior to their construction of the law. This was not Wight's position, however. Following Suarez, Grotius, and Locke, Wight held that prior to all political society, humans were bound by a law of nature, accessible to them through the exercise of right reason.[35] The creation of political society produces new municipal laws, but these do not extinguish natural law or its attendant obligations; to the contrary, natural law provides a deep moral foundation for such laws. All of this applied equally, in Wight's thinking, to international society as much as domestic society.[36] States do institute positive international law, codifying a host of rules and regulations in contractual treaties and conventions. But these coexist with natural law, which informs their precepts and undergirds their obligations. Nowhere is this clearer than in his discussion of the most fundamental of all international legal obligations: the sanctity of promises, *pacta sunt servanda*. 'Utilitarian reasons may be adduced as to the sources of authority for this principle', Wight argues, 'but the oldest and profoundest answer is that the observance of agreements represents an ethical norm: it

---

[33] Ibid., p. 91.
[34] Martin Wight, *Power Politics*, 2nd edn. (Harmondsworth: Penguin, 1986), p. 107.
[35] Martin Wight, *International Theory: The Three Traditions* (New York: Holmes and Meier, 1992), p. 234.
[36] For an excellent examination of natural law in Wight's thinking, see William Bain, 'Rival Traditions of Natural Law: Martin Wight and the Theory of International Society', *International History Review*, 36.5 (2014), 943–960.

conforms to an inherent standard of justice'.[37] Although in principle all humans have the reason required to access natural law, Wight saw belief in the existence of such law as a quality of Western Christian civilization, albeit one rapidly eroding. The essence of natural law is the natural unity of humankind, but other civilizations had imagined such unity only in political terms. 'It seems to be the West', Wight wrote, 'that originated the doctrine that mankind is a natural unity and not simply an imperial unity: that men form a community by virtue of their human character and not simply by virtue of submission to a single ruler'.[38]

As noted above, Wight worried that modern international society had 'outrun cultural and moral community'.[39] Like other founders of the English School, he feared that decolonization was bringing a host of non-Western states into the international system, states that lacked the civilizational values that had sustained the European society of states. Wight was no supporter of colonialism: his early writings were highly critical of the violence and exploitation of imperial rule.[40] He worried, however, that postcolonial states had no attachment to Western values. More than this, he criticized their revolutionary engagement with international society, their resentment of Western power and civilization. In an extraordinary comparison, he wrote that the 'Bandung powers and the Axis powers are united in history through a common resentment of Western civilization; and by a familiar and elementary psychological mechanism, the resentment is combined with a passionate desire to imitate'.[41] This dilution born of expansion was preceded and compounded, Wight believed, by the internal erosion of Western international society. Apostasy, the renunciation of religious belief, was replacing Christianity with secularism, robbing natural law of its theological foundations. This had two effects, both corrosive of international society: it freed power politics of whatever moral

---

[37] Wight, *International Theory*, p. 238.

[38] Martin Wight, 'The Disunity of Mankind', *Millennium: Journal of International Studies*, 44.1 (2015), 129.

[39] Wight, *Systems of States*, p. 34.

[40] Ian Hall, 'Martin Wight, Western Values, and the Whig Tradition of International Thought', *International History Review*, 36.5 (2014), 966.

[41] Quoted in Hall, *International Thought of Martin Wight*, p. 129. For a critique of Wight's position on Bandung, see Richard Devetak, Tim Dunne, and Ririn Tri Nurhayati, 'Bandung 60 Years On: Revolt and Resilience in International Society', *Australian Journal of International Affairs*, 70.4 (2016), 358–373.

constraints had existed and it allowed the emergence of parochial loyalties, most dangerously to the nation-state. 'Modern man in general', Wight lamented, 'has shown a stronger loyalty to the state than to church or class or any other international bond'.[42] Society among states was squeezed from two directions, therefore. The 'sense of unity has become rarefied as a multitude of powers have developed their independence of one another, and agreement on moral standards has been weakened by doctrinal strife within Europe and the expansion of the states-system beyond Europe'.[43]

The culturalism expressed in Wight's work is echoed to various degrees in the writings of other members of the English School. Herbert Butterfield and Wight shared many of the same views, and, as we shall see, there are culturalist strands to Bull's and Watson's work. Beyond Wight, though, it was Adda Bozeman who provided the clearest articulation of the culturalist position.[44] In *The Future of Law in a Multicultural World*, published in 1971, Bozeman advanced a conception of culture strikingly reminiscent of 1930s anthropology. 'Cultures are different', she wrote, 'because they are associated with different modes of thought ... The successive generations of any given society will be inclined to think in traditionally preferred groves, to congregate around certain constant, change resistant themes, and to rebut, whether intentionally or unconsciously, contrary ideas intruding from without.'[45] It is these different ways of thinking, Bozeman claimed, that shape a culture's institutional practices. 'Just as one has to know that the dharma is the basic theme in traditional international life and thought before one can appreciate the fact that the Indian Kingdom ... is rightly associated with the commitment to wage war, so must one know that the typically European idea of a "law of nature" could not have evolved before "law" as such had been carefully set apart from "nature".'[46] Because of this connection between cultural ideas and

---

[42] Wight, *Power Politics*, p. 25.   [43] Ibid., p. 26.

[44] An earlier version of this discussion of Bozeman's thought was published in Reus-Smit, 'International Law and the Mediation of Culture', pp. 69–70.

[45] Adda Bozeman, *The Future of Law in a Multicultural World* (Princeton, NJ: Princeton University Press), p. 14.

[46] Adda Bozeman, 'The International Order in a Multicultural World', in Hedley Bull and Adam Watson (eds.), *The Expansion of International Society* (Oxford: Oxford University Press, 1984), p. 390.

institutional practices, Bozeman was deeply sceptical about the viability of global international order:

An international system is as solid as the concepts that combine to compose it. Such concepts are solid only if they are meaningful in different local orders that are encompassed by the international system. We do not have such a globally meaningful system because world society consists today as it did before the nineteenth century of a plurality of diverse political systems, each an outgrowth of culture specific concepts.[47]

The biggest casualty in all of this is international law. For Bozeman, the very idea of the rule of law is a Western cultural artefact. '[L]aw has been consistently trusted in the West as the main carrier of shared values, the most effective agent of social control, and the only reliable principle capable of moderating and reducing the reign of passion, arbitrariness, and caprice in human life'.[48] European powers, in their long age of political ascendance, transplanted the rule of law into the international arena, establishing international law as 'the leading European reference for the conduct of relations between states without which "international order" could not even had been imagined in the West'.[49] The globalization of the system of sovereign states has, however, separated international law from its original cultural foundations, with Bozeman portraying the global cultural condition as one of fragmentation and incommensurability. There is a profound gap, she wrote, 'between the inner normative orders of the vast majority of states on the one hand, and the substantive concepts of established international law and organizing on the other'.[50] The net effect, she concluded, was an intensified power politics beneath the thin veneer of an increasingly ineffectual legalistic order.[51]

Hedley Bull

The shadow of Wight's thinking looms large over Bull's perspective on international relations. Indeed, a truism of the English School's self-narration is that Bull, as a new appointee to the Department of International Relations at the London School of Economics, learned IR by attending Wight's now-legendary introductory lectures. The two

---

[47] Ibid., p. 404.   [48] Bozeman, *Future of Law*, p. 38.
[49] Bozeman, 'International Law in a Multicultural World', p. 406.
[50] Bozeman, *Future of Law*, p. 181.   [51] Ibid., p. 186.

were also long-time members of the British Committee on International Theory, together exerting a profound influence over the English School's early thought. It is not surprising, then, that among Wight's ideas that permeated Bull's thinking, aspects of his culturalism found expression.

After identifying a number of international systems that were clearly, in his view, also international societies, Bull echoed Wight almost directly: 'A common feature of these historical international societies is that they were all founded upon a common culture or civilization, or at least some elements of such a civilization.'[52] He went on to identify two ways in which a common culture facilitates international society. First, it enables communication and fosters understanding, aiding 'the definition of common rules and the evolution of common institutions'.[53] Second, it 'may reinforce the sense of common interests that impels states to accept common rules and institutions with a sense of common values'.[54] Like Wight, Bull also worried about the fate of global international society, where a common culture was at best thin, at worst entirely absent. He distinguished between diplomatic culture ('the stock of ideas and values possessed by the official representatives of states') and international political culture ('the intellectual and moral culture that determines the attitudes towards the states system of the societies that compose it').[55] While acknowledging the existence of a worldwide diplomatic culture, he saw it as anaemic, lacking 'a common moral culture or common values'.[56] More significantly, he saw this diplomatic culture as precariously isolated, 'not powerfully reinforced by an international political culture favourable to the working of the states system'.[57] The success of global international society depended in part, he believed, on this cultural vacuum being filled. The best chance of this lay with the spread of the cosmopolitan culture of modernity, the Western roots of which he readily admitted. He hoped that this culture could 'provide the world international society of today with the kind of underpinning enjoyed by the geographically smaller and culturally more homogeneous international societies of the past'.[58]

These echoes of Wight's culturalism should not be read in isolation: Bull's overarching perspective on international relations was pluralist,

---

[52] Bull, *Anarchical Society*, p. 16.   [53] Ibid., p. 16.   [54] Ibid.
[55] Ibid., pp. 316–317.   [56] Ibid., p. 317.   [57] Ibid.   [58] Ibid.

reflecting influences on his thought other than Wight. As an under-graduate at the University of Sydney, Bull studied with the 'Australian realist' philosopher, John Anderson, to whom he declared his 'greatest intellectual debt'.[59] As Renee Jeffrey details, Bull inherited from Anderson a deep-seated philosophical realism, a fierce scepticism about religion, and, most importantly for our purposes, a view of society that emphasized conflicting interests and discounted solidaristic ties.[60] When later studying at Oxford, Bull came under the influence of H. L. A. Hart, the renowned legal positivist. Hart rejected classical natural law theory, insisting that law was a social artefact. But in a move that would resonate through Bull's work, he granted natural law a 'minimal content'. Humans have a natural will to survive, and without this there would be no imperative for social association, and no reason to accept legal rules voluntarily.[61] While positing this natural interest in society and underlying rationale for legal rules, Hart rejected any suggestion that law, as a positive system of rules, could, or should, always instantiate broader moral values.[62] In addition to these intellectual influences, Bull's antipodean character is said to have deeply coloured his perspective on international relations. In Tim Dunne's words, 'Bull was a hybrid of two political cultures which, whilst sharing certain affinities to a liberal constitutionalist tradition, nevertheless exhibited quite different positions on key postwar issues, from the personal to the international political.'[63]

The difference between Wight's culturalism and Bull's pluralism is evident in the priority he attached to interests over values as foundations of international society. While stating as a fact that 'all historical international societies have had as one of their foundations a common culture',[64] Bull thought this culture played a secondary, not a primary role: it could, as we saw above, '*reinforce* the sense of common *interests* that impels states to accept common rules and institutions with a sense of common *values*'.[65] Independent of any common

---

[59] Ibid., p. x.

[60] Renee Jeffery, 'Australian Realism and International Relations: John Anderson and Hedley Bull on Ethics, Religion, and Society', *International Politics*, 45.1 (2008), 63–65.

[61] H. L. A. Hart, *The Concept of Law*, 2nd edn. (Oxford: Clarendon Press, 1994), p. 193.

[62] Ibid., pp. 185–186.   [63] Dunne, *Inventing International Society*, p. 137.

[64] Bull, *Anarchical Society*, p. 316.   [65] Ibid., p. 16. Emphasis added.

culture, Bull held that individuals (and states) shared certain 'elementary goals of social life' that could be met only through society: principally, the goals of physical security, sanctity of promises, and stability of possession. The reality of human existence gave all individuals (and states) these interests, along with an understanding that they could be met only through reciprocal cooperation:

> Thus the facts of human vulnerability to violence and proneness to resort to it lead men to the sense of common interests in restricting violence. The fact of human interdependence for material needs leads them to perceive a common interest in ensuring respect for agreements. The facts of limited abundance and limited human altruism lead them to recognize common interests in stabilising possession. This sense of common interests may be a consequence of fear. It may derive from a rational calculation that the limitations necessary to sustain elementary goals of social life must be reciprocal.[66]

Bull acknowledged that the elementary goals could arise from something other than fear or rational calculation, that they could 'express the ability of the individuals or groups concerned to identify with each other to the extent of treating each other's interests as ends in themselves and not merely as means to an end; that is to say, it may express a sense of common values rather than common interests'.[67] He was clear, though, that this happened only 'in some cases', and that society could emerge without a common culture. His oft-quoted claim that international society exists when states are 'conscious of common interests and common values' should thus be read in a particular way. It reflects in part his understanding of the historical record (hitherto, all societies of states have rested on common values), as well as his belief that a common culture could 'reinforce' society born of interests. It should not be read, however, as an insistence that international society requires such a culture, at least theoretically. The historical coincidence of international society with a common culture was enough, however, to fuel his anxiety about the newly emergent global order.

These views on the relationship between common interests and values in the constitution of international society are reflected in Bull's ambivalent attitude toward the Grotian perspective on international

---

[66] Ibid., p. 54.   [67] Ibid.

relations. Like Wight, Bull saw this perspective as an important *via media* between Hobbesian realism and Kantian idealism. It brought into focus, he argued, an important and enduring feature of international relations: the element of society between states.[68] As others have observed, Bull never saw this as the only element of international relations; it waxed and waned, and always coexisted with struggles for power, on the one side, and transnational solidarity, on the other.[69] He saw it as an especially important element, though: providing a modicum of order in a world of independent states. Yet despite this acceptance of the Grotian idea of international society, Bull's Grotianism was far thinner than Wight's. While he embraced the general idea of international society, and credited Grotius as one of its originators, he famously distinguished between two perspectives: one pluralist, the other solidarist. Grotius, he argued, was solidarist: he believed that there was a unity to humankind that undergirded the society of states, a unity manifest in natural law. This was the Grotius embraced by Wight, but one rejected by Bull. For most of his career Bull held a pluralist perspective on international society, portraying it as a practical association, in which states shared minimal common purposes, and created functional institutions that reflect those purposes. This is evident most clearly in his preference for positivist theories of international law over the naturalist theories favoured by Wight. He commended Lassa Oppenheim's positivism, for example, as 'a conception of international society founded upon the observation of the actual area of agreement between states and informed by a sense of the limitations within which in this situation rules may be usefully made rules of law'.[70]

Recall that Wight thought Western civilization undergirded international society in two ways: Christianity sustained the law of nations through natural law, and Western values that privileged the 'golden mean' informed the institutional practices of European states. Bull

---

[68] Hedley Bull, 'The Importance of Grotius in the Study of International Relations', in Hedley Bull, Benedict Kingsbury, and Adam Roberts (eds.), *Hugo Grotius and International Relations* (Oxford: Clarendon Press, 1992), p. 93.

[69] See, for example, Dunne, *Inventing International Society*, p. 138, and Richard Little, 'The English School's Contribution to the Study of International Relations', *European Journal of International Relations*, 6.3 (2000), 395–422.

[70] Hedley Bull, 'The Grotian Conception of International Society', in Kai Alderson and Andrew Hurrell (eds.), *Hedley Bull on International Society* (Basingstoke: Macmillan, 2000), pp. 115–116.

could never accept the first of these: he, like Anderson, discounted any claims about human solidarity grounded in the exercise of reason. Natural law had been an important moral and intellectual scaffold for the development of international society after the Wars of Religion, and Bull acknowledged its moral appeal, the idea that 'there are rules or principles, and rights and duties following from them, that are not the product of human will, artifice or convention ... but exist object- ively, in the nature of things'.[71] The influence of natural law faded during the nineteenth century, however, and ultimately Bull held that it fails 'to recognize that men in world politics are in conflict about the most basic moral ends, and that when this occurs there is sometimes no rational way of choosing between them'.[72] This leaves the second of Wight's civilizational influences: the pervasiveness of 'disciplined scep- ticism and canonized prudence'. Here Bull is closer to Wight. As we saw above, he argued that global international society lacks an 'intel- lectual and moral culture that determines the attitudes towards the states system of the societies that compose it', an 'international political culture' evident, he claimed, in the eighteenth- and nineteenth-century European society of states.[73]

This discussion of Bull's position on culture and international society has implications for how we read his later works, especially his essays on the 'revolt against the West'. At the beginning of the 1980s, just before his untimely death, Bull published a series of works that pondered the fate of international order in a global, postcolonial society of states. In addition to his collaborative study of the expansion of international society,[74] he was particularly concerned with 'the struggle of non-European or non-Western states, peoples and political movements to challenge the dominant position of the Western nations in the international system'.[75] In contrast to Wight, who saw in this struggle a 'common resentment of Western civilization', Bull saw it as multifaceted struggle for justice (for which he had some sympathy).

[71] Hedley Bull, 'Natural Law and International Relations', in Kai Alderson and Andrew Hurrell (eds.), *Hedley Bull on International Society* (Basingstoke: Macmillan, 2000), p. 158.
[72] Ibid., p. 168.   [73] Bull, *Anarchical Society*, p. 316.
[74] Hedley Bull and Adam Watson (eds.), *The Expansion of International Society* (Oxford: Oxford University Press, 1984).
[75] Hedley Bull, *Justice in International Relations: 1983–84 Hagey Lectures* (Waterloo: University of Waterloo Press, 1984), p. 19.

Far from being an attack on Western civilization, he highlighted how dependent Third World claims were on Western conceptions of justice. And of the five justice claims he highlighted, only two could be construed as cultural: racial equality and cultural liberation. The first he saw as couched entirely within the Western discourse of human rights, and after noting the second, he gave it no further consideration (unlike the other claims).[76] Unlike Wight, therefore, the revolt against the West did not set off cultural alarms bells for Bull; it was not, in essence, a civilizational challenge, and culture was not the primary glue holding together international society – common interests were. His worries about the revolt worked at this level. In a move often interpreted as his 'solidarist turn', he argued that unless Western states addressed Third World justice claims – especially for economic justice and greater decision-making power – postcolonial states would lose interest in the rules and institutions of international society: the glue of common interests would dissolve. So far, these states had embraced sovereignty, diplomacy, and international law, but 'it is not credible', Bull wrote, 'that such an order can be sustained unless states of the Third World, representing as they do the majority of the states and the greater part of the world's population, believe themselves to have a stake in it'.[77]

Bull's collaborator, Adam Watson, also pondered the future of the world's first global, multicultural, international society, and unsurprisingly his thought evinces a similar logic. His work is not framed by the crisp conceptual distinctions characteristic of Bull's, but he too differentiated between states systems and international societies, the latter giving social content to the former. Unlike Bull, though, he resisted drawing 'sharp distinctions between systems of independent states, suzerain systems and empires', preferring instead to place them on a continuum from systems of independent states, through hegemony, suzerainty, and dominion, to imperial systems.[78] Anticipating the current wave of scholarship that highlights the impulse for hierarchy in all international systems,[79] he held that these forms bled into one another, frustrating categorical distinctions. Like Wight and Bull, Watson

---

[76] Ibid., pp. 2–5.   [77] Ibid., pp. 32–33.
[78] Adam Watson, *The Evolution of International Society* (London: Routledge, 1992), pp. 13–16.
[79] For a critical overview of this literature, see Janice Bially Mattern and Ayse Zarakol, 'Hierarchies in World Politics', *International Organization*, 70.3 (2016), 623–654.

believed that 'hitherto all international societies with shared values and assumptions have evolved within the matrix of a dominant culture'.[80] He agreed with Bull, however, that important as such a culture was, common interests and a shared acceptance of rules and institutions were primary. In his comparison of a myriad of historical systems, he stressed the centrality of legitimacy to society. Not only did he think that the 'rules and institutions and the accepted practices of a society of substantially independent states need legitimate authority to ensure habitual compliance',[81] he saw it at work in more hierarchical systems as well: hegemony through to empire.[82] While a sense of legitimacy could derive from a common culture, or be reinforced by it, it could also emerge from the recognition and satisfaction of interests. This having been said, Watson clearly believed that an international society in which legitimacy rested solely on interests could only ever be thin. When he looked at the evolving global society of states, for example, he saw states drawn ever closer in webs of interdependence, but little in the way of common culture. As a consequence, he argued, a 'large number of states now accept only the regulatory aspects of the present society, and do not feel bound by values and codes of conduct derived in Europe. The legitimacy of the society is exceptionally far towards the independences end of the spectrum'.[83]

Robert Jackson

Of the founding thinkers of the English School, none was a categorical pluralist. It was not until the School's renaissance in the 1990s and 2000s that such a position received unqualified expression. In response to humanitarian crises in the Balkans, Rwanda, and Somalia, a new wave of English School authors debated the ethics of international intervention, dividing along reinvigorated pluralist and solidarist lines. This debate is notable in part because of the categorical pluralism it galvanized, but also because of the secularized solidarism that emerged in dialogue, a solidarism that sublimated its cultural roots in Christian natural law.

---

[80] Watson, *Evolution of International Society*, p. 307.   [81] Ibid., p. 17.
[82] On this theme, see Ian Clark, *Hegemony in International Society* (Oxford: Oxford University Press, 2011).
[83] Watson, *Evolution of International Society*, p. 300.

The most sustained articulation of the pluralist position is advanced
by Robert Jackson in *The Global Covenant*.[84] The unalloyed nature of
Jackson's pluralism reflects in part his selective engagement with Wight
and Bull, but also his debt to theorists from outside the English School
canon, most notably, Michael Oakeshott. Jackson is a latecomer to the
English School, discovering Wight only when researching his oft-cited
study of sovereignty and postcolonial states.[85] Reflecting on the impact
of this discovery, Jackson describes Wight's thought as 'an intellectual
world I have never left, or wanted to leave'.[86] Yet when listing the
aspects of Wight's work he considers most important, Wight's views
on the cultural foundations of international society receive little mention. He applauds Wight's essay on 'Western Values in International
Relations', but says nothing about its central civilizational claims.[87]
Similarly, he devotes considerable attention to Wight's Christianity,
but focuses on his views of human nature, not the relationship between
natural law and society.[88] This bracketing of Wight's views on culture
and international society is indicative of Jackson's broader engagement
with the English School's conception of international society. It is
noteworthy, in this regard, that he favours Alan James's definition of
international society, which he paraphrases in the following way: 'it is
a society of states which are "notional persons" (or corporate personalities) but obviously not real persons; it is a body of rules (protocol,
morals, and law) which define "proper behaviour" for its members;
and it is a channel of diplomatic communication between them'.[89]
What is missing from this definition is Wight's and Bull's emphases
on common values, however complex and ambivalent these might
have been.

Onto this interpretation of the English School, Jackson grafts Oakeshott's conception of society. Oakeshott distinguished between two
kinds of human association: prudential and procedural. The first characterizes relations between self-interested, power-maximizing actors,

[84] Robert Jackson, *The Global Covenant: Human Conduct in a World of States* (Oxford: Oxford University Press, 2000).
[85] Robert Jackson, *Quasi-States: Sovereignty, International Relations and the Third World* (Cambridge: Cambridge University Press, 1990).
[86] Robert Jackson, 'From Colonialism to Theology: Encounters with Martin Wight's International Thought', *International Affairs*, 84.2 (2008), 351.
[87] Ibid., p. 357.   [88] Ibid., pp. 360–363.
[89] Jackson, *The Global Covenant*, p. 102.

where cautionary, prudential ethics prevail. The second occurs where actors recognize each other's legitimacy and relate through common practices and mutual agreements.[90] While Oakeshott held that international relations was a purely prudential realm of power and interest, Jackson is committed to the idea of international *society*, arguing that states engage in both forms of association.[91] He insists, though, that this is a limited society, enlisting Terry Nardin's concept of a 'practical association'.[92] This 'is a relationship among those engaged in the pursuit of different and possibly incompatible purposes, and who are associated with one another, if at all, only in respecting certain restrictions on how each may pursue his own purposes'.[93] Such associations are held together by 'authoritative institutions', not common purposes: actors accept a limited set of functional rules that enable them to coexist and cooperate while pursuing their diverse ends.

When these two influences are combined – a distinctive reading of the English School canon with an Oakeshottian conception of society – Jackson ends up with a pluralism that exhibits none of Bull's ambivalence. This pluralism is manifest, he argues, at two levels. International society is organizationally plural: 'it is an association of multiple political authorities based on the values of equal sovereignty, territorial integrity, and non-intervention of member states'.[94] In addition to this 'jurisdictional pluralism', and largely as a consequence, Jackson sees international society as normatively plural. It is 'an arrangement in which the domestic affairs of states are their own affair, which means that statespeople and citizens are free to compose their own domestic values and orchestrate them in their own way'.[95] This unique international society arose not from cultural unity, Jackson holds, but from the religious turmoil of the Thirty Years' War. The traumas of continental war, and the irreconcilability of the underlying religious disputes, drove states to construct a secular political order in which sovereignty protected difference. At no time since has international society rested on solidaristic affinities, but Jackson considers its combination of jurisdictional and 'value pluralism' a unique institutional achievement. Stressing the 'unlimited heterogeneity in the history, politics, ideology, religion, language, ethnicity, culture, customs, traditions, of the member

[90] Ibid., pp. 116–118.   [91] Ibid., p. 119.
[92] Terry Nardin, *Law, Morality, and Relations of States* (Princeton, NJ: Princeton University Press, 1983).
[93] Ibid., p. 9.   [94] Jackson, *The Global Covenant*, p. 178.   [95] Ibid., p. 179.

states of global international society',[96] he commends 'modern international *societas*' as 'the most articulate institutional arrangement that humans have yet come up with in response to their common recognition that they must find a settled and predictable way to live side by side on a finite planetary space without falling into mutual hostility, conflict, war, oppression, subjugation, slavery, etc.'.[97]

In contrast to Wight and Bull, who worried in different ways and to different degrees about the future of international society in a culturally diverse world, Jackson sees this pluralist society as a unique solution to the problem of diversity. This does not mean, though, that he has no concerns about the expansion of international society to encompass postcolonial states; he does, they're just not cultural. Individual sovereign states emerged in Europe before they formed a pluralist international society. They established robust forms of civil association, and sufficient capacities for self-defence, in advance of their procedural ties: empirical sovereignty preceded juridical sovereignty.[98] This was reversed, however, after 1945. The assertion and recognition of a categorical right to self-determination allowed a host of postcolonial states to join international society, often evincing little if any capacity for empirical sovereignty. States gained all the rights of sovereignty, Jackson argues, but commonly lacked the most basic elements of political civility.[99] A key characteristic of pluralist international societies is that they institutionalize sovereignty: they ground it in mutual recognition and reinforce it with norms of sovereign equality and non-intervention. Yet post-1945 decolonization radically transformed the institution of sovereignty: a 'negative' sovereignty regime replaced the former 'positive' regime. This has produced a profound institutional disjuncture, in which civil association between states straddles a widespread lack of such association within them.[100] This has forced international society to overreach beyond its core pluralist norms to codify international human rights norms, which Jackson sees as an understandable, if ultimately futile, attempt to civilize 'quasi-states'.[101]

---

[96] Ibid., p. 403.   [97] Ibid., p. 181.   [98] Jackson, *Quasi-States*, pp. 34–40.
[99] Ibid., p. 42.   [100] Ibid., p. 162.
[101] Ibid., p. 146. For a critique of Jackson's argument about sovereignty and human rights, see Christian Reus-Smit, 'Human Rights and the Social Construction of Sovereignty', *Review of International Studies* 27.4 (2001), 519–538.

For pluralists like Jackson, the cardinal norms of international society are those of sovereign equality and non-intervention, the norms that protect the integrity of individual states and enable them to coexist. Any erosion of these norms, they fear, will undermine international order, placing even humanitarian interventions well beyond the pale. In Jackson's words, 'the stability of international society, especially the unity of the great powers, is more important, indeed far more important, than minority rights and humanitarian protections in Yugoslavia or another country – if we have to choose between those two sets of values'.[102] These views have been hotly contested, however, by solidarists within the English School. Here is not the place for a detailed exposition of their responses. What matters for us, though, is how they resuscitate solidarist strands of Grotian thought, but in a highly secularized way, evincing none of Wight's anxieties about the fate of ideas rooted in Western Christianity in a global, multicultural, international society. What we see, then, is a debate between a categorical pluralism, in which the problem of cultural diversity is transferred to the domestic realm by the institution of sovereignty, and a secularized solidarism confident in the universality of ideas once rooted in natural law.

Nicholas Wheeler's classic study of humanitarian intervention, *Saving Strangers*, is emblematic of this secularized solidarism. Wheeler's goals are twofold. The first is to determine whether states, when debating and engaging in humanitarian intervention, have been animated by solidarist purposes. Where Jackson casts solidarism as 'a moral vision but not yet a political reality',[103] Wheeler puts this to the test, asking '*how far states have recognized humanitarian intervention as a legitimate exception to the rules of sovereignty, non-intervention, and non-use of force*'.[104] By carefully specifying the relationship between argument, legitimacy, and outcomes, and through detailed case studies of key interventions, he shows that international society has indeed displayed solidarist tendencies. His second goal is normative, to provide a moral defence of solidarist arguments in favour of humanitarian intervention. Against pluralist and realist counterarguments, he defends the claim that '*states that massively violate human rights should forfeit their right to be treated as legitimate sovereigns,*

---

[102] Jackson, *The Global Covenant*, p. 291.   [103] Ibid., p. 112.
[104] Nicholas J. Wheeler, *Saving Strangers: Humanitarian Intervention in International Society* (Oxford: Oxford University Press, 2002), p. 2. Emphasis in original.

thereby morally entitling other states to use force to stop oppression.[105] Nothing I say here questions the veracity of this claim; my interest is in the structure of his argument. He argues that if four criteria are met, a humanitarian intervention can be considered legitimate:

First, there must be a just cause, or what I prefer to call a supreme humanitarian emergency, because it captures the exceptional nature of the cases under consideration; secondly, the use of force must be a last resort; thirdly, it must meet the requirement of proportionality; and, finally, there must be a high degree of probability that the use of force will achieve a positive humanitarian outcome.[106]

The first of these constitutes the solidarist core of Wheeler's argument: the proposition that humans have basic moral obligations to one another, and that preventing humanitarian catastrophes can be a 'just cause' to violate the pluralist norms of international society. The key question, though, is why we should think we have such obligations. When addressing this, Wheeler comes very close to natural law reasoning. Reason tells us, he implies, that a bystander who can rescue a drowning child has an obligation to do so. The same is true for humanitarian intervention.[107] Yet in contrast to the many other connections Wheeler makes back to earlier strands of solidarist thinking in the English School, nowhere does he tie such claims back to Wight's naturalist reading of Grotius. Recall that Wight believed in natural law, but worried about its purchase in a multicultural world where non-Westerners might not share these beliefs. Wheeler has none of these anxieties, partly because he shows empirically that states have intervened for solidarist reasons, but also because his solidarism is confident in its universality and sublimates its cultural influences.

Historical Narratives

These contrasting English School perspectives on culture, society, and order condition other aspects of the School's thinking. We have already seen how they inform arguments about order and justice, but they also affect how different scholars narrate the history of international society. Barry Buzan has usefully distinguished between two

---

[105] Ibid., pp. 12–13. Emphasis in original.   [106] Ibid., p. 34.   [107] Ibid., p. 49.

kinds of narratives that weave together culture and the evolving society of states. A 'vangardist' narrative 'emphasizes the centrality of Europe in the expansion story and projects a rather one-way view of cultural transmission from the West to the rest of the world'.[108] By contrast, a 'syncretist' narrative 'puts more emphasis on the interplay between civilizations during the expansion process, and takes a more fluid and interactive view of cultural transmissions generally'.[109] The English School's narrative is considered quintessentially vangardist, with syncretist accounts often cast in critique.[110] Yet on closer inspection, the English School's vangardism takes several forms, reflecting its contrasting perspectives on culture and international order.

The most frequently cited vangardist narrative is Bull and Watson's *The Expansion of International Society*, a narrative that reflects their culturally inflected pluralism. While acknowledging that non-European peoples shaped international society as it expanded,[111] Bull and Watson pay little attention to such influences, focusing instead on the global spread of an essentially European order. International society emerged in Europe between the fifteenth and eighteenth centuries, a product of elementary social imperatives, but deeply conditioned by the values of Western Christendom. The expanding society of states thus had a distinctly European 'character', even as it 'secularized' in the nineteenth century, as positive international law replaced naturalist conceptions. The engine of expansion was also distinctly European. European states had long interacted with polities across the globe, creating what Bull saw as an early global 'system'. But it was European imperialism that knit the world together, producing the 'economic and technological unification of the globe'.[112] It was the collapse of Europe's empires that transformed this into a global society of states.

---

[108] Barry Buzan, 'Culture and International Society', *International Affairs*, 86.1 (2010), 3.

[109] Ibid.

[110] Two notable examples are John Hobson, *The Eastern Origins of Western Civilization* (Cambridge: Cambridge University Press, 2004), and Tim Dunne and Christian Reus-Smit, *The Globalization of International Society* (Oxford: Oxford University Press, 2017).

[111] Hedley Bull, 'The Emergence of a Universal International Society', in Hedley Bull and Adam Watson (eds.), *The Expansion of International Society* (Oxford: Clarendon Press, 1985), p. 123.

[112] Hedley Bull and Adam Watson, 'Introduction', in Bull and Watson (eds.), *The Expansion of International Society*, p. 2.

The cultural elements of Bull and Watson's account recede at this point, replaced by a more rationalist story of reconciled interests. International society is a rule-governed order, and it expanded by admitting new rule-observant members. This became more complicated in the nineteenth century, when aspiring members were increasingly non-European. In his contribution to *Expansion*, Gerrit Gong put it this way: 'the European powers faced the challenge and difficulty of drawing the non-European countries into their system of international relations in an orderly and humane way'.[113] To deal with this problem, European states codified the notorious 'standard of civilization', setting down legal criteria that aspiring polities had to meet if they were to join the society of states. That this standard was as much a legal rationale for imperialism as it was a mechanism for its orderly dissolution receives little attention in *Expansion*. Greater emphasis is placed on the willingness of non-European polities to join the club of states, embracing its pluralist institutions. 'While non-European communities in some cases were incorporated in the international system against their will', Bull wrote, 'they have taken their places in international society because they themselves have sought the rights of membership in it, and the protection of its rules, both *vis-à-vis* the dominant European powers and in relation to one another'.[114] As we have seen, Bull worried that global international society lacked adequate cultural foundations, but he believed the requisite common interests existed, vulnerable as they were to conflicts over justice.

On either side of this account sit two other historical narratives: one by Wight, the other by Jackson. Wight's is a pessimistic narrative of international social decline. Theologically, he was committed to an eschatological view of history, in which the prospect of immanent judgement and redemption was entwined with a secular history of repeated crises. On the latter, he cited Christ's teaching, arguing that the 'picture of human history this suggests is of mankind, not marching steadily up out of the shadow into broad sunshine, but always going on through the murk and obscurity produced by man's misuse of his moral freedom'.[115] Historiographically, he was opposed to progressivist history, holding that it reduced past lives to teleological stepping

[113] Gerrit W. Gong, 'China's Entry into International Society', in Bull and Watson (eds.), *The Expansion of International Society*, p. 171.
[114] Bull, 'The Emergence of a Universal International Society', p. 124.
[115] Cited in Hall, *The International Thought of Martin Wight*, p. 35.

stones, denying their richness and unique purposes for the sake of false tales of human progress.[116] Wight dated the emergence of European international society from the Council of Constance (1414–1418), the point at which the 'political and cultural unity' of *Respublica Christiana* began to fragment into a system of independent polities.[117] Over the next three centuries, he argued, the key features of European international society clarified: territorially defined sovereign states, mutual recognition, great power balancing, diplomatic exchange, and international law. As we have seen, Wight considered the last of these fundamental, as international law rested on natural law, and natural law was prior to society. This early period between the Council of Constance and the Peace of Utrecht (1713–1715) was thus the heyday of international society for Wight, as natural law was still assumed to undergird international law (as evident in the writings of Suarez, Vitoria, and Grotius). The nineteenth century ushered in a new phase, however. The naturalist understanding of international law was displaced by a positivist understanding, in which the law of nations derived from the consent of states. This distancing of international society from the notion of an underlying unity to humankind coincided with the rise of European nationalism, which placed loyalty to the nation over identification with Western civilization. The most extreme manifestation of this loyalty was revolution. As the French and Russian revolutions demonstrated, revolutions are partly about national liberation and partly about ideological export, posing a profound challenge to the legitimacy of international society.[118] The net result of these processes was the dominance of power politics, a dominance that wreaked havoc on the twentieth century. Wight saw flickers of natural-law thinking in the League of Nations and the Nuremburg Trials, but he saw the United Nations as a continuation of the power politics that drove the two world wars. It is 'a body within which the tripartite struggle of the Communist powers, the status quo powers and the have-not powers can go on. This might almost be said to define its nature', he concluded.[119] A third world war was all but inevitable. Across this broad span of history, as international society had secularized internally and globalized externally, Wight saw 'the effective transformation

---

[116] Ibid., p. 53.   [117] Wight, *Systems of States*, p. 129.
[118] Wight, *Power Politics*, pp. 81–94.   [119] Ibid., p. 233.

of the international community from one based on a common ethos to one whose principle is inclusiveness'.[120] Jackson's historical narrative could not be more different. In contrast to Wight's story of decline born of civilizational erosion, Jackson's is one of rational pluralism. His starting point is the Peace of Westphalia, which Wight had rejected because it obscured the long processes of 'doctrinal conflict' that shaped the evolution of international society.[121] For Jackson, however, Westphalia constitutes 'the pluralist moment', the threshold between a Europe wracked by religious conflict, where culture supervened on the political, and a Europe where cultural differences were confined to the domestic realm. After 120 years of religious conflict, and thirty years of devastating continental war, the Treaties of Westphalia weakened the transnational authority of the Holy Roman Empire and the papacy, instituted a nascent order of sovereign states, and made questions of religion matters of state. The net result, Jackson argues, was the 'reconstitution of European politics from that of a *universitas*, based on solidarist norms of Latin Christendom, to that of a *societas*, based on the pluralist norms of state sovereignty, on political independence'.[122] But where Wight lamented the erosion of these solidarist norms, Jackson sees the new *societas* as a momentous human achievement, a unique and lasting solution to the problem of order in diversity. 'The *societas* of sovereign states is the idea and institution that expresses the morality of difference, recognition, respect, regard, dialogue, interaction, exchange, and similar norms that postulate coexistence and reciprocity between independent political communities', and so far this 'has proved to be the only generally acceptable and workable basis for world politics'.[123]

For Jackson, the history of international society is one of institutional robustness and adaptation. The *societas* of sovereign states, he contends almost euphorically, 'adapted to the scientific revolution of the seventeenth century', 'adjusted to the Enlightenment', 'accommodated the industrial revolution of the nineteenth century', 'witnessed the mass movement of millions of people', 'took on board the doctrine of nationalism and the national state', accommodated republics and monarchies, 'withstood the two world wars', 'survived the Russian

---

[120] Ibid., p. 294.   [121] Wight, *Systems of States*, p. 114.
[122] Jackson, *The Global Covenant*, p. 165.   [123] Ibid., p. 168.

Revolution' and 'the Nazis and the fascists', 'answered the demands for Third World decolonization', 'responded to the nuclear age', and 'became blind to distinctions of race and culture and ideology', as well as religion and gender.[124] Jackson attributes this extraordinary resilience partly to the decentralization of international society, but more importantly to the unassailable of logic of its pluralism. It is 'hard to think about convincing alternative images of international life', he writes, 'without employing the ideas and language associated with the society of states. They are too basic and too deeply ingrained in our thought.'[125]

Pushing the Boundaries

The discussion so far has focused on select canonical or emblematic thinkers. Not only do their writings reveal, in well-elaborated forms, the principal ways in which the English School has thought about culture and international society/order, but the writings of foundational thinkers, especially Wight and Bull, serve as enduring reference points for new work, providing a conceptual language and analytical framework that deeply informs and structures the School's ongoing debates. Having said this, though, there have been important attempts to push the boundaries of these debates, especially on questions of culture and international order.

We saw in the Introduction, for example, that Hurrell directly challenges Wight's culturalism, and he goes on to deny that international orders grow out of shared cultural values, and rejects the idea that the world is divided into 'a limited number of cultures, each with its own immutable core'.[126] In a complementary line of argument, Iver Neumann and Jennifer Welsh have long criticized the idea that international society grew out of a culturally coherent and independent West, arguing that European cultural identity was always a social construct: 'the very idea of what Europe was from the beginning defined partly in terms of what it was *not*. In other words, the Other, i.e., the non-European barbarian or savage, played a decisive role in

---

[124] Ibid., p. 420. [125] Ibid., p. 421.
[126] Hurrell, *On Global Order*, pp. 43–44.

the evolution of European identity and in the maintenance of order among European states.'[127] Edward Keene has further explicated this relationship between the 'Western' society of states and the non-European world, showing how the European powers used the principle of sovereignty to govern relations among themselves, and the principle of imperial paramountcy in their relations with others, creating a bifurcated international order.[128] Others, like Yongjin Zhang and Barry Buzan, have challenged the English School's traditional focus on European historical experiences, arguing that sophisticated international orders have existed elsewhere, and well before European expansion. 'East Asian states and peoples', for example, 'had historically chosen and established complex institutions and practices informed by their history and culture in dealing with challenges of security, conflict, co-existence and cooperation.'[129] New scholarship is also questioning earlier understandings of the 'revolt against the West', showing how postcolonial states were neither passive recipients of preexisting international norms nor revolutionaries seeking a radical transformation of international society; their goal was to make international society genuinely pluralist, attempting to strip it of its civilizational biases and colonial hierarchies.[130]

Many of these attempts to push the boundaries of the English School resonate with the argument I develop in Chapter 6, in particular Hurrell's position on the ubiquity of cultural diversity, Neumann and Welsh's stress on the interactive construction of cultural identities, Keene's emphasis on the civilizational ordering of international society, and Zhang and Buzan's exploration of non-Western orders. Moreover, Devetak, Dunne, and Nurhayati's reconsideration of the agency of

[127] Iver B. Neumann and Jennifer M. Welsh, 'The Other in European Self-Definition: An Addendum to the Literature on International Society', *Review of International Studies*, 17.4 (1991), 329. Also see Iver B. Neumann, *Uses of the Other: 'The East' in European Identity Formation* (Minneapolis: University of Minnesota Press, 1998).

[128] Edward Keene, *Beyond the Anarchical Society* (Cambridge: Cambridge University Press, 2002).

[129] Yongjin Zhang and Barry Buzan, 'The Tributary System as International Society in Theory and Practice', *Chinese Journal of International Relations*, 5.1 (2012), 12. Also see Shogo Suzuki, Yongjin Zhang, and Joel Quirk, *International Orders in the Early Modern Period* (London: Routledge, 2014).

[130] Devetak, Dunne, and Nurhayati, 'Bandung 60 Years On'. Also see Ian Hall, 'The "Revolt against the West" Revisited', in Dunne and Reus-Smit (eds.), *The Globalization of International Society*, pp. 345–361.

postcolonial states complements my past work on struggles for individual rights and the expansion of the international system.[131]

Yet to varying degrees, and in various ways, this revisionist scholarship never fully shakes off the problematic assumptions of foundational thinkers. To begin with, the treatment of culture in this literature is far from consistent. Hurrell's insistence that all cultural formations are inherently diverse, for example, sits uncomfortably with Zhang and Buzan's Wightian claim that the Chinese 'Tributary' order was 'unquestionably informed mostly, if not exclusively, by Chinese culture and civilization'.[132] Second, this literature, like all work in the English School, struggles to escape the conceptual distinction between solidarist and pluralist international societies. For example, in arguing that postcolonial states at the Bandung Conference (1955) sought a genuinely pluralist international society, Devetak, Dunne, and Nurhayati hold that such a society is 'designed to facilitate cooperation among diverse – and seemingly incompatible – cultures, traditions and values'.[133] In Chapter 6 I argue that while the idea of a pluralist international society might be a valuable normative ideal,[134] its practical expression is near-impossible to achieve. In *Moral Purpose* I argued that international societies are membership associations: they recognize some polities as legitimate and others as illegitimate, and these decisions are always based on substantive political, social, or cultural criteria – pluralism is always pluralism of the elect.[135] Adding to this critique, I will argue in Chapter 6 that any historical example of states seeking to construct what they see as a pluralist order has to be located within the long history of order builders seeking to organize cultural diversity, in the modern order and elsewhere. Pluralism, whatever its concrete manifestation, is just another diversity regime. Understanding this is crucial, as it raises key questions that the English School – old and new – has largely neglected. If there was a move to construct a pluralist diversity regime after decolonization, what new configurations of power and articulations of cultural difference was it

---

[131] Reus-Smit, *Individual Rights*.
[132] Zhang and Buzan, 'The Tributary System', p. 18.
[133] Devetak, Dunne, and Nurhayati, 'Bandung 60 Years On', p. 359.
[134] For a thoughtful articulation and defense of this ideal, see Jennifer M. Welsh, 'A Normative Case for Pluralism: Reassessing Vincent's Views on Humanitarian Intervention', *International Affairs*, 78.5 (2011), 1193–1204.
[135] Reus-Smit, *Moral Purpose*, pp. 36–39.

seeking to accommodate? If all diversity regimes generate political and cultural hierarchies, what patterns of inclusion and exclusion did this purportedly pluralist regime create?[136] And, finally, what grievances have these hierarchies produced, and what is their likely impact on the future of the modern international order?

Conclusion

The English School has enjoyed a remarkable renaissance since the end of the Cold War. This is partly because a new generation of scholars took the horse by the reins, clarifying and driving forward key concepts and theoretical insights. It is also because the School's master concept – international society – resonated so strongly with the constructivist move to reimagine international relations as a social realm. Added to this, the School's 'classical approach' to the study of politics challenged the axioms of American social science, placing a premium on the art of interpretation and a historical sensibility. This not only gave the School a distinctive intellectual profile; it invited connections with other schools of thought. Constructivists latched onto 'international society', liberals enlisted Bull's conception of international order, scholars of diverse stripes aligned with the order versus justice debate, and critical theorists saw potential in the School's non-materialist ontology and interpretive methodology. Most recently, revisionists within the School have joined the push for a more global IR discipline, reconceiving the evolution of today's global international society as a process not of expansion but of interactive globalization.[137]

There is one claim for the English School, however, upon which the argument advanced in this chapter casts doubt. Some have commended the School for its insightful treatment of culture in world politics. Two decades ago Roger Epp drew out the hermeneutic undercurrents of the School's thought, claiming that it presents 'an understanding

---

[136] What of the fate of indigenous peoples, for example? See Paul Keal, *European Conquest and the Rights of Indigenous Peoples* (Cambridge: Cambridge University Press, 2003).

[137] Dunne and Reus-Smit (eds.), *The Globalization of International Society*, conclusion.

of international relations that is less about structure or what Wight called "mechanics" than it is about the diffuse, imprecise domain of culture'.[138] More recently, Andrew Linklater has presented an ambitious critical historical sociology of harm conventions in world politics, building a bridge between Wight's argument about the cultural foundations of international societies and Norbert Elias's sociology of civilizing processes. Wight brought to this relationship an understanding of the dynamics of international societies, along with an appreciation that 'a pre-existing sense of belonging to a shared culture or civilization smoothed the way to creating an international society'.[139] What Wight lacked, Linklater argues, was a grasp of the civilizing process: 'he did not discuss how societies came to have specific values in common or explain how shared "civilized" beliefs influenced – and were shaped by – the ways in which states were bound together in an international society'.[140] It was insights into this civilizing process that Elias brought to the table.

These claims about the English School arguments about culture and international society sit uncomfortably with the analysis presented in this chapter. As noted in the introduction to this chapter, the School is distinguished by its enduring interest in the relationship between culture and order. Yet it evinces two markedly different positions: Wight's culturalism and Jackson's pluralism, with Bull's work advancing elements of both. As we have seen, these inform very different narratives of international history, stressing different dynamics and phases, with different messages of pessimism or optimism. Most importantly, the School is torn between two equally unsustainable positions. On the one hand, Wight's understanding of culture is a quintessential example of the default conception critiqued in Chapter 1. Western civilization appears as a coherent, neatly bounded cultural entity, with natural law and Western values not just undergirding the society of states but constituting it. Linklater is right that Wight is blind to processes of cultural construction, but he fails to acknowledge how mired Wight is in 1930s to 1950s anthropology and sociology, a heritage Elias never fully escapes either. On the other hand, Jackson's pluralism brackets

---

[138] Roger Epp, 'The English School on the Frontiers of International Society: A Hermeneutic Recollection', *Review of International Studies*, 24.5 (1998), 49.
[139] Andrew Linklater, *Violence and Civilization in the Western States-Systems* (Cambridge: Cambridge University Press, 2017), p. 4.
[140] Ibid.

culture altogether. Religious conflict is the background to Westphalia's pluralist moment, but once sovereignty resolves this conflict, culture drops out of Jackson's theoretical framework and historical narrative. A new wave of English School writings has sought to push beyond these limited perspectives, accepting most notably the inherent diversity of all cultural formations. Yet this is far from universally accepted, with other scholars still employing the old default conception of culture. The pluralist position is also alive and well in much of the current literature, even if appears alongside more innovative insights. Overall, the English School's engagement with culture is commendable only when set against other mainstream theories of international relations, not against contemporary theory and research in specialist fields.

4 | *Culture as Norms*

Constructivists should be at the forefront of discussions about culture in world politics. After all, their most basic ontological assumption is that intersubjective meanings make the natural and social worlds knowable, constituting social existence at the most fundamental level, and rendering the physical world meaningful. They also describe these meanings frequently as 'culture' or 'cultural', suggesting a sustained interest in such phenomena. Yet the dominant strands of constructivist thought have approached culture in two very distinctive ways, both of which are problematic. The first of these disaggregates culture into individual norms and traces the effects of these norms on behavior. Whatever the merits of this as a methodological strategy – and I concede they are many – it obscures the broader web of multiple, tangled, and at times contradictory meanings in which individual norms are embedded: the actual normative environment that constitutes knowledgeable social agents, and the world through which they navigate. The second approach treats culture as deep structure, as a foundational set of meanings – 'social epistemes', 'social imaginaries', 'lifeworlds' – that constitutes institutional forms and practices and enables meaningful communication. While this approach steps back and takes a more macro perspective on culture, it reproduces the default conception critiqued in Chapter 1. Culture appears again as unitary, coherent, and deeply constitutive.

My early work on fundamental institutions combines both of these approaches. The title of my first book is *The Moral Purpose of the State: Culture, Social Identity, and Institutional Rationality in International Relations*. Clearly, I thought that culture was sufficiently central to highlight. Yet culture is seldom mentioned again: it doesn't even appear in the index. What I discuss instead is how deep constitutional social norms shaped the nature of fundamental institutions in different historical international societies. When I use the term 'culture' in the subtitle, therefore, what I really mean is norms: particular

119

norms, with very specific causal effects. These are not the issue-specific norms explored by most constructivists, however; they are foundational norms, hegemonic beliefs about the moral purpose of the state, the organizing principle of sovereignty, and procedural justice – beliefs essential to the lifeworlds in which international societies emerge. I would now place far greater emphasis on how such beliefs become hegemonic in highly variegated cultural contexts, but when I wrote *Moral Purpose* I explicitly, if mistakenly, saw my argument as akin to Wight's claim that international societies emerge in unitary cultural contexts.[1]

This chapter explores these two approaches to culture. The first section revisits the core social theoretic ideas undergirding constructivism, showing how they are derived from three principal intellectual sources: the sociology of Durkheim and Weber, the symbolic interactionism of Berger and Luckman, and the linguistic and communicative theories of Wittgenstein, Searle, and Habermas. The second section argues that these resources have been mobilized in two main constructivist projects: the norms project and the institutional structure project. Each evinces forms of 'normative monism', obscuring the complexity of culture by treating either single norms or unitary deep structure as causal. I examine both projects in detail, tracing the persistent tendency of mainstream constructivists to either atomize or homogenize culture. This need not have been the case, though. It has only been possible, I argue in the third section, because scholars have relied on insights from Durkheimian sociology, symbolic interactionism, and sociological institutionalism, while neglecting insights from linguistic and communicative sources, sources that are, at least in principle, compatible with more sophisticated understandings of culture. Furthermore, recent theoretical innovations in practice theory, which enlist social theoretical resources underappreciated in early constructivist theorizing, also suggest a more complex cultural terrain.

Social Theory

Constructivists have insisted time and again that constructivism is not a theory of international relations; it is a set of social theoretic propositions that apply equally to all domains of social interaction and, when

---

[1] Reus-Smit, *Moral Purpose*, p. 37.

mobilized systematically, can inform heuristically powerful international theory. In this respect, constructivism is considered no different from rational-choice theory (discussed in Chapter 5). Both consist of propositions about 'the nature of human agency and its relationship to social structures, the role of ideas and material forces in social life, the proper form of social explanations, and so on'.[2] And these contending propositions can be enlisted in the construction of any number of substantive constructivist and rationalist theories of international relations: some 'grand', some 'middle range', some explaining large-scale historical change or continuity, and others focused on very specific forms of conflict or cooperation.

Three Propositions

The core social theoretic propositions undergirding constructivism are ontological: they concern the nature of the social world, the nature of humans as social beings, and the relationship between the two. These propositions lead to associated epistemological and methodological propositions, but most constructivists treat ontology as primary, and as we shall see, not all agree that their social ontology has particular epistemological or methodological implications: some constructivists are committed interpretivists, others are methodological conventionalists.

Constructivism's key ontological proposition is that the natural and social worlds are 'meaningful'. In a minimal sense, the social world is 'full' of intersubjective meanings: values, norms, practices, etc. These 'social facts' are not natural: they 'depend on human agreement that they exist and typically require human institutions for their existence'.[3] More fundamentally, humans know their worlds – natural as well as social – only through shared meanings. Constructivism, as Friedrich Kratochwil observes, is directly at odds with empiricism. Instead of treating things in the world as 'simply given and correctly perceived

---

[2] Wendt, *Social Theory of International Politics*, p. 5.
[3] John Gerard Ruggie, 'What Makes the World Hang Together? Neo-Utilitarianism and the Social Constructivist Challenge', *International Organization*, 54.4 (1998), 856.

by our senses', constructivism sees them as 'the product of our conceptualizations'.[4] This does not mean that constructivists deny the physical or material world's reality, the fact that it exists independent of the meanings we attach to it. Unlike poststructuralists, constructivists are ontological realists. 'While accepting the notion that there is a real world out there', Emanuel Adler argues, 'they nevertheless believe that it is not entirely determined by physical reality and is socially emergent'.[5] Physical reality defines the limits of feasible human action, Wendt argues.[6] Or as Martin Hollis put it, 'life in a desert full of oil differs from life in a tundra full of bears'.[7] Yet physical reality is also socially emergent, in the sense that we know it only through our conceptualizations: the intersubjective meanings we attach to things in the natural world determine what they *are* for us. A 'species' is not a natural form; it is a human categorization of a biological phenomenon, just as a 'planet' is a human categorization of an astronomical phenomenon. Recent shifts in this latter categorization have literally changed the nature of what Pluto *is*. Until 2006 it was the ninth planet in our solar system, but then the definition of a planet changed, and Pluto became a 'dwarf planet'.

A second constructivist proposition is that our meaningful social world is constitutive, in the sense that it has 'the power to establish or give organized existence to something'.[8] For rationalists, intersubjective meanings, in the form of institutional rules and norms, are regulatory: they enable or constrain actors in the pursuit of their exogenously determined interests. For constructivists, by contrast, meanings also shape actors' social identities, which in turn inform their interests. Identities are actors' self-understandings of who they are, and 'actors acquire identities – relatively stable, role-specific understandings and expectations about self – by participating in . . . collective

---

[4] Friedrich Kratochwil, 'Constructivism: What It Is (not) and How It Matters', in Donatella Della Porta and Michael Keating (eds.), *Approaches and Methodologies in the Social Sciences* (Cambridge: Cambridge University Press, 2008), p. 81.
[5] Emanuel Adler, 'Seizing the Middle Ground: Constructivism in World Politics', *European Journal of International Relations*, 3.3 (1997), 324.
[6] Wendt, *Social Theory of International Politics*, p. 111.
[7] Martin Hollis, *Models of Man: Philosophical Thoughts on Social Action* (Cambridge: Cambridge University Press, 1977), p. 26.
[8] *Oxford English Dictionary*, 3rd edn. (Oxford: Oxford University Press, 2010), p. 373.

meanings'.[9] In other words, actors, from ballet dancers to sovereign states, become who they are by internalizing and enacting the inter-subjective meanings that structure their social worlds. And because these meanings are multiple, and the social domains actors engage are varied, actors commonly have several social identities, which become more or less salient in different social contexts: the identity of professor coming to the fore within the university, for example, compared with the identity of the parent at parent–teacher meetings. Understanding the social constitution of identities is important for constructivists because they see identities as the primary source of interests. Where rationalists bracket interest formation and focus on how actors pursue their interests strategically, constructivists see as necessarily incomplete any explanation that fails to account for why actors advance the interests they do. Actors' interests derive primarily from their social identities, constructivists argue. 'When we say that professors have an "interest" in teaching, research, or going on leave, we are saying that to function in the role identity of "professor" they have to define certain situations as calling for certain actions.'[10] At the international level, historically the United States' interests (and actions) have been shaped by its social identity as a liberal hegemon, an identity consti-tuted both domestically and internationally. It was not just hegemony that affected the post-1945 order, John Ruggie contends, but *American hegemony*.[11]

To this point, constructivism appears highly structural. Unlike neorealism and world systems theory, the structures are not material; they are intersubjective. Their effects are no less significant, though. Intersubjective meanings confront actors as structural phenomena, and these phenomena constitute actors as knowledgeable social agents, giving them role identities that inform their interests. This apparent structuralism is qualified, however, by a third constructivist propos-ition. While intersubjective structures constitute actors' identities and interests, these structures exist only because of the routinized practices of actors. They 'define the meaning and identity of the individual actor

---

[9] Alexander Wendt, 'Anarchy Is What States Make of It: The Social Construction of Power Politics', *International Organization*, 46.2 (1992), 397.

[10] Ibid., p. 398.

[11] John Gerard Ruggie, 'Multilateralism: The Anatomy of an Institution', in John Gerard Ruggie (ed.), *Multilateralism Matters: The Theory and Praxis of an Institutional Form* (New York: Columbia University Press, 1993), p. 31.

and patterns of appropriate economic, political, and cultural activity engaged in by those individuals',[12] but it 'is through reciprocal interaction that we create and instantiate the relatively enduring social structures in terms of which we define our identities and interests'.[13] Constructivists are 'structurationists', therefore: they see agents and structures as mutually constituted. Anthony Giddens, whose work informs constructivism in this area, speaks of the 'duality of structure'. 'The constitution of agents and structures are not two independently given sets of phenomena, a dualism, but represent a duality ... [T]he structural properties of social systems are both medium and outcome of the practices they recursively organize'.[14] The institution of marriage is a structure of intersubjective meanings that has historically constituted the gendered social identities of husband and wife, but as movements for marriage equality are now demonstrating, this stands only so long as actors reproduce traditional meanings. Similarly, for millennia the institution of empire constituted the hierarchical identities of colonizer and colonized, but twentieth-century decolonization delegitimized not just particular empires, but the meanings that licensed imperial hierarchies in general.[15]

Early constructivists held that these ontological propositions had epistemological and, in turn, methodological implications. Two epistemological issues are at stake. First, if the natural and social worlds are indeed meaningful, then much of what they comprise is not comprehensible from a positivist epistemological standpoint. For an explanation to count as valid from a positivist standpoint, independent and dependent variables have to be isolated, and the causal relationship between the two measured. An example would be a billiard cue striking a ball, the former being the independent variable, the latter the dependent. Yet intersubjective meanings don't work this way – their causality is not force-like; they constitute actors' identities, give meaning to social and natural forms, and define, warrant, and justify action.

---

[12] John Boli, John Meyer, and George Thomas, "Ontology and Rationalization in the Western Cultural Account', in George Thomas et al. (eds.), *Institutional Structure: Constituting State, Society, and the Individual* (London: Sage, 1989), p. 12.

[13] Wendt, 'Anarchy Is What States Make of It', p. 406.

[14] Anthony Giddens, *The Constitution of Society: Outline of a Theory of Structuration* (Berkeley: University of California Press, 1984), p. 25.

[15] See Reus-Smit, *Individual Rights*, pp. 154–157.

Furthermore, meanings are not external forces acting on individuals; they are communicated, enacted, and reproduced by the very actors and actions they condition.[16] Second, if we only know the natural and social worlds through our conceptualizations, then we can never 'test' our theories against an independent reality, natural or social. Constructivism's ontology thus challenges 'the positivist notion that science creates warranted knowledge by simply "discovering" a ready-made world. Precisely because we never test against "nature" directly – not even in the natural sciences – but only against other theories, "nature" itself can hardly "answer" us, even if asked in experiments, unless it uses, so to speak, our language.'[17] Taken together, these issues encouraged early constructivists to follow Weber in seeking an interpretive epistemology, and associated methodological strategies, that were compatible with the role of intersubjective meanings in constituting social life. As we shall see below, this call for ontological and epistemological symmetry was abandoned with the rise of norms research.

Intellectual Sources

The above propositions should be seen as points of coalescence: core ideas on which leading constructivists have converged, despite drawing on very different intellectual sources. Finnemore and Onuf, Kratochwil and Sikkink, Ruggie and Wendt, and Adler and Katzenstein all treat these as characteristically constructivist positions. Yet the social theories they draw on differ markedly. Over time, constructivists have drawn on a myriad of sources, from Nietzsche to Bourdieu. Three sources were particularly influential on early constructivist thought, though: the sociology of Durkheim and Weber; the symbolic interactionism of Mead, Blumer, and Berger and Luckman; and the linguistic and communicative theories of Wittgenstein, Searle, and Habermas. How these were read and enlisted set the

---

[16] Friedrich Kratochwil and John Gerard Ruggie, 'A State of the Art on an Art of the State', *International Organization*, 40.4 (1986), 753–775; and Friedrich Kratochwil, 'Regimes and the "Science" of Politics: A Reappraisal', *Millennium: Journal of International Studies*, 17.2 (1988), 263–284.

[17] Friedrich Kratochwil, 'Sociological Approaches', in Christian Reus-Smit and Duncan Snidal (eds.), *The Oxford Handbook of International Relations* (Oxford: Oxford University Press, 2008), p. 449.

course for mainstream constructivism, with significant implications for its understandings of culture.

Durkheim's influence appears most prominently in Ruggie's account of large-scale international change. In his oft-cited critique of Waltz's theory of international politics, Ruggie holds that Waltz misunderstood the concept of 'differentiation'. As we saw in Chapter 2, Waltz argues that political structures have three dimensions: an ordering principle, the functional differentiation of the units, and the distribution of capabilities. In international political structures, only the last of these changes. A change in the ordering principle is rare, and would transform a system fundamentally from anarchy to hierarchy; and states are functionally undifferentiated – they are 'like-units' – and this is reinforced by the logic of anarchy. This leaves variations in the capabilities of states – shifts in polarity – as the only significant axis of change. Yet Ruggie argues that when properly conceived the differentiation of units also varies. Waltz misread Durkheim, he claims, 'giving an infelicitous interpretation to the sociological term "differentiation", taking it to mean that which denotes *differences* rather than that which denotes *separateness*'.[18] It's not whether states are like-units that matters; it's how they stand in relation to one another. Understood in this way, the differentiation of units can be seen as a key axis of large-scale international change. Indeed, it was a shift in how units were separated that gave rise to the modern international system. Medieval Europe was an anarchy: a segmented political system, just like the modern system that replaced it. What differed was the principle on which political units were differentiated. Medieval Europe was heteronomous; it comprised multiple units of authority with non-exclusive, non-territorial jurisdictions. In the modern system, by contrast, units are differentiated on the principle of sovereignty: states are centralized political authorities, claiming exclusive jurisdiction within their territories. A key axis of variation in any social system, Durkheim argues, is 'how the constituent elements in a society are grouped'.[19] And because Waltz fails to understand this, Ruggie contends, he is blind to the dimension of change that produced the system he seeks to theorize. More than this, Waltz ignores a key engine of

[18] John Gerard Ruggie, 'Continuity and Transformation in the World Polity: Toward a Neorealist Synthesis', *World Politics*, 35.2 (1983), 273–274.

[19] Emile Durkheim, *The Rules of Sociological Method* (New York: Free Press, 1982), p. 135.

change highlighted by Durkheim: increases in 'dynamic density' – 'the quantity, velocity, and diversity of transactions that go on within society'.[20] Such increases, Ruggie argues, '*can* be linked to a societal restructuring of property rights and political organization, which had the domestic and international consequences' that produced the modern system.[21]

A decade after this initial revision of Waltz's conception of international structure, Ruggie introduced a second Durkheimian concept: the idea of collective conscience or mentality. In the wake of the Cold War, and in the midst of accelerating globalization, he sought a framework in which to comprehend 'the possibility of fundamental discontinuity in the international system'.[22] His reference point is again the transition from medieval heteronomy to modern sovereignty, and he reiterates his position that '[w]ithout the concept of differentiation ... it is impossible to define the structure of modernity in international politics'. Indeed, now he goes further to insist that 'modes of differentiation are nothing less than the focus of the epochal study of rule'.[23] He does more, though, than simply offer differentiation as a lens through which to understand post–Cold War change: he tries to account for the medieval-modern transformation, hoping that this might identify key dimensions of contemporary change. The modern system of sovereign states – that 'peculiar form of sociopolitical individuation' – was the product of three developments, he argues: changes in material environments, strategic behaviour, and social epistemology. It is the last of these that he considers most important, as the shift from a heteronomous to a sovereign mode of differentiation was possible, he holds, only because 'the mental equipment that people drew upon in imagining and symbolizing forms of political community itself underwent fundamental change'.[24] He conceptualizes these different forms of mental equipment as 'social epistemes', seeking a middle ground between Weber's characterization of society as webs of meaning and the focus in French sociology, from Durkheim to Foucault, on *mentalities collective*. The latter is crucial for Ruggie, as it suggests a deep constitutive structure of ideas informing social organization. Durkheim distinguished between two kinds of social solidarity: one resting on 'mechanical conscience',

---

[20] Ruggie, 'Continuity and Transformation', p. 281. [21] Ibid., p. 282.
[22] John Gerard Ruggie, 'Territoriality and Beyond: Problematizing Modernity in International Relations', *International Organization*, 47.1 (1993), 143–144.
[23] Ibid., pp. 151–152. [24] Ibid., p. 157.

which exists 'when the collective conscience completely envelops our whole conscience'; the other founded on 'organic conscience', where a division of labour requires that 'the collective conscience leave open a part of the individual conscience in order that special functions may be established there, functions it cannot regulate'.[25] While 'civilization' depends on a division of labour and the existence of organic conscience, Durkheim held that mechanical conscience – the conscience of the collectivity – was essential to social cohesion. Foucault makes no reference to collective conscience, emphasizing instead the existence of deep, culture-wide 'epistemes' that enable the ordering of the natural and social worlds by defining 'the conditions of possibility'.[26] These vary from one civilization to another, and fundamental historical 'discontinuities' occur within civilizations when one episteme supplants another:[27] precisely what Ruggie sees happening in the transformation from medieval heteronomy to the modern system of sovereign states.

As we have seen, constructivists don't just argue that intersubjective structures affect how actors comprehend the world; they argue, more specifically, that these structures constitute actors' identities and interests. Their principal influence here is symbolic interactionism, most notably the work of Mead, Blumer, and Berger and Luckman. Wendt introduced their thought in his critique of Waltz's theory of international politics, reconceiving the structure of the international system and challenging the purported logic of anarchy. His conclusion has become one of the most quoted phrases in IR: 'Anarchy is what states make of it.' But to reach this position, he had to make two theoretical moves. The first is to give the structure of the international system social content. Like Ruggie, he leans on Durkheim, but this time it is the idea of 'collective representations': the 'knowledge structures held by groups which generate macro-level patterns of individual behavior over time'.[28] Anarchy – the simple absence of central government – has no logic, Wendt argues; its effects depend entirely on the structure of knowledge in which it is embedded: its 'cultural' context and content.

[25] Emile Durkheim, *The Division of Labor in Society* (New York: Free Press, 1997), p. 84.
[26] Michele Foucault, *The Order of Things: An Archaeology of the Human Sciences* (New York: Vintage Books, 1973), p. xxii.
[27] Ibid., pp. xxii–xxiii.
[28] Wendt, *Social Theory of International Politics*, pp. 161–162.

His second move is to treat this structure as constitutive. The inter-subjective meanings it comprises do not just affect actors' epistemic frames – how they know the world around them – they constitute actors' social identities: 'the sets of meanings that an actor attributes to itself while taking the perspective of others, that is, as a social object'.[29] For symbolic interactionists, how humans respond to objects depends on the meanings they attach to them, and these meanings are produced and reproduced through social interaction. This is true not only of 'external' objects – physical, social, or abstract – but also of the self. As Blumer explains, 'in order to become an object to himself a person has to see himself from the outside. One can do this only by placing himself in the position of others and viewing himself from that position.'[30] Humans do this by role taking: by assuming institutionally defined 'types' of self. 'Institutions are embodied in individual experience by means of roles', Berger and Luckman argue. 'By playing roles, the individual participates in the social world. By internalizing these roles, the same world becomes subjectively real to him.'[31] For Wendt, this means that the effects of anarchy are determined not only by the surrounding structure of knowledge but, most importantly, by the role identities this structure constitutes. To show that there is no single logic of anarchy, he imagines three different cultures of anarchy, each characterized by dominant role identity: 'enemy' in a Hobbesian culture, 'rival' in a Lockean, and 'friend' in the Kantian.[32]

Constructivists acknowledge that interests can have multiple sources, not all of which relate to actors' identities. 'Sometimes situations are unprecedented in our experience', Wendt argues, 'and in these cases we have to construct their meaning, and thus our interests, by analogy or invent them de novo'.[33] Most of the time, however, it is our institutionally referential role identities that generate our interests. As we navigate our way through the world, we determine the meaning of situations with reference to who we are, assessing, often

[29] Alexander Wendt, 'Collective Identity Formation and the International State', *American Political Science Review*, 88.2 (1994), 385.
[30] Herbert Blumer, *Symbolic Interactionism: Perspective and Method* (Berkeley: University of California Press, 1986), pp. 12–13.
[31] Peter L. Berger and Thomas Luckman, *The Social Construction of Reality: A Treatise in the Sociology of Knowledge* (New York: Anchor Books, 1966), p. 74.
[32] Wendt, *Social Theory of International Politics*, pp. 257–258.
[33] Wendt, 'Anarchy Is What States Make of It', p. 398.

unconsciously, what a situation means for *us*: what it consists of, what is at stake, what our interests are in that situation. 'Without the binding thread of identity', Nelson Foote contends, 'one could not evaluate the succession of situations. Literally, one could say there was not value in living, since value only exists or occurs relative to particular identities – at least value as experienced by organisms which do not live in the mere present, as animals presumably do, devoid of self and unaware of impending death.'[34] Added to this, the process of identification – the development of role identities shared with others – is essential to the development of collective interests and values. As Foote explains, 'it is only through identification as the sharing of identity that individual motives become social values and social values, individual motives'.[35] Constructivists are not opposed to the concept of 'self-interest', therefore. Indeed, they lay claim to a richer understanding, insisting that explaining behaviour with reference to self-interest demands some account of how a particular conception of self informed a particular constellation of interests.

Durkheimian- or Foucauldian-type arguments about social epistemes defining the epistemological field of view, and the symbolic interactionist thesis that meanings constitute actors' identities, in turn shaping their interests, all assume that processes of constitution are cognitive. Social epistemes condition what actors can see, and how they order their social and natural universes. Intersubjective meanings shape actors' identities as they learn social roles, and identities shape interests by rendering situations meaningful. Because intersubjective meanings ground all of these processes, cognition is not something isolated in individual minds. Moreover, these constitutive processes all depend on social interaction: intersubjective meanings are produced and reproduced by communication and shared practices; actors construct their identities through engagement with others; and while interests may derive from identities, they are also situational, clarified as actors navigate through their social and natural environments.

A third strand of constructivism highlights the centrality of language and communication to processes of social constitution, drawing in particular on the work of Wittgenstein, Austin, Searle, and Habermas.

---

[34] Nelson Foote, 'Identification as the Basis for a Theory of Motivation', *American Sociological Review*, 16.1 (1951), 20.

[35] Ibid.

Humans are not merely 'suspended in webs of significance', as Geertz famously argued. For constructivists like Onuf and Kratochwil, these webs are suspended in, and mobilized by, language. Key here is Onuf's claim that '[c]onstructivism begins with deeds. Deeds done, acts taken, words spoken – These are all that facts are.'[36] In the third section, I discuss the importance of this idea to recent developments in practice theory, but early constructivists were primarily concerned with what it meant for understanding the social role of language. Onuf's claim highlights two things: that spoken words, or language, constitute facts, and that language is a kind of deed, a form of action. To sustain these ideas, Onuf draws on Wittgenstein's later writings, in which Wittgenstein rejected his earlier view of language as a form of representation, arguing instead that the meanings that inhere in language exist solely in its use. How, Wittgenstein asked, are what words 'signify supposed to come out other than in the kind of use they have'?[37] He uses the example of the words 'five slabs' expressed on a building site. They have different meanings depending on whether they are a report – 'I counted five slabs' – or an order – 'get me five slabs'.[38] (Any Australian will know that the meaning of 'five slabs' is even more complicated, where a 'slab' might refer to a piece of concrete or a large pack of beer.) The meanings that attend words, Wittgenstein argued, are determined by the 'language games' in which they are expressed, by the amalgams of 'language and activities into which it is woven'.[39] The language games humans navigate are multiple, and language acquisition is a process of learning the rules that define and structure these games. This is the first sense in which linguistic constructivists see human action as rule governed: language constitutes social life, and language is constituted by rules. Human action is rule governed in a second way, though. As Kratochwil explains, 'with the exception of pure reflexes or unthinking conditioned behavior – it [human action] becomes understandable against the background of norms embodied in conventions and rules which give meaning to an action. Thus, not only must an actor refer to rules and norms when he/she wants to make a choice, but the observer, as well, must understand the normative structure

---

[36] Nicholas Greenwood Onuf, *World of Our Making: Rules and Rule in Social Theory and International Relations* (New York: Routledge, 2012), pp. 35–36.
[37] Ludwig Wittgenstein, *Philosophical Investigations*, 4th edn. (Oxford: Blackwell, 2009), p. 43.
[38] Ibid., p. 51.   [39] Ibid., p. 42.

underlying the action in order to interpret or appraise choices.'[40] These two senses in which human action is rule governed are closely related: rules and norms are particular kinds of speech acts, and the words that communicate them are only meaningful within particular rule-governed language games.

When explaining how rules and norms shape human action, linguistic constructivists draw primarily on speech act and communicative action theories. When actors say they 'promise', 'argue', 'apologize', 'approve', 'condemn', or 'consent', they are not just describing an action; they are performing that action. Moreover, each of these speech acts, along with thousands of others, refers implicitly to a background set of rules or norms that give that act meaning, to both the speaker and others. In Kratochwil's words, '[o]nly with reference to the rules and norms constitutive of a practice does, for instance, the utterance of "I do" in a marriage ceremony mean that I have committed myself'.[41] Speech-act theory illuminates these workings, showing how rules and norms – formal and informal, legal and social – do not just regulate actions; they also constitute them as meaningful practices. Yet rules and norms are far from determinate. Their meanings can be unclear: does saying 'I do' in a wedding commit one to love and cherish or love and obey? Also, in any given situation, multiple, at times conflicting, rules and norms might apply. In such cases, actors argue over normative applicability and meaning: 'they try to figure out in a collective communicative process ... whether norms of appropriate behavior can be justified, and which norms apply under given circumstances'.[42] But as Habermas explains, arguing is itself a norm-governed practice. If communicative action is to succeed, and not collapse into strategic action or outright conflict, 'a communicatively achieved agreement must be based *in the end* on reasons'.[43] Parties have to justify the norms they favour, as well as their normative interpretations. In this process, not all reasons have equal standing; only those that resonate

---

[40] Friedrich Kratochwil, *Rules, Norms, and Decisions: On the Conditions of Practical and Legal Reasoning in International Relations and Domestic Affairs* (Cambridge: Cambridge University Press, 1989), p. 11.

[41] Ibid., p. 7.

[42] Thomas Risse, '"Let's Argue!": Communicative Action in World Politics', *International Organization*, 54.1 (2000), 7.

[43] Jürgen Habermas, *Theory of Communicative Action* (Boston: Beacon Press, 1984), p. 17.

with preexisting, mutually recognized higher order values are considered valid. '[O]nly those persons count as responsible', Habermas argues, 'who, as members of a communicative community, can orient their actions to intersubjectively recognized validity claims'.[44] The most fundamental of these higher order values are rooted in the parties' shared lifeworld, 'the storehouse of unquestioned cultural givens from which those participating in communication draw agreed-upon patterns of interpretation for use in their interpretive efforts'.[45] Without this shared cultural storehouse, communicative action is incomprehensible.

Normative Monism

In its formative years – either side of the end of the Cold War – constructivism was a building project, in which its core ontological propositions were constructed out of the intellectual resources detailed above. Over time this initial phase of construction passed and constructivists turned to application: working within their ontological framework to answer a variety of empirical questions – from the end of apartheid and the nature of multilateralism to weapons taboos and revolutions in sovereignty. Theoretical innovation has continued, but with notable exceptions, such as work on the intersection of empirical and normative theory,[46] the 'practice turn',[47] and reconceptualizations of power,[48] most of this has involved refining the original propositions or crafting middle-range theoretical explanations. The broad trend, as Onuf observes, is that 'constructivism has both slowed down as a theoretical project and spread out as a research enterprise'.[49]

[44] Ibid., p. 14.
[45] Jürgen Habermas, *Moral Consciousness and Communicative Action* (Cambridge, MA: MIT Press, 1990), p. 135.
[46] See Richard Price (ed.), *Moral Limit and Possibility in World Politics* (Cambridge: Cambridge University Press, 2008).
[47] See Emanuel Adler and Vincent Pouliot (eds.), *International Practices* (Cambridge: Cambridge University Press, 2011).
[48] The most recent contributions to this reconceptualization are Ayse Zarakol (ed.), *Hierarchies in World Politics* (Cambridge: Cambridge University Press, 2017); and Peter J. Katzenstein and Lucia Seybert (eds.), *Protean Power: Exploring the Uncertain and Unexpected in World Politics* (Cambridge: Cambridge University Press, 2018).
[49] Nicholas Onuf, 'Constructivism at the Crossroads; or, the Problem of Moderate-Sized Dry Goods', *International Political Sociology*, 10.2 (2016), 115.

This enterprise has distinctive strands, however. Constructivist research has coalesced into two principal projects: the norms project and the institutional structure project. Both privilege certain social theoretical sources over others, evince coherent lineages of ideas, and are animated and structured by distinctive internal debates.

Within these projects, two approaches to culture are evident. The norms project disaggregates culture, breaking it up into individual norms, the causal effects of which can then be studied. The institutional structure project treats culture as deep structure, the intersubjective foundation on which social orders are constructed. Though different in key respects, both approaches are forms of normative monism; they begin with a coherent normative entity and then trace its causal effects through a variety of mechanisms: epistemic framing, socialization, argument, etc. In the norms project, these entities are individual rules or norms; in the institutional structure project, they are social epistemes or lifeworlds. The development and persistence of these forms of monism flies in the face of early calls for culture to be conceived as 'contested and polymorphic'.[50] In focusing on the causal effects of single rules and norms, the norms project brackets the complex normative terrain that actors actually navigate. And the institutional structure project reproduces the default conception of culture, attributing the nature of international orders to underlying cultural structures: unitary, coherent, and constitutive.

The Norms Project

That constructivists should be interested in the nature and effects of norms is hardwired into their ontology. Their starting assumption is, after all, that the social world is structured by intersubjective meanings, and among these meanings, rules and norms constitute actors' role identities and enable them to navigate social life. If human action is rule governed, then studying norms is essential to understanding such action. The norms project is not just the study of norms, however; it is a particular way of studying norms, driven in significant measure by the methodological imperative to operationalize culture.

---

[50] Yosef Lapid, 'Culture's Ship: Returns and Departures in International Relations Theory', in Yosef Lapid and Friedrich Kratochwil (eds.), *The Return of Culture and Identity in IR Theory* (Boulder, CO: Lynne Rienner, 1996), p. 8.

The pioneers of norms research were clear about this imperative. When summarizing the principal claims advanced in *The Culture of National Security*, Ronald Jepperson, Wendt, and Katzenstein repeatedly qualify their references to 'cultural and institutional environments' with the phrase 'in this volume, most often norms'.[51] Katzenstein explains this move in his own work on the police and military in postwar Japan, arguing that '"culture" is not a helpful analytical tool for empirical research; instead it is more useful to analyze particular aspects of culture (here, social and legal norms)'.[52] In *National Interests and International Society*, Martha Finnemore distinguishes between holistic approaches to social structure, which emphasize system-wide shared knowledge and intersubjective meanings, and her preferred variety of constructivism that focuses on particular 'social elements': rules or norms. The advantage of this approach, she argues, is that it 'identifies a different socially constructed variable as causal and describes the causal process'.[53] In their widely cited review of early constructivist norms research, Finnemore and Kathryn Sikkink differentiate between earlier work on the normative dimensions of world politics and the more rigorous new wave. The virtue of this new work, they argue, is its determination 'to specify ideational causal claims and mechanisms clearly, think seriously about the microfoundations on which theoretical claims about norms rest, and evaluate those claims in the context of carefully designed historical and empirical research'.[54]

In addition to disaggregating culture into individual norms, the norms project reduces culture to norms, bracketing other kinds of intersubjective meanings that comprise cultural environments. Norms are commonly defined as 'shared (thus social) understandings of standards of behavior',[55] 'shared expectations about appropriate behavior

[51] Ronald L. Jepperson, Alexander Wendt, and Peter Katzenstein, 'Norms, Identity, and Culture in National Security', in Peter J. Katzenstein (ed.), *The Culture of National Security: Norms and Identity in World Politics* (New York: Columbia University Press, 1996), p. 52.

[52] Peter J. Katzenstein, *Culture Norms and National Security: Police and Military in Postwar Japan* (Ithaca, NY: Cornell University Press, 1996), p. 2.

[53] Martha Finnemore, *National Interests and International Society* (Ithaca, NY: Cornell University Press, 1996), p. 17.

[54] Martha Finnemore and Kathryn Sikkink, 'International Norm Dynamics and Political Change', *International Organization*, 52.4 (1998), 890.

[55] Audie Klotz, *Norms in International Relations* (Ithaca, NY: Cornell University Press, 1996), p. 14. For similar definition, see Finnemore, *National Interests*, p. 22.

held by a community of actors',[56] or 'collective expectations about proper behavior for a given identity'.[57] And they are seen as having regulatory and constitutive effects, prescribing or proscribing forms of behaviour and producing and reproducing role identities. One does not have to deny that social life is rule governed, however, to see that in any cultural context rules and norms are embedded in, and inextricably connected to, a host of other intersubjective meanings. Indeed, constructivists outside the norms project pay special attention to these meanings. Social life is structured by social epistemes, by shared ideas about the nature of things and how they work, by collective assumptions about cause and effect, by beliefs in the divine (or that there is no divine); even emotions are said to have intersubjective foundations.[58] None of these is easily conceived as a 'shared expectation of behavior', and together they burst the boundaries of the conception of culture that contributors employed in *The Culture of National Security*, where '*culture* refers both to a set of evaluative standards, such as norms or values, and to cognitive standards, such as rules or models defining what entities and actors exist in a system and how they operate and interrelate'.[59]

Having disaggregated culture into individual norms, the norms project has focused on how norms, as atomized meanings, emerge, shape behaviour, and die. Finnemore and Sikkink distilled from the first wave of norms research the idea that norms have a life cycle; they go through phases of 'emergence', 'cascade', and 'internalization'. This distinction is important, they argue, because 'different social processes and logics of action may be involved at different stages in a norm's "life cycle"'.[60] In the initial phase of norm emergence, communicative processes of persuasion are crucial as '[n]orm entrepreneurs attempt to convince a critical mass of states (norm leaders) to embrace new norms'.[61] In the norm cascade phase, socialization via imitation is more important than argument, as 'a combination of pressure for conformity, desire to enhance international legitimation, and the desire of state leaders to enhance self-esteem facilitate norm cascades', understood as the spread

[56] Finnemore, *National Interests*, p. 22.
[57] Jepperson, Wendt, and Katzenstein, 'Norms, Identity, and Culture', p. 54.
[58] See Emma Hutchison, *Affective Communities in World Politics: Collective Emotions after Trauma* (Cambridge: Cambridge University Press, 2016).
[59] Jepperson, Wendt, and Katzenstein, 'Norms, Identity, and Culture', p. 56.
[60] Finnemore and Sikkink, 'International Norm Dynamics', p. 895.   [61] Ibid.

of a norm from leaders to followers.[62] In the final implementation phase, norms assume a taken-for-granted quality, eventually emerging as new 'standards of appropriateness', possibly becoming focal points for the development of new, contradictory norms. Neglected in early norms research, this idea that norms can in time be supplanted has become the focus of more recent work on norm death. Not only does the rise of new norms often mean the demise of others, but sometimes hard-won norms, which still appear morally progressive and justified, seem to lose their purchase; the norm against torture is a possible example.[63]

This early work on the life cycle of norms was complemented by research on their effects, in particular their role in bringing about domestic political change. Much of this work focuses on human rights, with two key volumes edited by Thomas Risse, Stephen Ropp, and Kathryn Sikkink being both emblematic of this work and indicative of how it has evolved. *The Power of Human Rights* introduces the widely cited 'spiral model' to describe how human rights norms, when mobilized by transnational advocacy networks, can change national practices. The spiral circles through five phases, each characterized by a shift in the target state's position, from repression and denial through tacit concessions to norm acceptance and rule-consistent behaviour.[64] Movement through these phases is driven by a 'boomerang' process, in which '[n]ational opposition groups, NGOs, and social movements link up with transnational networks and INGOs who then convince international human rights organizations, donor institutions, and/or great powers to pressure norm-violating states'.[65] A decade and a half after the publication of this first volume, Risse, Ropp, and Sikkink published *The Persistent Power of Human Rights*, seeking to explain why states move from a simple commitment to human rights norms to compliance with those norms. While the original spiral model encompassed norm compliance, they acknowledged that they had failed to

---

[62] Ibid.
[63] For a critique of this literature, see Sarah Percy and Wayne Sandholtz, 'Do Norms Really Die?' (unpublished paper).
[64] Thomas Risse and Kathryn Sikkink, 'The Socialization of International Human Rights Norms into Domestic Practices: Introduction', in Thomas Risse, Stephen C. Ropp, and Kathryn Sikkink (eds.), *The Power of Human Rights: International Norms and Domestic Change* (Cambridge: Cambridge University Press, 1999), p. 20.
[65] Ibid., p. 18.

fully theorize the move from commitment to compliance and paid insufficient attention to cases where states got 'stuck', never moving beyond bare acceptance. Their principal innovation in the new volume is to integrate rationalist and norms-based arguments, showing how different modes of social action interact: coercion, shifting incentives, persuasion, and capacity building. Their 'central point is that the logic of consequences and the cost–benefit calculations of utility-maximizing egoistic actors are often embedded in a more encompassing logic of appropriateness of norm-guided behavior as institutionalized in the contemporary international human rights regime'.[66] This focus on compliance has been criticized for neglecting processes of implementation. Implementation, Alexander Betts and Phil Orchard argue, is 'a *process* which furthers adoption of the new norm', whereas compliance 'is an *act* whereby the state follows an existing norm'.[67] To fully understand this process, they contend, implementation must be seen as primarily a 'state-level' or 'organization-level' process, and attention focused on how ideational, material, and institutional factors constitute and constrain norms.[68]

In all of this work – whether focused on norm emergence, institutionalization, diffusion, commitment, compliance, implementation, or some other dynamic – the norms project has been consistent in isolating single norms and tracing their effects. Norms researchers readily admit that individual norms exist in complex normative environments, populated by multiple, often contradictory, norms. In Finnemore's words, '[t]ensions and contradictions among normative principles in international life mean that there is no set of ideal political or economic arrangements towards which we are all converging'.[69] Indeed, Finnemore and Sikkink warned that 'the danger in using norm language is that it can obscure distinct and interrelated elements of social institutions if not used carefully'.[70] Yet norms researchers engage this complexity in bite-sized pieces, showing how the emergence and

[66] Thomas Risse and Stephen Ropp, 'Introduction and Overview', in Thomas Risse, Stephen Ropp, and Kathryn Sikkink (eds), *The Persistent Power of Human Rights* (Cambridge: Cambridge University Press, 2013), p. 13.
[67] Alexander Betts and Phil Orchard, 'Introduction: The Normative Institutionalization-Implementation Gap', in Alexander Betts and Phil Orchard (eds.), *Implementation and World Politics: How International Norms Change Practice* (Oxford: Oxford University Press, 2013), p. 6.
[68] Ibid., pp. 12–18.   [69] Finnemore, *National Interests*, p. 135.
[70] Finnemore and Sikkink, 'International Norm Dynamics', p. 891.

effectiveness of a chosen norm was affected by its relationship to discrete other norms. Stories about single norms thus become tales of normative dyads or triads, in which the focus norm is able to emerge because it resonates naturally with preexisting norms or because it has been related to them explicitly. In his account of banning of anti-personnel landmines, Richard Price calls these processes 'grafting', which he defines as 'the genealogical heritage and conscious manipulation involved in such normative rooting and branching'.[71] By focusing on these processes, norms researchers have offered powerful accounts of key norms, from racial equality and weapons taboos to decolonization and sovereignty.[72] It bears noting, however, that this approach to the complex cultural universes in which norms emerge is driven by the same methodological imperative as the initial focus on single norms: the need to isolate individual norms, specify their relations, and demonstrate their causal effects.

The relationship between individual norms and broader cultural contexts is also a concern of the 'localization' literature. Pioneered by Amitav Acharya, this literature focuses on how international norms are taken up by local actors, translated in relation to preexisting cultural norms, and institutionalized in a new form, often amplifying prior norms. Acharya calls these processes localization, which he defines as 'the active construction (through discourse, framing, grafting, and cultural selection) of foreign ideas by local actors, which results in the former developing significant congruence with local beliefs and practices'.[73] Challenging moral cosmopolitan approaches to norm diffusion, which privilege the international and transnational teaching of universal norms, and approaches that emphasize the 'fit' between international and domestic norms, ignoring local 'match-making', Acharya shows how '[l]ocal actors borrow and frame external norms in ways that establishes their values to the local audience',

---

[71] Richard Price, 'Reversing the Gun Sights: Transnational Civil Society Targets Land Mines', *International Organization*, 53.3 (1998), 628.

[72] Klotz, *Norms in International Relations*; Price, 'Reversing the Gun Sights'; and Daniel Philpott, *Revolutions in Sovereignty* (Princeton, NJ: Princeton University Press, 2001).

[73] Amitav Acharya, 'How Ideas Spread: Whose Norms Matter? Norm Localization and Institutional Change in Asian Regionalism', *International Organization*, 58.2 (2004), 245. For another approach to the localization of global norms, see Lisbeth Zimmerman, *Global Norms with a Local Face* (Cambridge: Cambridge University Press, 2017).

how norms 'may be reconstructed to fit with local beliefs and practices even as local beliefs and practices may be adjusted in accordance with the external norm', and how '[n]ew instruments and practices are developed from the syncretic normative framework in which local influences remain highly visible'.[74] The great strengths of this perspective are its emphasis on local agency and the mutually constitutive relationship it posits between international and local norms. It also suggests that international norms are mobilized and reconstituted within complex, highly variegated local cultural contexts. Yet in his empirical accounts of localization processes in contemporary Southeast Asia, Acharya follows other norms researchers, focusing on discrete relations between small numbers of individual norms. For example, after the Cold War international ideas of common security were successfully localized as a new norm of cooperative security because ASEAN leaders reframed them in relation to three preexisting regional norms.[75] Interestingly, when Acharya steps out of the norms project to examine broader civilizational interactions between India and 'classical' Southeast Asia, localization is presented as a mutually constitutive relationship between complex universes of meaning and practice, not discrete norms in dyadic or triad relations.[76]

The Institutional Structure Project

The second project around which constructivist research has coalesced focuses on the nature and evolution of international institutional structures. It is useful here to distinguish between three levels of institutions (a distinction I return to in Chapter 6). Issue-specific institutions or 'regimes' are the rules, norms, and decision-making practices that govern state conduct in particular issue areas, such as trade, security, or human rights. Fundamental institutions are the basic institutional practices that states employ to facilitate coexistence and solve coordination and collaboration problems, with international law and multilateralism privileged in the modern era. Constitutional institutions are the metavalues that define the units of legitimate political authority and how they stand in relation to one another, the institution of sovereignty

[74] Acharya, 'How Ideas Spread', p. 251.   [75] Ibid., pp. 254–260.
[76] Amitav Acharya, *Civilizations in Embrace: The Spread of Ideas and the Transformation of Power; India and Southeast Asia in the Classical Age* (Singapore: Institute for Southeast Asian Studies, 2012).

being the prime example.[77] These institutions are hierarchically ordered, with constitutional institutions defining the units engaged in fundamental institutional practices, and these practices are enacted every time issue-specific institutions are created. The institutional structure project is primarily concerned with constitutional and fundamental institutions, leaving issue-specific institutions to the norms project.

As anticipated above, it was Ruggie who pioneered research on the constitutional metavalues that structure international systems. The most basic feature of any international system, he argues, is how political units are differentiated. This is not about whether they are the same or different but, rather, how they are arranged. And this is determined not by struggle and competition (or not only), but by intersubjective '*principles on the basis of which the constituent units are separated* from one another'.[78] Understanding this is crucial, he contends, because historically different international systems have been structured by different principles, and a shift in these principles is the defining characteristic of systems change: 'change in the nature of the actors or diverse entities that compose an international system'.[79] As we have seen, Ruggie sees the shift from medieval heteronomy to modern sovereignty as a key example of such change. Both systems were anarchic, but their units differ fundamentally, as do their jurisdictional powers and relations.

What interests me here is how Ruggie explains the shift from heteronomy to sovereignty, as this reveals the normative monism at the heart of his argument. In the norms project, normative monism involves the selection of a single norm and the tracing of its causal effects. In Ruggie's work, and in the institutional structure project more broadly, it involves the identification of a deep, system-wide set of intersubjective meanings – a collective mentality or social episteme – that structures the systemic distribution of authority. As we have seen, Ruggie attributes the modern sovereign order to three factors: changing material conditions, shifts in strategic behaviour, and the rise

---

[77] This typology is detailed in Reus-Smit, *Moral Purpose*, pp. 12–15.

[78] Ruggie, 'Continuity and Transformation', p. 274.

[79] Gilpin, *War and Change*, p. 39. Note here that when Gilpin refers to a change in the nature of the actors, he is not referring to their functions, as did Waltz. Rather, he is referring to their nature as units of political authority – their legitimate powers and jurisdictions. This invariably brings him closer to Ruggie, as variations in such powers affects how units stand in relation to one another.

of a new social episteme, the last of which he considers especially important. Building on Michael Walzer's claim that the state has to be 'personified before it can be seen, symbolized before it can be loved',[80] Ruggie argues that the shift from heteronomy to sovereignty was possible only because of an epistemic revolution. Centrally important here was the Renaissance rediscovery of single-point perspective in art, which involved a fundamental change in the rendering of reality. The world came to be seen from 'a *single* point of view, the point of view of a *single* subjectivity, from which all other subjectivities were differentiated and against which all other subjectivities were plotted in diminishing size and depth toward the vanishing point'.[81] This epistemic transformation was not confined to art: it reordered political authority. Medieval paintings of cities, with their seemingly random layering of buildings, reflect the same decentring that characterized the heteronomous political landscape, populated, as it was, by multiple centres of authority with non-exclusive, overlapping jurisdictions. Similarly, after the Renaissance, Ruggie argues, '[w]hat was true in the visual arts was equally true in politics: political space came to be defined *as it appeared from a single fixed viewpoint*. The concept of sovereignty, then, was merely the doctrinal counterpart of the application of single-point perspectival forms to the spatial organization of politics'.[82] A nice example of this is Louis XIV's claim that a king is 'of rank superior to all other men, he sees things more perfectly than they do'.[83]

This kind of normative monism is also apparent when constructivists address the nature and origins of fundamental institutions: multilateralism, international law, etc. My own early work merits a brief discussion here. My goal in *The Moral Purpose of the State* was to explain why different international societies have privileged different kinds of fundamental institutions or basic institutional practices.[84] Since the nineteenth century, multilateralism and positive international law have predominated, but very different practices were privileged in absolutist Europe, Renaissance Italy, and ancient Greece. When I was

[80] Michael Walzer, 'On the Role of Symbolism in Political Thought', *Political Science Quarterly*, 82.2 (1967), 194.
[81] Ruggie, 'Territoriality and Beyond', p. 159.   [82] Ibid.
[83] Quoted in R. W. Harris, *Absolutism and Enlightenment; 1660–1789* (London: Blandford Press, 1967), p. 76.
[84] Reus-Smit, *Moral Purpose*, pp. 4–5.

writing, two explanations for the rise of multilateralism existed, neither of which was satisfactory. Rationalists argued that states adopt multilateralism to solve problems of collaboration, coordination, suasion, and assurance, but admitted that 'at this level of analysis the outcomes remain indeterminate. Multiple feasible solutions exist for each problem.'[85] To overcome this indeterminacy, constructivists attributed the post-1945 proliferation of multilateral institutions to America's identity as a liberal hegemon, in particular, to its determination to construct institutions that embodied the architectural principles of the New Deal regulatory state.[86] The problem, however, is that international society's embrace of multilateralism began in the nineteenth century, well before American hegemony.[87] To account for the modern privileging of multilateralism, and the predominance of other institutional forms earlier, I made the characteristic move of the institutional structure project – I stressed the importance of deep intersubjective structures: in particular, hegemonic beliefs about the moral purpose of the state, the organizing principle of sovereignty, and pure procedural justice. These meanings form a coherent normative system, I argued: beliefs about the moral purpose of the state provide the justificatory foundations for the organizing principle of sovereignty, and they carry with them ideas about how social rules and norms can legitimately be defined.[88] 'Constitutional structures', as I called these deep meanings, took root first in the social interactions of individuals and communities, producing in time particular kinds of legitimate states: ancient Greek city-states, Renaissance republics, absolutist monarchies, constitutional democracies, etc. Once this has occurred, these ideas get transplanted into international society, defining the terms of legitimate statehood and rightful state action, in particular, the kinds of institutional practices states deem appropriate for solving problems of coexistence and collaboration.

[85] Lisa Martin, 'The Rational State Choice of Multilateralism', in John Gerard Ruggie (ed.), *Multilateralism Matters: The Theory and Praxis of an Institutional Form* (New York: Columbia University Press, 1993), p. 92.
[86] Anne-Marie Burley, 'Regulating the World: Multilateralism, International Law, and the Projection of the New Deal Regulatory State', in John Gerard Ruggie (ed.), *Multilateralism Matters: The Theory and Praxis of an Institutional Form* (New York: Columbia University Press, 1993), pp. 125–156; and John Gerard Ruggie, *Winning the Peace: America and World Order in the New Era* (New York: Columbia University Press, 1996.
[87] Reus-Smit, *Moral Purpose*, p. 24.   [88] Ibid., p. 33.

Nineteenth- and twentieth-century multilateralism, I argued, is not just a rational solution to cooperation problems, or a product of *American* hegemony; it is an expression of far deeper assumptions about how constitutional democracies legislate rules and norms.[89]

The normative monism of this argument is readily apparent: a deep and coherent structure of intersubjective meanings constitutes states and their basic institutional practices. The monism evident in my own early work differs from Ruggie's in three respects, though. First, our deep structures are different. Ruggie's are very deep: the meanings he emphasizes are social epistemes, the most basic cognitive frames determining how actors know their worlds. These then affect how actors imagine political space, especially the distribution of political authority: heteronomy, then sovereignty. My deep structures are closer to the surface. Indeed, they are at the same level as the organizing principles Ruggie seeks to explain. But where he sees sovereignty, I embed sovereignty in a broader cluster of meanings about the moral purpose of the state and procedural justice, and then use these to explain the nature of fundamental institutions. Second, while both of us stress the constitutive relationships between our respective deep structures and what we seek to explain (unit differentiation in Ruggie's case, and fundamental institutional forms in mine), we emphasize different constitutive mechanisms. For Ruggie, the mechanism is social cognition: a socially constructed epistemic frame determines how actors imagine political space. An element of this is also at work in my argument: states in all of my international societies came to imagine some practices as normative and others as beyond the pale. The principal mechanism I emphasize, however, is communicative action. Leaning heavily on Habermas, I argue that states produce and reproduce fundamental institutions through processes of moral argument, and in doing so they appeal to higher order values that such institutions are meant to serve. Deep constitutional structures provide these values, the communicative touchstones that states invoke when arguing about appropriate institutional practices. Finally, where Ruggie's social epistemes are intersubjective universals within a given social order, I stressed the hegemonic, not totalizing, nature of constitutional structures. Contrasting conceptions of the moral purpose of the state always exist, I argued, even if they take a counter-hegemonic form.[90] The

---

[89] Ibid., chapter 6.   [90] Ibid., p. 33.

problem is that I took the hegemonic status of particular constitutional structures as given, ignoring how they emerged ascendant from highly complex ideational terrains.

Arguably the best recent contribution to the institutional structure project is Andrew Phillips's *War, Religion, and Empire*, an ambitious attempt to explain how international orders collapse, grounded in a detailed comparison of the fates of medieval Christendom and East Asia's Sinosphere.[91] To gain this empirical reach, Phillips adopts an expansive conception of international order, following Ruggie in not assuming that international orders are organized on the principle of sovereignty (a move I also make in Chapter 6). International orders, he writes, are 'systemic structures that cohere within culturally and historically specific social imaginaries, and that are composed of an *order-producing* normative complex and its fundamental institutions', both of which 'rest in turn on a permissive *order-enabling* material foundation'.[92] In this conception, 'fundamental institutions' include the basic units of political authority and how they stand in relation to one another (sovereignty, suzerainty, or heteronomy), as well as the authoritative norms and practices that enable coexistence and cooperation (systems of law, legitimate modes of violence, etc.). These institutions are informed and licensed by the 'normative complex', which consists of the values that legitimize political authority.[93] Undergirding an order's normative complex and fundamental institutions are deeper 'social imaginaries' – 'tacit assumptions, images, and symbols'[94] – and enabling 'material foundations': principally, commercially and technologically determined modes of 'violence interdependence'.[95]

Drawing on detailed analyses of the collapse of the pre-Westphalian order of Latin Christendom and the demise of the Qing Chinese order, Phillips argues that international orders fall after sustained 'systemic crises', crises generated by challenges to foundational social imaginaries and the advent of disruptive military innovations. Long periods of 'institutional decay', 'ideological dissent and cultural innovation', and heightened 'violence interdependence' are followed by acute crises,

---

[91] The following account of Phillips's argument draws on my discussion in Reus-Smit, 'Cultural Diversity and International Order', pp. 13–16.

[92] Andrew Phillips, *War, Religion, and Empire: The Transformation of Orders* (Cambridge: Cambridge University Press, 2011), pp. 23–24.

[93] Ibid., pp. 26–27.   [94] Ibid., p. 24.   [95] Ibid., p. 46.

where ideological shocks coincide with military change.[96] In an explicit attempt to meld realist and constructivist insights, Phillips argues that 'international orders are transformed when they experience systemic legitimacy crises occasioned by a combination of institutional decay, disruptive military innovations, and ideological shocks that terminally destabilize existing social imaginaries and thus shatter the normative consensus upon which international orders depend.'[97] In the pre-Westphalian order, this was manifest in the conjunction of Reformation theology and the introduction of modern artillery, the increased use of mercenaries, and the enhanced financial resources of European monarchs.[98] In nineteenth-century Qing China, it was the ideological and geopolitical challenges of the encroaching West, combined with the domestic upheaval of the Taiping Rebellion.[99]

Like Ruggie's argument, as well as my own, the normative monism of Phillips's argument is all too apparent. He posits a hierarchy of institutions: 'fundamental institutions' that rest on a deeper 'normative complex', which rest in turn on underlying 'social imaginaries'. The last of these constitutes the deep structure, informing and rendering possible the principles of legitimacy that comprise the normative complex, as well as organizing principles and functional norms that inhere in fundamental institutions. Coming very close to Ruggie's idea of social epistemes, Phillips argues that social imaginaries 'encompass our most basic and mostly unarticulated assumptions about social reality, extending to those that condition our experience of categories as allegedly basic as time, space, language and embodiment'.[100] Collectively held assumptions such as these, he argues, are essential to the viability of an order's normative complex, as they provide 'a primary condition of possibility for orders' constitution and operation'.[101]

Before proceeding it is important to note that while most contributions to the institutional structure project evince versions of this normative monism, there are notable exceptions that are more sensitive to the complexity of the cultural contexts in which international institutions evolve. Mlada Bukovansky's study of the impact of the

---

[96] Ibid. Richard Ned Lebow also argues that a breakdown in the prevailing 'cultural equilibrium' can generate crises in political orders. See his *A Cultural Theory of International Relations* (Cambridge: Cambridge University Press, 2008), pp. 96–108.
[97] Ibid., pp. 43–44.   [98] Ibid., p. 84.   [99] Ibid., p. 175.   [100] Ibid., p. 24.
[101] Ibid., p. 25.

American and French revolutions on the nature of international society is the best example.[102] Together, these revolutions transformed the terms of international legitimacy, replacing previously ascendant ideas of monarchical sovereignty with popular or democratic sovereignty. Bukovansky's account of this change stresses the importance of 'international political culture', but it is not culture conceived as a deep, constitutive structure. To begin with, although she alludes to culture in general as 'the intersubjective structure of overall pattern of knowledge and beliefs held by a society at any given time',[103] she is concerned with a more specific stratum of culture: international 'political' culture. This she defines as 'a set of propositions about legitimacy, identity, and power, and the rules about behavior derived therefrom'.[104] Her crucial move, however, is to treat culture as inherently contradictory, not coherent. 'Political culture', she writes, 'is made up of ideas and propositions that may be related to one another in various ways: Two types of relationships are particularly significant to this analysis: the relationship of contradiction and that of complementarity.'[105] This is important, she argues, because it is the contradictions and complementarities within political culture that drive change. 'When the rules and norms of a political culture contradict each other, this constitutes an opportunity for certain types of social action; the same can be said for complementarities.'[106] Demonstrating this argument, Bukovansky shows how the ideas of enlightenment culture were first mobilized by European monarchies to extend their rule, but the contradictions within this culture enabled 'counterattacks on the legitimacy of the expansion of absolutist power',[107] ultimately justifying a particular kind of popular, though not necessarily democratic, sovereignty.

Lost Opportunities, Promising Leads

The normative monism that characterizes the norms and institutional structure projects, and the impact this has had on how mainstream constructivists understand culture, need never have taken root, or at least not in unproblematized form. While driven by the methodological

[102] Mlada Bukovansky, *Legitimacy and Power Politics: The American and French Revolutions in International Political Culture* (Princeton, NJ: Princeton University Press, 2002).
[103] Ibid., p. 22.   [104] Ibid., p. 16.   [105] Ibid., p. 30.   [106] Ibid., pp. 30–31.
[107] Ibid., p. 13.

imperative to operationalize culture, it is also a product of how certain
intellectual sources have been privileged over others. This privileging
is not the same in the norms and institutional structure projects, but
both neglect insights from linguistic and communicative action theory,
insights that point toward more complex understandings of culture.
There is another neglect, however, that is now being corrected, also
suggesting a richer view of culture. When Onuf argued that '[c]onstruc-
tivism begins with deeds. Deeds done, acts taken, words spoken',[108]
he and other linguistically inclined scholars focused on the role speech
acts play in constituting social life. But buried within this statement
is an emphasis on social practices more generally, which were also
stressed by Wittgenstein (Onuf's principal inspiration). As I explain
below, practices are now the focus of a new wave of constructivist
scholarship, and because in any social context practices are multiple,
overlaid, and do not form neatly bounded arrangements, practice
theory challenges, however implicitly, the default conception of culture
as coherent, bounded, and singularly constitutive.

Of the three sources discussed above – Durkheimian sociology,
symbolic interactionism, and linguistic and communicative action
theory – the norms project relies primarily on the second. From the
background structure of knowledge, individual norms are selected, and
these work their effects by constituting actors' role identities and, in
turn, their interests. The principal mechanisms linking norms, identities, and interests are persuasion and socialization. When discussing
the first of these, norms researchers enlist elements of communicative
action theory, stressing how actors argue about normative interpretation and applicability. This is communicative action theory 'lite',
though. There is little acknowledgement of the theory's deeper claims
about the linguistically constituted nature of reality or of the multiplicity of language games that constitute any social environment. This
reflects the methodological conventionalism of the norms project.
Bracketing these deeper claims is necessary if the proposition that
constructivism does 'not depend exceptionally upon any specialized
separate "interpretive methodology"',[109] a revisionist claim directly at
odds with foundational theory that stressed the linguistic construction

---

[108] Nicholas Greenwood Onuf, *World of Our Making: Rules and Rule in Social
Theory and International Relations* (New York: Routledge, 2012), pp. 35–36.
[109] Jepperson, Wendt, and Katzenstein, 'Norms, Identity, and Culture', p. 67.

of reality. When norms researchers turn to socialization, they rub shoulders with Durkheimian sociology, but socialization through learning and imitation is very different from socialization via epistemic constitution: the first involves already knowledgeable actors internalizing new norms through social interaction; the second entails the prior constitution of actors' cognitive horizons.

The institutional structure project enlists a different mix of ideas, but again marginalizes linguistic and communicative theory. Ruggie set the tone with his early use of Durkheimian sociology, using it to establish unit differentiation as a key axis of international change and, mixed with Foucauldian ideas, to conceive of the deep social epistemic structures that shape international institutional architectures. Nowhere in the relationship between social epistemes and the foundational institutions that determine unit differentiation – heteronomy or sovereignty – does communicative action feature; the mechanism at work is socially constituted cognition. As social epistemes change, actors come to see and inscribe the political landscape in new ways. My early work was less concerned with shifts in unit differentiation than with how sovereignty, as a distinctive form of differentiation, has been justified historically. These justifications, which invoke historically contingent ideas of the moral purpose of the state to license sovereignty, have been crucial, I suggested, in determining the kinds of fundamental institutions societies of states privilege. As we have seen, I use Habermasian communicative action theory to explain the necessary relationship between sovereignty and conceptions of the moral purpose of the state, and how the constitutional structures they form license basic institutional practices. But this is bounded communicative action: it is confined to the justificatory relations between elements of constitutional structures, and then relations between these structures and fundamental institutions. I ignore entirely the broader, highly complex terrain of language games that constitutes international social life. Phillips's argument evinces a logic much closer to Ruggie's, with socially constituted cognition reappearing as the principle link between strata of intersubjective meanings. Social imaginaries, normative complexes, and fundamental institutions are linked by ideological unity, not argument or discursive construction. Phillips stresses that '[a]uthoritative power operates through the medium of practices of communicative action', but the imaginaries, normative complexes, and fundamental institutions that define orders provide the arena in which such action takes place: they themselves are held together by the ideological resonance and complementarity that characterizes prevailing cultural life-worlds.[110]

Had constructivists paid more attention to linguistic and communicative theories, the normative monism that characterizes their principal projects might have been less sustainable, and a door would have opened to richer understandings of culture. The idea that social life is constituted by a multiplicity of language games, and that actors construct themselves and their social worlds through speech acts, articulated through discourse and argument, suggests a highly complex cultural universe of meanings and practices: neither a world of single norms, nested in dyadic or triadic relations, nor a world of coherent deep cultural structures. Interestingly, though, even those constructivists who place the greatest emphasis on argument as an engine of international change fail to fully embrace this more complex understanding. Neta Crawford's magisterial *Argument and Change in World Politics* is a case in point. Seeking to explain the demise of colonialism in world politics – a demise that fundamentally reordered political authority globally – Crawford calls for an emphasis on processes, especially communicative processes such as 'political argument, persuasion, and practical reason'.[111] Beliefs and culture, she argues, enable such processes: 'without them actors could not understand the arguments that others make, nor could actors successfully argue with others'.[112] This is not Swidler's idea of culture as a toolkit, however. Culture is not a highly variegated set of meanings from which actors can draw when arguing; it is an intersubjective background condition, essential to the very practice of arguing. More than this, Crawford reaches back to Benedict's writings, accepting her claim that culture is 'a more or less consistent pattern of thought and action', and defining it as 'the beliefs, symbols, and practices that social groups are convinced of or in great measure take for granted'.[113] There is a crucial difference, however, between Benedict's and Crawford's positions. Where Benedict thought individuals live in *a* culture, Crawford sees them living in multiple cultures, simultaneously. Cultures exist, she writes,

[110] Phillips, *War, Religion, and Empire*, pp. 21–33.
[111] Neta Crawford, *Argument and Change in World Politics: Ethics, Decolonization, and Humanitarian Intervention* (Cambridge: Cambridge University Press, 2002), p. 2.
[112] Ibid.   [113] Ibid., p. 59.

in 'epistemic communities, formal organizations, bounded political communities (nations and states), civilizations, and global cultures', she writes. This is, however, a multilayered version of IR's default conception of culture, and either individuals navigate their way through an array of distinct and coherent cultural arenas, each enabling their own internal forms of argument, or these cultures are nested hierarchically, with deeper cultural systems – say civilizations – providing macroframeworks of meaning that enable argument at other levels (which I think is closest to Crawford's position).

If mainstream constructivists have built on insights from Durkheimian sociology and symbolic interactionism but neglected ideas from linguistic and communicative theories, those who have enlisted these theories – including myself – initially did so quite narrowly: focusing on language games, speech acts, and communicative action (as a form of linguistic interaction). Neglected in this focus was Wittgenstein's insistence that meanings do not inhere in words themselves; they exist in, are learnt through, and are communicated by social practices. Not only are language games and speech acts themselves practices, but non-linguistic practices also embody and convey meanings, including the meanings of words.[114] Pioneers like Adler, Kratochwil, and Onuf have always been attuned to this, but recently it has become the focus of a 'practice turn' in constructivism, adding perhaps a third major 'project'.[115] Emanuel Adler and Vincent Pouliot define practices as 'socially meaningful patterns of action which, in being performed more or less

---

[114] For an excellent account of this theme in Wittgenstein's thought, see Kjell S. Johannessen, 'The Concept of Practice in Wittgenstein's Later Philosophy', *Inquiry*, 31.3 (1988), 357–369.

[115] Works that have been part of this wave include Emanuel Adler and Vincent Pouliot, 'International Practices', *International Theory*, 3.1 (2011), 1–36; Christian Bueger, 'Pathways to Practice: Praxiology and International Politics', *European Political Science Review*, 6.3 (2014), 383–406; Alena Drieschova, 'Peirce's Semeiotics: A Methodology for Bridging the Material-Ideational Divide in IR Scholarship', *International Theory*, 9.1 (2017), 33–66; Anna Leander, 'Practices (Re)producing Order: Understanding the Role of Business in Global Security Governance', in M. Ougaard and A. Leander (eds.), *Business and Global Governance* (New York: Routledge, 2009), pp. 57–77; Jennifer Mitzen, 'Anchoring Europe's Civilizing Identity: Habits, Capabilities and Ontological Security', *Journal of European Public Policy*, 13.2 (2006), 270–285; Iver Neumann, 'Returning Practice to the Linguistic Turn: The Case of Diplomacy', *Millennium: Journal of International Studies*, 31.3 (2002), 627–651; and Vincent Pouliot, *International Security in Practice: The Politics of NATO–Russia Diplomacy* (Cambridge: Cambridge University Press, 2010).

competently, simultaneously embody, act out, and possibly reify background knowledge and discourse in and on the material world'.[116] So understood, practices challenge the most fundamental of our theoretical dichotomies, as they are both ideational and material (they embody meanings in concrete ways of doing), and simultaneously agentic and structural (actors encounter them as social facts, but they are produced and reproduced through patterned actions). In addition to this, a focus on practices challenges IR's most basic politico-spatial distinctions, most notably, between the international, the domestic, and the transnational. The social and political topography of the world is shaped by, and manifest in, shifting constellations of practices. And to the extent that international, domestic, and transnational realms exist, they are contingent accomplishments of social practices. This argument articulates with a claim about agency. If world politics is structured by practices, and if these practices are inherently social, the crucial agents are communities of practice. 'A community of practice', write Adler and Pouliot, is 'a domain of knowledge that constitutes like-mindedness, a community of people that "creates the social fabric of learning," and a shared practice that embodies "the knowledge the community develops, shares, and maintains'.[117]

Like linguistic and communicative theories – and for much the same reasons – this new wave of constructivist scholarship challenges the normative monism of the norms and institutional structure projects, and points to a more complex view of culture than the default conception. For Adler and Pouliot, a focus on practices belies any notion that culture might reside in individuals' minds, or even solely in the realm of language or discourse. Culture, they argue, should be seen 'as bundles of ideas and matter that are linguistically, materially, and intersubjectively mediated in the form of practices'.[118] What interests me, though, is that because practices are multiple, overlapping, and not aligned in neat packages, practice theory necessarily conceives culture as polyvalent. In Adler's words, 'culture ceases to be a homogeneous normative or institutional structure and becomes disaggregated into diverse practices and their carriers, the latter of which carry multiple, overlapping, contesting, and differing cultural epistemic backgrounds'.[119] This is a

[116] Emanuel Adler and Vincent Pouliot, 'International Practices: Introduction and Framework', in Adler and Pouliot (eds.), *International Practices*, p. 6.
[117] Ibid., p. 17.   [118] Ibid., p. 13.
[119] Emanuel Adler, correspondence with the author, 16 November 2017.

significant improvement on the normative monism found in the norms and institutional structure projects. Two cautions, though. First, there is a risk in focusing on meaning-making through doing that the constitution and reconstitution of practices through the linguistic mobilization of ideas is unnecessarily discounted. Key moments of international change have been driven by such processes – the long struggle for decolonization is but one example – and recasting such moments as stories of shifting or clashing practices would at best obscure some of their essential dynamics. Second, while insisting that practices exist in 'constellations' or 'assemblages', Adler and Pouliot also suggest that research might focus on individual practices, proposing that these evolve through a 'practice lifecycle'.[120] Whatever the merits of such an approach, practice theorists should be careful not to reproduce the normative monism that characterizes norms research.

Conclusion

Among mainstream scholars of international relations, constructivists invoke the language of culture the most. They describe their arguments as cultural, they emphasize cultural variables, and they weigh the heuristic power of their theories against non-cultural alternatives. Given constructivism's relative youth, one might expect this interest to have translated into a relatively sophisticated understanding of culture, fully engaged with post-1970s arguments in anthropology, sociology, and political theory. Yet the lack of constructivist engagement with these literatures is striking, and when constructivists do look to these fields for conceptual insights, it is to debates of the 1950s or earlier. Drawing primarily on Durkheimian sociology and symbolic interactionism, they have treated culture in two very distinctive ways, either disaggregating it into individual norms or treating it as a deep structure, powerfully constitutive in effect. The first of these is blind to culture in its full complexity, missing how individual norms are enmeshed in complex, often contradictory, webs of intersubjective meanings and practices, not all of which are usefully characterized as norms. And the second simply reproduces the default conception of culture critiqued in previous chapters. Whether at the foundational level of social epistemes, imaginaries, or lifeworlds, or the next level up

[120] Adler and Pouliot (eds.), 'Introduction', p. 19.

of constitutional norms and values, a coherent, integrated, and thickly constitutive field of intersubjective meanings is imagined.

As we have seen, both approaches to culture are forms of normative monism; they take a single norm, or a single normative complex, and then trace its causal effects. This is a product, in part, of the intellectual resources they draw upon, but also of the imperative to operationalize constructivist claims about the effects of social meanings methodologically. If constructivists are to engage culture in a more sophisticated way, however, they have to abandon these forms of normative monism. They have to locate – theoretically and methodologically – individual norms within wider, heterogeneous complexes of meanings and practices, and recognize that actors are always navigating these broader terrains. And they have to break with the assumption that deep structures of intersubjective meanings are singular and coherent wholes. Such structures, anthropologists and sociologists now understand, are more commonly highly diverse, even contradictory. This raises a crucial theoretical challenge for constructivists, though. Normative monism allows constructivists to talk about meanings being both strategic resources and constitutive forces that shape actors' identities and interests (norm X was invoked by actors in justificatory struggles, for example, and/or it constituted actors' role identities). But once the focus shifts to broader, highly diverse complexes of meanings and practices, this becomes more challenging. As Swidler has shown, this move is compatible with seeing culture as a strategic resource – a diverse 'toolkit' of meanings and practices[121] – but it is harder to grasp its constitutive power, its role in shaping actors as knowledgeable social agents. There is a huge opportunity here, though, as complex cultural environments can be expected to constitute diverse, multilayered social identities, something constructivists have at times acknowledged but struggled to accommodate within their monist approaches.

---

[121] Swidler, 'Culture in Action'.

5 Rational Culture

For many, rational choice theory is an unlikely site for excavating ideas about culture. If realism's default materialism pushes culture to the margins, rational choice goes one step further, discounting the causal significance of social structural phenomena, and insisting that economic, political, and social outcomes are the products of individuals' instrumentally rational choices and strategies. Inverting Durkheim's axiom that 'society is not the mere sum of individuals, but ... their association represents a specific reality which has its own characteristics',[1] rationalists stress the primacy of maximizing individuals, and see society as at best the wrong starting point, at worst a metaphysical myth. Moreover, rationalists are often cast as materialists, accused of reducing individuals' preferences to economic gain and material advantage. Between its discounting of social structures, portrayal of individuals as instrumentally rational, and privileging of material preferences, what room is left in rational choice theory for culture?

Quite a bit, as it turns out. Rationalists do emphasize maximizing individuals, attribute social outcomes to the strategic interaction of such individuals, and are sceptical about the causal power of intangible social facts. Yet within these parameters they have crafted a distinctive perspective on culture. To grasp this perspective, it is useful to distinguish between 'thin' and 'thick' versions of rational choice theory. Contrary to some interpretations,[2] the thin version is usefully conceived as a parsimonious set of deep ontological assumptions. The thick version takes several forms, each constituting a distinctive rational choice theory. All are augmentations or modifications of the

---

[1] Emile Durkheim, *The Rules of Sociological Method* (New York: Free Press, 1982), p. 129.
[2] See, for example, James Fearon and Alexander Wendt, 'Rationalism v. Constructivism: A Skeptical View', in Walter Carlsnaes, Thomas Risse, and Beth A. Simmons (eds.), *Handbook of International Relations* (London: Sage, 2002), p. 53.

core ontological assumptions, more complex edifices constructed to overcome the indeterminacy of these foundational assumptions. Within these theories, three arguments about culture are apparent. The first provides a rationalist account of culture (qua norms), the second reduces culture to preferences, and the third integrates culture as common knowledge, essential to the solution of coordination problems. In each case, understandings of culture evince distinctive rationalist DNA, developed as they are within a framework of foundational ontological commitments.

Of these arguments, it is the one about common knowledge that interests me most. In prominent articulations, this argument has striking affinities with the default conception of culture that reappears time and again in theories of IR. Shared cultural meanings and practices play a crucial role in enabling stable social interaction, as culture instantiates and communicates the common knowledge individuals need to solve the myriad of coordination problems that social existence entails. Rational choice theorists say little directly about culture and international order, but the logic is clear: shared culture can be expected to facilitate order, while cultural diversity is likely to fragment the common knowledge essential to international coordination. Like other expressions of the default conception, this view struggles to accommodate the heterogeneous nature of all cultural formations and the fact that historically international orders have emerged in highly complex, even contradictory, cultural environments. This having been said, though, the argument can be reconfigured in productive ways. The construction of international orders is, in significant measure, an exercise in social coordination, and rational choice theorists are correct that such coordination requires common knowledge. In the heterogeneous cultural contexts in which international orders emerge, however, cultural meanings and practices have to be choreographed to generate the requisite common knowledge. Indeed, order builders have a powerful incentive to organize diversity, to order difference in ways that facilitate particular forms of coordination while impeding others (an imperative I return to in Chapter 6).

The following discussion is divided into two main sections. The first section identifies a small number of core rationalist propositions, differentiates between thin and thick theories, and surveys notable examples of the latter. It is here that I make the case that rational choice theories build out from a discrete set of ontological assumptions that structure subsequent elaborations. Against this background, the second section details the three principal ways in which rationalist theories have understood and incorporated culture: the rational choice of norms, culture as preferences, and culture as common knowledge. I focus principally on the last of these, detailing its affinity with the default conception of culture while drawing out its potential in revised form.

Before proceeding, a note on my approach. Rationalist theories are sometimes presented in textual form, at other times in more formal, mathematical forms. While rationalists argue persuasively that formal articulations perform an 'important service by helping us to work out the underlying logic and clarifying the grounds for different claims',[3] the following discussion engages primarily with textual expressions of rationalist theories: largely because the 'thick' approaches considered here necessarily entail textual articulation, but also (and quite frankly) because of the limits of my own competencies.

The Elements of Rational Choice Theory

Four Assumptions

Like constructivism, rational choice theory is not a substantive theory. Its underlying assumptions can be crafted into any number of specific theories, explaining any number of things, at times with contradictory results. But where constructivism is commonly described as an 'analytical framework', rational choice theory is most often presented as a 'methodology'. What is meant by this somewhat confusing appellation is that rational choice offers a distinctive way of understanding social life: it provides a series of internally coherent starting assumptions on which heuristically powerful explanations can be constructed.

Duncan Snidal provides a concise summary of this way of comprehending social life. Rational choice, he writes, is 'a methodological approach that explains both individual and collective (social outcomes) in terms of *individual goal seeking under constraints*'.[4] The assumptions that undergird this approach have been unpacked in a

---

[3] Duncan Snidal, 'Rational Choice and International Relations', in Walter Carlsnaes, Thomas Risse, and Beth A. Simmons (eds.), *Handbook of International Relations*, 2nd edn. (London: Sage, 2013), p. 92.

[4] Snidal, 'Rational Choice and International Relations', p. 87.

number of ways, but four seem especially important. First, where realists are groupists, as we saw in Chapter 2, rationalists are individualists: they treat individual human actors as the irreducible units of analysis. In its strongest, methodological individualist form, this view holds that 'the social world is ultimately the *result* of many individuals interacting with one another and that any theory that fails to accept this basic premise rests on mysterious metaphysical assumptions.'[5] In the study of international relations, this immediately confronts a problem: sovereign states, not individuals, are usually considered the principal actors. Various attempts have been made to accommodate this, by treating states 'as if' they were individuals (a move not restricted to rationalists), by aggregating intrastate preferences to produce a coherent national interest, or by focusing on peak decision makers within states.[6] For purists, only the last of these is satisfactory, as it alone avoids the 'black box' problem (assuming the integrity of an individual actor, where in fact that actor can be disaggregated into actual, irreducible individuals).[7]

Second, individuals are assumed to have a coherent set of preferences that they pursue strategically. Preferences are conceived as products or amalgams of desires and beliefs, the former encompassing individuals' wants and needs, and the latter, their understandings of their social and physical environments. 'The idea is simple', Lina Eriksson explains: 'people have desires (goals, wishes, etc.) and beliefs (convictions, vague ideas, etc.), and based on these they choose the alternative that best satisfies their desire (achieves their goal), given what they believe about various actions' possible consequences and their likelihood'.[8] Individuals are assumed to have multiple preferences that are rank ordered. The stability of these preference orders is secured by a series of assumed conditions, the most important of which is that preferences are transitive; that is, if an individual prefers A to B

---

[5] Christian List and Kai Spiekermann, 'Methodological Individualism and Holism in Political Science: A Reconciliation', *American Political Science Review*, 107.4 (2013), 629.

[6] Bruce Bueno de Mesquita, *The War Trap* (New Haven, CT: Yale University Press, 1981).

[7] Raymond Boudon, 'Rational Choice Theory', in Bryan S. Turner (ed.), *The New Blackwell Companion to Social Theory* (Oxford: Basil Blackwell, 2009), p. 180.

[8] Lina Eriksson, *Rational Choice Theory: Potential and Limits* (Houndmills: Palgrave Macmillan, 2011), p. 28.

and B to C, they must also prefer A to C.[9] For many rationalists, this assumption of a stable rank ordering of preferences is essential to rational choice's predictive power, as variation in an individual's preferences, or fluidity in their rank ordering, undermines the theory's *ex ante* capacity to predict behaviour.[10] This impulse has also encouraged some rationalists to assume that all individuals have certain primary, substantive preferences, most notably, economic gain (a legacy of rational choice's origins in economics, but a position now denied by most political scientists).[11]

Third, rationalists assume that individuals pursue their preferences within environmental constraints. The most important of these constraints is the array of other individuals' preferences and choices. Because individuals have to navigate these other preferences to realize their own, and because preferences often partially conflict, rationalists treat bargaining as the principal mode of social interaction. Environmental constraints are not limited to the prevailing array of preferences, though: other social constraints exist as well. Principal among these are institutions (broadly defined), which rationalists see as both bargaining outcomes and, once in existence, regulatory constraints on the pursuit of preferences. Added to all of this, individuals face material constraints that impose 'hard' limits on the range of feasible outcomes. The United States, as rational actor, may want to end North Korea's nuclear program, for example, but the latter's extant nuclear capability severely limits the former's options. Two things should be noted at this point. Rationalists are less concerned with the objective

---

[9] Keith Dowding identifies three assumed conditions: that preferences be reflexive, complete, and transitive. See his 'Rational Choice Theory', in Mark Bevir (ed.), *The Sage Handbook of Governance* (London: Sage, 2011), p. 36.

[10] A classic statement is provided by Gary Becker: 'The assumption of stable preferences provides a stable foundation for generating predictions about responses to various changes, and prevents the analyst from succumbing to the temptation of simply postulating the required shift in preferences to "explain" all apparent contradictions to his predictions'. See Gary Becker, *The Economic Approach to Human Behavior* (Chicago, IL: University of Chicago Press, 1976), p. 5. For a useful discussion, see Bruce Bueno de Mesquita, 'Ruminations on Challenges to Prediction with Rational Choice Models', *Rationality and Society*, 15.1 (2003), 136–147.

[11] For an example of this narrow reading of preferences, see John C. Harsanyi, 'Rational Choice Models of Political Behavior vs. Functionalist and Conformist Theories', *World Politics*, 21.4 (1969), 524.

nature of constraints than with individuals' subjective beliefs about them.[12] Indeed, some of the most important beliefs that inform preferences are beliefs about environmental constraints.

Finally, rationalists assume that individuals are rational in how they pursue their preferences. In short, this means that an actor is rational when, faced with multiple alternatives that lead to outcomes, they choose the alternative that best realizes their preferences.[13] Jon Elster explains this in greater detail:

> In order to justify and explain behaviour, rational-choice theory appeals to three distinct elements in the choice situation. The first element is the feasible set, i.e. the set of all courses of action which (are rationally believed to) satisfy various logical, physical, and economic constraints. The second is (a set of rational beliefs about) the causal structure of the situation, which determines what courses of action will lead to what outcomes. The third is a subjective ranking of the feasible alternatives, usually derived from a ranking of outcomes to which they (are expected) to lead. *To act rationally, then, simply means to choose the highest-ranked element in the feasible set.*[14]

Because of this rationality assumption, rational choice is often described as both a positive/empirical theory and a normative theory. It is said to provide not only a way of understanding or predicting human behavior but also a consequentialist basis on which to determine how individuals ought to act. Pushing back against claims that rational choice has little to offer normative theory, Snidal holds that 'rational choice began as a normative enterprise and lends itself readily to normative analysis, at least along the utilitarian lines from which it developed'.[15]

Thin and Thick

These four assumptions – individual actors as the units of analysis, stable and ordered preferences, environmental constraints on action, and instrumental rationality – can be treated as foundational to rational choice theory. Yet as John Ferejohn points out in an oft-cited

---

[12] Jon Elster, 'Introduction', in Jon Elster (ed.), *Rational Choice* (New York: New York University Press, 1986), p. 4.
[13] Duncan Luce and Howard Raiffa, *Games and Decisions: Introduction and Critical Survey* (New York: Wiley, 1957), p. 50.
[14] Elster, 'Introduction', p. 4.
[15] Snidal, 'Rational Choice and International Relations', p. 102.

chapter, not all rational choice theories are the same: some are 'thin', and some are 'thick'. Different authors invoke this distinction in different ways, but John Goldthorpe picks up on three key aspects of variation.[16]

Thin and thick theories differ, first of all, in how they treat goals and beliefs. In thin theories, as Ferejohn stresses, 'the theorist assumes only that agents are (instrumentally rational), that they efficiently employ the means available to pursue their ends'.[17] Such theories have been widely criticized, as '[t]hey can be made consistent after the event ... with nearly any kind of behavior'.[18] In thicker theories, by contrast, 'the analyst posits not only rationality but some additional description of agent preferences and beliefs'.[19] Not all thick theories are the same, though. Some, seeking generalizable theory, attribute universal goals, such as economic or material gain, to all individuals, and assume with regard to beliefs that individuals have perfect information about their environments. A more common approach, especially outside economics, has been to acknowledge that individuals can have all manner of goals (normative as well as material), to make only formal assumptions about these goals (that they are transitive, for example), and to treat the formation of goals as exogenous to the theory (something it cannot explain, and that can only be known through empirical analysis). Individuals' beliefs about their environments are treated in a similar way, as subjective and imperfect.[20]

A second difference between thin and thick rationalist theories – not included in Ferejohn's original distinction – concerns how they see rationality in action: Is it situationally or procedurally determined, or both? In thin theories, if we take economic theory as an example, rational action is heavily conditioned by the situational constraints of the environment. '[R]ationality in action is understood essentially as a response or *re*action to the situation – that is, a market situation of some kind – that actors face'.[21] Thicker versions of rational choice

[16] John H. Goldthorpe, 'Rational Action Theory for Sociology', *British Journal of Sociology*, 49.2 (1998), 167–192.
[17] John A. Ferejohn, 'Rationality and Interpretation: Parliamentary Elections in Early Stuart England', Working Paper No. 44, Centre for Law and Economic Studies, Columbia University School of Law, 2000, pp. 5–6.
[18] Michael Hechter and Satoshi Kanazawa, 'Sociological Rational Choice Theory', *Annual Review of Sociology*, 23 (1997), 195.
[19] Ferejohn, 'Rationality and Interpretation', p. 6.
[20] Goldthorpe, 'Rational Action', p. 171.   [21] Ibid., p. 173.

have rejected this, directing attention to the psychological procedures that guide individual choice.[22] Herbert Simon pioneered this approach, arguing that the computational capacities of individuals to process information about their environments did not match the assumptions of thin theory. Choice situations are often highly complex, individuals have cognitive limits, pressures of time constrain choice. The net result, Simon argued, is that individual rationality is bounded and choices are often satisficing not optimizing, arguments popularized in IR by Robert Keohane.[23] A number of scholars have challenged the dichotomous separation of psychological and situational determinates, arguing that the two are in fact interconnected. For example, Raymond Boudon argues that individual cognition is determined not only by internal psychological processes but also by the 'cognitive context in which they move'.[24] Scientists might be proven to have previously held false beliefs, like the Sun orbits around the Earth, but for Boudon these beliefs were not irrational, given the cosmological milieu of the time.

The third variation within thin and thick rationalist theories concerns their ambitions: To what extent do they claim to be general, as opposed to special, theories of action? I say 'within' these theories because in this case differences cut across the thin and thick forms. For example, Gary Becker's conception of rational choice is very thin, assuming only 'maximizing behavior, market equilibrium, and stable preferences', but he sees it as 'comprehensive' and 'applicable to all human behavior'.[25] Attempts to 'thicken' rational choice, by relaxing assumptions about the nature of preferences, introducing more sophisticated understandings of the psychology of choice, and broadening the range of situational determinants, can also be read as efforts to bolster rational choice's standing as a general theory of action. A more common position, however, is to treat rational choice as a special but

---

[22] The most recent expression of this is the special issue of *International Organization* on the behavioral revolution and international relations. For an overview, see Emilie M. Hafner-Burton, Stephan Haggard, David A. Lake, and David G. Victor, 'The Behavioral Revolution and International Relations', *International Organization*, 71.S1 (2017), S1–S31.

[23] Herbert A. Simon, 'A Behavioral Model of Rational Choice', *Quarterly Journal of Economics*, 69.1 (1955), 99. Applied to international relations, see Robert Keohane, *After Hegemony* (Princeton, NJ: Princeton University Press, 1984).

[24] Raymond Boudon, 'Beyond Rational Choice Theory', *Annual Review of Sociology*, 29 (2003), 12.

[25] Becker, *The Economic Approach to Human Behavior*, pp. 5, 8.

privileged theory: 'special' in the sense that its domain is necessarily limited, that there will always be aspects of human behaviour and features of social life that it struggles to accommodate, and 'privileged' in the sense that it constitutes the best starting point for social explanation. It is 'not just one theory of action among others', Goldthorpe argues, 'but rather *the* theory with which attempts at explaining social action should start and with which they should remain for as long as possible'.[26] This appears to be the position of most rational choice scholars in IR (but so too is it the position of realists and constructivists).

These differences between thin and thick forms of rational choice are evident in the differences between expected utility theory and prospect theory, both of which seek to explain choice under conditions of risk. The former assumes that individuals are utility-maximizers, with stable preferences, who can identify the options presented by their environments, along with their attendant probabilities and risks, and, on this basis, can make optional choices.[27] In a series of seminal articles, Amos Tversky and Daniel Kahneman admitted the normative parsimony of this thin theory, but argued that it misunderstood how actual individuals make choices, advancing prospect theory as an alternative. Its central insight is that the choices individuals make is determined, in significant measure, by how decision problems are framed. For example, Tversky and Kahneman asked a group of respondents to choose between surgery or radiation treatment for lung cancer, giving them statistical data on the risks of each. When the data were presented in terms of mortality rates, as opposed to survival rates (which are logically equivalent), those favouring radiation over surgery jumped from 18 per cent to 44 per cent.[28] Building on insights such as this, prospect theory holds that individual choices vary depending on whether a decision problem is framed as one of gains or losses, and 'that individuals tend to be risk-averse with respect to gains and risk-acceptant with respect to losses'.[29] This version of rational choice is 'thick' in two respects: it makes assumptions about the psychology of

[26] Goldthorpe, 'Rational Action', p. 184.

[27] Jack Levy, 'An Introduction to Prospect Theory', *Political Psychology*, 13.2 (1992), 173.

[28] Amos Tversky and Daniel Kahneman, 'Rational Choice and the Framing of Decisions', *Journal of Business*, 59.4 Part 2 (1986), S254–S255.

[29] Levy, 'An Introduction to Prospect Theory', p. 174.

choosing, and in emphasizing the role of framing, it suggests that choice is in part situationally determined (someone or something other than the individual has to be doing the framing).

The Question of Ontology

There is considerable debate about how the core assumptions of rational choice theory should be understood: are they deep ontological suppositions about the nature of the social universe or simply analytical tools for theorizing economic, political, and social life? Elsewhere I have made the former case, arguing that all theories rest on foundational ontological assumptions, and that constructivism and rational choice have very different foundations, placing limits on the degree to which they can be mixed and matched. This view is countered by those who shun ontology talk, and prefer to treat all theoretical assumptions as analytical tools that stand only so long as they are heuristically useful, and that can be combined with a wide range of other assumptions without contradiction. In a highly cited chapter, James Fearon and Alexander Wendt make this case. While admitting that constructivism and rational choice make different ontological assumptions (a central theme of Wendt's *Social Theory of International Relations*), they argue that focusing on such differences obscures fruitful points of convergence. Practically, scholars working in both traditions spend little time thinking about their underlying ontological commitments, and instead approach social life with sets of constructivist or rationalist analytical tools. Seeing theories in this way, as analytical tools, takes much of the heat out of debates and allows problem-driven researchers to see similarities as well as differences. Rationalists are not necessarily materialists, for example, and constructivists accept that norms are often used strategically.[30]

Nothing I say here challenges the idea that focusing on ontology can accentuate differences and obscure similarities between theoretical approaches. And nowhere do I deny that constructivism and rational choice contain complementary ideas that can be fruitfully combined; in fact, I attempt precisely this in Chapter 6. These approaches do rest on different ontological assumptions, though, and highlighting these can serve several valuable purposes. For some, addressing ontology is

---

[30] Fearon and Wendt, 'Rationalism v. Constructivism'.

important because ontology affects epistemology and, in turn, meth-odology.[31] While I am inclined to see ontology and epistemology as mutually constituted, I leave this issue aside. A more important reason to highlight ontology, at least for this project, is that the ontological assumptions of a theoretical approach condition how it is elaborated in specific theories. Like the foundations of a building, ontological assumptions anchor theories and limit the kinds of theoretical archi-tecture that can be constructed. Put differently, ontological assump-tions affect how theoretical approaches are 'built out', and this is as true of constructivism as it is of rational choice.

Following Norman Blaikie, I define social ontology as 'the claims or assumptions that a particular approach to social enquiry makes about the nature of social reality – claims about what exists, what it looks like, what units make it up and how these units interact with one another'.[32] There will be debate about which assumptions in rational choice theory form its ontological foundations, but the four discussed above are compelling candidates: the ontological primacy of the indi-vidual, the stable ordering of individuals' preferences, environments conceived as constraints on choice, and the instrumental rationality of the individual. Substantively, these are the kinds of assumptions Blaikie is talking about, but there are other reasons for treating them as ontological. For example, leading rational choice scholars refer to them as unquestionable social realities. Arguing from 'first principles', Jon Elster takes it as 'trivially and boringly true' that 'all social phe-nomena' 'must be understood within an individualist framework'.[33] Second, and most importantly for our purposes, rational choice theor-ists reason as though these assumptions were foundational, treating them as touchstones from which to elaborate and reference points to which they return.

My purpose in characterizing the core assumptions of rational choice theory as ontological is not to draw the discussion onto metatheoretical terrain; my goal is far more prosaic. To properly understand how rational choice scholars understand and incorporate

---

[31] See Colin Hay, 'Political Ontology', in Robert E. Goodin (ed.), *The Oxford Handbook of Political Science* (Oxford: Oxford University Press, 2011), p. 460.

[32] Norman Blaikie, *Approaches to Social Inquiry* (Cambridge: Polity Press, 1993), p. 6.

[33] Jon Elster, 'Rationality and Social Norms', *European Journal of Sociology*, 32.1 (1991), 114.

cultural phenomena, we need to recognize that they do so within a framework of foundational assumptions (as do constructivists and any other theorists). Other authors might define these assumptions slightly differently, or identify more or less than my preferred four. I am confident, though, that these capture the ontological core of rational choice, and that it is to some version of these that rational choice scholars – thin and thick – cleave. In practice, this means two things for how rationalists view culture. It affects, first, how they *conceive* cultural phenomena: what they think social norms are, for example, and what powers they attribute to them. It also affects, second, where they *locate* such phenomena in the social universe. Are common cultural values social priors, conditioning identities and interests, or are they focal points in coordination games between preconstituted individuals?

The Nature and Place of Culture

Rational choice theorists address culture in three ways. At the most superficial level, they treat it as something to be explained, a dependent variable amenable to rationalist theorizing. Social norms are the principal target here. At a deeper level, rationalists treat cultural values as individuals' preferences, as goals to be pursued or beliefs about feasible options. At the deepest level, they treat culture as common knowledge, essential to individuals solving coordination problems. In each case, the basic logic of rationalist theory is retained. Rules and norms are presented as rational institutional solutions, regulatory rather than constitutive in their effects. Cultural values are incorporated as the non-material preferences of individuals, but are treated as though they were subjective, their intersubjective status and effects bracketed. Arguments about common knowledge come closer to accommodating intersubjectivity, and as noted in the Introduction, these arguments have striking affinities with the default conception of culture that recurs in other theories. Yet culture is thinner here, and exists at a different level. Cultural knowledge is common – in the sense that individuals know it, know that others know it, and know that others know that they know it – and this enables coordination. Yet common knowledge is not the same as collective knowledge, which is how culture is usually understood in the default conception. As I explain below, collective knowledge is macro-structural and constitutive, whereas the common knowledge of rational choice theory is more localized (related to coordination in specific domains of social inter-action) and not thought to constitute individuals' identities or interests (which are treated as exogenous).[34]

Social Norms as Dependent Variables

Where constructivists refer to social norms as cultural phenomena, rationalists avoid such language, describing them instead in institu-tional terms. But to the extent that culture consists, in part, of shared standards of behaviour, social norms are one place where culture enters rational choice theory. In IR, rationalist accounts of social norms first developed in the 1980s literature on 'international regimes'. In an effort to explain the persistence of institutional cooperation after the perceived decline of US hegemony, rationalists argued that an enduring need to cooperate drove states to create and maintain regimes, quite independent of the power and will of the hegemon. Regimes were 'defined as principles, *norms*, rules, and decision-making procedures around which actor expectations converge in a given issue-area',[35] and these institutional complexes were said to overcome, at least in part, impediments to cooperation inherent to the anarchic international system.

Regime theory was the first instalment of an ongoing rational insti-tutionalist project within IR. Animated by the broader goal of showing how cooperation between self-interested actors is possible under anarchy, this project has had several expressions, the most prominent of which have been showcased as special issues of *International Organization*. The early work on international regimes was followed by a widely cited inquiry into legalization in world politics, which was soon followed by a study of rational institutional design. The recent special issue on the 'Behavioral Revolution and International Rela-tions' is the project's most recent instalment, this time probing the psychological determinants of rational institutional choice. While these studies have taken institutionalism in different directions, they evince

---

[34] On the differences between common and collective knowledge, see Wendt, *Social Theory of International Politics*, pp. 141–164.

[35] Stephen D. Krasner, 'Structural Causes and Regime Consequences: Regimes as Intervening Variables', *International Organization*, 36.2 (1982), 185. Emphasis added.

the same underlying rationalist logic, and they understand and explain social norms in broadly equivalent ways.

The rationalist argument about regimes has been well canvassed and needs only summarizing here. Cooperation between self-interested individuals is always difficult, especially in the absence of a central authority and persistent uncertainty about the intentions of others. But while these problems are overcome, in significant measure, by the sovereign state, no such authority exists internationally. Even when states (qua individuals) have common interests, they struggle to reach mutually beneficial agreements because of these constraints inherent to anarchy.[36] While decentralized cooperation in anarchy is possible,[37] it is extremely fragile and self-interested states construct regimes to make it more likely. These amalgams of principles, norms, rules, and decision-making procedures provide an institutional context in which states can reach specific cooperative agreements. They enable such agreements by increasing information, lowering transaction costs, and impeding cheating.[38]

How, though, are social norms understood in rationalist arguments such as this, and what role do they, in particular, play? On the first of these, rationalists conceive norms as behavioural regularities sustained by social sanctions. As Phillip Pettit explains, a norm exists when there is a behavioural regularity in a population to which 'nearly everyone conforms', when 'nearly everyone approves of nearly everyone else's conforming and disapproves of nearly anyone else's deviating', and when 'the fact that nearly everyone approves and disapproves on this pattern helps to ensure that nearly everyone conforms'.[39] For rationalists, social norms do not emerge because individuals hold prior beliefs about right and wrong, or at least not primarily. Rather, norms are established by self-interested individuals when their uncoordinated, yet individually rational choices, lead to suboptimal outcomes for all. The classic illustration is the Prisoner's Dilemma game. Two members of a

---

[36] Robert O. Keohane, 'The Demand for International Regimes', in Stephen D. Krasner (ed.), *International Regimes* (Ithaca, NY: Cornell University Press, 1983), p. 148.

[37] See Robert Axelrod, *The Evolution of Cooperation* (Harmondsworth: Penguin, 1990).

[38] Robert O. Keohane, *After Hegemony: Cooperation and Discord in the World Political Economy* (Princeton, NJ: Princeton University Press, 1984), p. 88.

[39] Phillip Pettit, '*Virtus Normativa*: Rational Choice Perspectives', *Ethics*, 100.4 (1990), 731.

criminal gang have been arrested and are being held in solitary confinement. Prosecutors lack sufficient information to convict them on the principal charge, so they offer each prisoner the opportunity to either betray the other or remain silent. If A and B betray each other, both will serve two years. If A betrays B, but B remains silent, A will walk free and B will serve a long term. And if A and B both remain silent, they will both serve one year (on a lesser charge). The optimal joint outcome for the prisoners is to remain silent, but if they are rational actors the incentive structure will lead each of them to betray the other. Rationalists have shown, however, that when the game is played repeatedly, and individuals know each other's past choices and worry about their future ones, the possibility of cooperation emerges.[40] The problem is, though, that in repeated games there are almost always multiple equilibria (stable configurations of individuals' choices), and individuals may not be able to coordinate on one of them to achieve a good joint outcome. Social norms develop in these contexts, providing socially sanctioned behavioural guides that enable individuals to coordinate their choices.

Elinor Ostrom offers a classic statement of this view of social norms. She set out to explain the emergence of cooperative institutions for the management of 'common-pool resources', and most of her empirical cases lacked effective central authority (and are thus akin to the context of international relations). In each case, Ostrom writes, '[e]xtensive norms evolved ... that narrowly define "proper" behavior. Many of these norms make it feasible for individuals to live in close interdependence on many fronts without excessive conflict. Further, a reputation for keeping promises, honest dealings, and reliability in one arena is a valuable asset. Prudent, long-term self-interest reinforces the acceptance of norms or proper behavior.'[41] Rationalists offer several reasons why norms have this effect. Norms provide focal points around which choices can converge. As Ostrom observes, 'actions that are considered wrong among a set of individuals interacting together over time will not even be included in the set of strategies contemplated by the individual'.[42] Norms also lower

[40] Axelrod, *The Evolution of Cooperation*, pp. 10–11.
[41] Elinor Ostrom, *Governing the Commons: The Evolution of Institutions for Collective Action* (Cambridge: Cambridge University Press, 1990), pp. 88–89.
[42] Ibid., p. 35.

transaction costs. Norms give a majority of individuals rights to criticize non-compliant behaviour, and when would-be non-compliers recognize this right, 'the action is inhibited without any transaction occurring'.[43] Finally, rationalist IR scholars argue that the social norms of a regime facilitate more specific agreements because, irrespective of their specific content, they promote reciprocation: the willingness of individuals to accept short-term losses in some agreements in return for long-term gains across future agreements.[44]

In addition to social norms in general having rational origins, rationalists hold that variations in the form norms take is also a product of rational selection. For example, in the early 2000s rationalists noted the increasing legalization of international institutions, a key dimension of which was a growing preference for formal legal rules over informal social norms. Of the three dimensions of institutional legalization they observed – strengthened obligations, heightened precision, and the delegation of enforcement to authoritative third parties – the first two relate specifically to the nature of norms.[45] Legal rules are precise and have strong obligations, they argued, whereas softer, informal norms are less binding and more ambiguous. For rational actors, the former have certain attractions: they 'reduce transaction costs, strengthen the credibility of their commitments, expand their available political strategies, and resolve problems of incomplete contracting'.[46] This does not mean, however, that rational states will always prefer legal rules to social norms, as legalization entails significant costs. States will often choose 'softer' norms if they think they can realize their preferences at lower cost. The fact that international institutions vary in their reliance on legal rules or social norms reflects the complex cost–benefit calculations that lie behind institutional choices and interstate bargaining.[47]

---

[43] James S. Coleman, *Foundations of Social Theory* (Cambridge, MA: Harvard University Press, 1990), pp. 261–262.

[44] Keohane, 'The Demand for International Regimes', p. 114.

[45] Kenneth W. Abbott, Robert O. Keohane, Andrew Moravcsik, Anne-Marie Slaughter, and Duncan Snidal, 'The Concept of Legalization', *International Organization*, 54.3 (2000), 404–408.

[46] Kenneth W. Abbott and Duncan Snidal, 'Hard and Soft Law in International Governance', *International Organization*, 54.3 (2000), 422.

[47] Ibid., p. 434.

Culture as Preferences

One of the most common critiques of rational choice theory is that cultural ideas, values, and practices are granted a highly circumscribed causal role. As we have seen, rationalists treat social norms as things to be explained, and integrate them as intervening variables between maximizing individuals and cooperative outcomes. Yet culture works at a much deeper level, critics argue. Individuals are cultural beings; they hold and pursue cultural values and beliefs. Not only do such values work at the very beginning of the rationalist causal chain – in the very utilities individuals seek to maximize – their origin in broader cultural formations pushes that chain back, suggesting a primary causal role for structural meanings and practices. By starting with instrumentally rational individuals, critics hold, rational choice casts preferences too narrowly, excluding the cultural goals that very often animate individuals, and brackets the social origins of those goals. 'For rationalists', Katzenstein argues, 'actors deploy culture and identity strategically, like any other resource, simply to further their own self-interests'.[48]

Rationalists have responded to such criticisms in two ways. First, they have defended the integrity of their individualist theory, acknowledging that individuals' preferences may be shaped by a wide range of social structural factors, including shared cultural meanings and practices, but bracketing these factors, along with wider processes of preference formation. Substantive rationalist theories, which seek to explain particular outcomes, commonly attribute preferences to key actors, inferring them from the actors' behaviour.[49] The origins of such preferences are treated as exogenous, however, as beyond the explanatory scope of the theory. Second, and more importantly for our purposes, rationalists have sought to integrate cultural factors within the framework of their existing theoretical commitments. They have done this by relaxing any theoretical assumptions about the substantive

---

[48] Peter J. Katzenstein, 'Introduction: Alternative Perspectives on National Security', in Peter J. Katzenstein (ed.), *The Culture of National Security* (New York: Columbia University Press, 1996), p. 17.

[49] Rationalist are, however, acutely aware of the problems that attend revealed preference arguments. On these problems, see Botond Koszegi and Matthew Rabin, 'Mistakes in Choice-Based Welfare Analysis', *American Economic Review*, 97.2 (2007), 477–481.

content of individuals' preferences and by stressing the importance of common knowledge to social coordination. I address the first of these here, and the second in the following section.

Rationalists have insisted repeatedly that rational choice makes no assumptions about the substantive content of individuals' preferences. Particular theorists, especially in economics, have defined preferences narrowly: Harsanyi's claim that all individuals are motivated principally by economic gain and social acceptance is a case in point.[50] It is more common today, however, for rationalists to forswear such limits. While rational choice theories seek to explain 'both individual and collective (social) outcomes in terms of *individual goal-seeking under constraints*', Snidal writes, 'the goals are *not* restricted to self-regarding or material interests but could include other-regarding and normative or ideational "goals"'.[51] As we have seen, rationalists treat preferences as amalgams of desires and beliefs, but Fearon and Wendt argue that 'there is nothing in the model which requires that "Desire" be material. It *may* be material, but then again it may not; rational choice theory, as a theory of choice given desires and beliefs, is strictly speaking agnostic on this question.'[52]

Theoretically, rationalists have employed two strategies to broaden the range of preferences. The first is to define instrumental rationality expansively. On a narrow reading, this form of rationality combines two things: egoistic (often material) self-interest and means–ends choices. The instrumentally rational person, in common parlance, is thus someone who makes means–ends choices to achieve selfish (even base) goals. Moves to broaden the scope of instrumental rationality retain means–ends choosing, but jettison the narrow reading of interests. Individuals are instrumentally rational, Stephen Quackenbush claims, whenever they 'act in accordance with their motivations, regardless of what those motivations may be . . . Instrumental rationality makes no normative judgements about preferences. That is, whether one's preferences are "good" or "evil", "instrumental" or "expressive", or anything else has no impact on one's instrumental rationality.'[53] The second strategy imagines other forms of individual rationality, sitting alongside instrumental rationality. The idea that

---

[50] Harsanyi, 'Rational Choice Models', p. 524.
[51] Snidal, 'Rational Choice and International Relations', p. 87.
[52] Fearon and Wendt, 'Rationalism v. Constructivism', p. 59.
[53] Quackenbush, 'The Rationality of Rational Choice', pp. 94–95.

individuals are utility-maximizers operating under constraints is retained, but differences in motives are implicated in different kinds of rationality. The most commonly cited example is 'axiological rationality', where the utilities individuals pursue are socially derived 'expressive' values.[54]

If we take the standard rationalist formula, culture can enter preferences at either of two points: as desires or beliefs. Recall that desires are valued ends, which under an expanded conception of rationality include all manner of goals and wishes: from wealth or security to salvation or justice. Beliefs, by contrast, are understandings of environmental constraints, and perceptions of feasible options. Substantive rationalist theories have integrated culture at both of these points. It should be noted, however, that such integrations are less than common, for as Margaret Levi notes, the 'real action' for rational choice does not 'come from the internal considerations of the actor but from the constraints on her or his behavior'.[55] This having been said, a good example of the integration of culture at the level of desires can be found in debates among rationalists about how best to accommodate religion. The most prominent approach treats religion as a dependent variable, as something to be explained. There are some ends that individuals want that cannot be realized in life, and religion, the argument goes, facilitates an exchange between individuals and their gods for the delivery of those ends.[56] This view has been challenged, however, by other rationalists who think religion also affects individuals' desires. Religion, on this view, fuels in individuals 'an emotional devotion to a moral cause', and this speaks to the normative, or axiological, dimensions of rationality.[57] If we turn to the integration of culture at the level of beliefs, a good example is Richard Herrmann's recent argument about how national attachments give

[54] Boudon, 'Rational Choice Theory', p. 6.
[55] Margaret Levi, 'Reconsiderations of Rational Choice in Comparative and Historical Analysis', in Mark Lichbach et al., *Comparative Politics: Rationality, Culture, and Structure* (Cambridge: Cambridge University Press, 2009), p. 128.
[56] See R. Stark and W. S. Bainbridge, *A Theory of Religion* (New York, NY: Peter Lang, 1987); and R. Stark and R. Finke, *Acts of Faith: Explaining the Human Side of Religion* (Berkeley: University of California Press, 2000).
[57] Colin Jerolmack and Douglas Porpora, 'Religion, Rationality and Experience: A Response to the New Rational Choice Theory of Religion', *Sociological Theory*, 22.1 (2004), 158.

individuals 'motivated beliefs', affecting how they interpret and navigate international contexts.[58]

While rationalist IR scholars now take it as axiomatic that rational choice theory makes no assumptions about the substantive content of individuals' preferences, allowing all kinds of goals to be accommodated, the move has met with stiff criticism. From within rationalism itself, scholars argue that rational choice loses all predictive power if preferences aren't defined a priori. Defending a modified version of Harsanyi's claim that individuals seek economic gain or social acceptance, Phillip Pettit holds that 'the explanatory and predictive project of rational choice theory is in jeopardy in the absence of some substantive postulate about people's desires'.[59] From outside rationalism, Donald Green and Ian Shapiro level the same criticism. '[W]hat is gained by avoiding controversial assumptions about human nature can come at a considerable cost from the standpoint of measurement and empirical testing of rational choice hypotheses. If the content of preferences is not specified, it becomes enormously difficult to determine, for example, whether a changed outcome in the majority vote of a committee reflects the presence of stable but cyclical preferences among voting members, changes in their preferences over time, or some other phenomenon.'[60] In the end, a lot hinges on where substantive preferences are integrated in rational choice theory. Some, like Harsanyi, want them assumed a priori, while others prefer to introduce them as empirical assumptions in specific rationalist explanations.

Culture as Common Knowledge

Of the principal ways in which culture is accommodated in rational choice theory, it is the idea that culture provides the common knowledge required to solve coordination problems that interests me most. First, this is where rationalists come closest to invoking the default

---

[58] Richard K. Hermann, 'How Attachments to the Nation Shape Beliefs about the World: A Theory of Motivated Reasoning', *International Organization*, 71.S1 (2017), S61–S84.

[59] Philip Pettit, 'Institutional Design and Rational Choice', in Robert E. Goodin (ed.), *The Theory of Institutional Design* (Cambridge: Cambridge University Press, 1996), p. 63.

[60] Donald P. Green and Ian Shapiro, *The Pathologies of Rational Choice: A Critique of Applications in Political Science* (New Haven, CT: Yale University Press, 1994), p. 18.

conception of culture detailed and critiqued in Chapter 1, and where, unreflectively invoked, their ideas would appear to support Wight-like claims that a common culture is needed to sustain international order. In modified form, however, the idea can be harnessed in very different ways. It may well be true that social coordination requires common knowledge, and that cultural meanings and practices can provide or convey such knowledge. This is entirely compatible, though, with conceiving culture as inherently diverse. In heterogeneous cultural contexts, order builders have powerful incentives to organize culture – to construct and choreograph meanings and practices and to enable and legitimate certain forms of social coordination while foreclosing others (an idea I enlist in Chapter 6).

To understand this particular rationalist argument about culture, we first need to grasp the nature of coordination problems. Such problems exist when individuals have common interests, but where they can realize these optimally only if they coordinate their choices. These problems are most pronounced when individuals have little or no chance to communicate, as this greatly reduces the means of coordination. Thomas Schelling provided a classic account of such problems, arguing that they exist when 'two or more parties have identical interests and face the problem not of reconciling interests but only of coordinating their actions for their mutual benefit, when communication is impossible'.[61] Understanding the logic of these problems is important for two reasons, he argued. First, Schelling's principal concern was military strategy, and such strategy was played out in 'mixed games', characterized by 'both conflict and mutual dependence'.[62] While these games differ from pure coordination games, Schelling insisted that coordination problems were nonetheless inherent to mixed games, and that key features of coordination games also characterize problems of divergent interests. Much was to be learned, therefore, by first properly comprehending coordination problems.[63] Second, although Schelling specified a lack of communication as a feature of coordination problems, he held that defining aspects of these problems were also 'powerfully present even in explicit bargaining'.[64] Again, understanding the logic of pure

[61] Thomas C. Schelling, *The Strategy of Conflict* (Cambridge, MA: Harvard University Press, 1980), p. 54.
[62] Ibid., p. 89.   [63] Ibid., p. 54.   [64] Ibid., p. 67.

coordination problems could shed important light on more complex forms of social interaction and bargaining.

Schelling's principal insight is that to solve coordination problems, individuals rely on mutual expectations. To demonstrate this, he imagines a game in which two individuals, sitting in separate rooms and unable to communicate, are both given a stack of new, hundred-dollar notes. They are asked to divide their stacks in two, and told that they if divide them in exactly the same way they can keep the money. To secure this prize the players have to coordinate their choices, but they cannot do this through communication. In such situations, Schelling argues, individuals rely on their expectations of one another: how Woodrow divides the pile will be determined by how he expects Elly to divide her pile, knowing that her choice will be shaped by her expectations of him, which she knows are affected by his expectations of her.[65] Commonly, these mutual expectations coalesce around 'focal points', or what Schelling also terms 'coordinators'. 'Most situations', Schelling holds, 'provide some clue for coordinating behavior, some focal point for each person's expectation of what the other expects him to expect to be expected to do'.[66] A focal point for Woodrow and Elly might be aesthetic symmetry, where they expect one another to divide their stacks into simple but *elegant* halves. Or it might be a shared principle of fairness, where they expect each other to treat their choice as though it were a distributional choice, thus dividing their stacks into *equal* halves. Either way, mutual expectations are essential to coordinating Elly's and Woodrow's choices and realizing their interests, and such expectations are guided by focal points of some kind. This insight, Schelling argues, is not restricted to pure coordination problems; it applies equally to mixed games, characterized by common and divergent interests, and to games involving explicit bargaining. In such situations, '[e]ach party's strategy is guided mainly by what he expects the other to accept or insist on; yet he knows that the other is guided by reciprocal thoughts ... These infinitely reflexive expectations must somehow converge on a single point, at which each expects the other not to expect to be expected to retreat.'[67]

The source of mutual expectations is 'common knowledge', rationalists contend. Fairness works as a focal point only if it is a principle that Woodrow accepts, he knows Elly accepts, he knows that Elly

---

[65] Ibid., p. 57.   [66] Ibid.   [67] Ibid., p. 70.

knows that he accepts, and so forth. Focal points that are not common knowledge cannot inform mutual expectations or, in turn, coordinate individuals' choices. Rationalists understand common knowledge in a very distinctive way, however. For knowledge to be common, Ostrom explains, it is required 'that all participants know x, that the participants know that each of the others knows x, and that the participants know that each of the others know that each of the others knows x' – and on and on ad infinitum.[68]

So defined, common knowledge differs from the 'collective knowledge' emphasized by constructivists. Both are intersubjective, in the sense that they comprise knowledge that is shared between individuals. They differ, therefore, from subjective forms of knowledge, which reside solely in individual minds: my deeply held, but totally unrecognized, view that aliens facilitated the Peace of Westphalia, for example. Both common knowledge and collective knowledge are structural, as well. Not only do they condition individuals' behaviour; their existence is not dependent on the beliefs of particular individuals.[69] For instance, the knowledge shared among Australians that we drive on the left side of the road stands irrespective of whether there are radical libertarians who see this as an unacceptable encroachment by the state on individuals' freedoms. Common and collective knowledge differ in two important respects, though. First, and most importantly, the collective knowledge emphasized by constructivists is constitutive: it doesn't just regulate or coordinate individuals' choices; it creates those individuals as knowledgeable social actors. It informs their role identities and helps inform their interests. Rationalists do not attribute this to common knowledge. It facilitates coordination by informing mutual expectations, but individuals enter the game with exogenously determined identities and interests, and common knowledge has little bearing on these. Second, if both common and collective knowledge are structural, the former has a macro quality lacking in the latter. Because

[68] Ostrom, *Governing the Commons*, p. 223. A classic expression of the view of knowledge is found in R. J. Aumann, 'Agreeing to Disagree', *Annals of Statistics*, 4.6 (1976), 1236.
[69] My reading of rationalist understandings of common knowledge differs from Wendt's on this count. He argues, erroneously in my view, 'that with each change in belief, or each change in membership, the cultural forms constituted by common knowledge literally become different'. Wendt, *Social Theory of International Politics*, p. 161.

constructivists think collective knowledge constitutes social identities, and because identities stand in complex relations of self and other, collective knowledge has broad social reach. By contrast, rationalists present common knowledge as far more localized, as pertaining to social coordination in particular issue areas or domains of interaction.

If the first way that rationalists integrate culture is at the level of preferences, the second is via the proposition that common knowledge informs mutual expectations. Common knowledge need not be cultural. Woodrow and Elly may both know that Elly likes symmetry, know that they share this knowledge, and thus form mutual expectations on this basis. Rationalists argue, however, that in any social order culture is likely to be a major source of common knowledge. Michael Chwe's *Rational Ritual* develops this argument in some detail. Challenging the notion that rationality and culture belong to separate realms, Chwe argues that cultural rituals are crucial sites for the generation, expression, and communication of common knowledge. Cultural meanings come in many forms, and are expressed, mobilized, and embodied in multiple ways. At a minimum, such meanings can provide the substance of common knowledge: the particular values, beliefs, and ideas that individuals share. Cultural rituals do more than this, though. They can, of course, be engines of meaning creation, but their principal role is translating meanings into common knowledge. Indeed, Chwe defines rituals in terms of this function. 'Public rituals', he writes, 'can thus be understood as social practices that generate common knowledge'.[70]

Where cultural rituals are often presented as emotion-laden practices – animated by expressive beliefs and attachments, and stimulating action by accentuating collective feelings – Chwe sees them as coldly rational.[71] They exist for a rational reason – the generation of common knowledge – and their nature and structure serves this function. Rituals are public; they are visible to, and engaging of, smaller or larger groups of individuals. Moreover, '[r]itual language', Chwe argues, 'is often patterned and repetitive',[72] ensuring that participants get the message. Together, these characteristics are particularly effective in generating common knowledge: 'when a person

---

[70] Michael Suk-Young Chwe, *Rational Ritual: Culture: Coordination, and Common Knowledge* (Princeton, NJ: Princeton University Press, 2001), p. 3.
[71] Ibid., p. 4.   [72] Ibid.

hears something repeated, not only does she get the message, she knows it is repeated and hence knows that it is more likely that others have heard it'.[73] While this suggests that the discursive element of cultural rituals is decisive, the physical or aural aspects of cultural rituals are often the principal engines. Chwe highlights the role of ritual dancing, for example, which 'can be understood as allowing individuals to convey meaning to each other through movement ... [G]roup dancing is also an excellent common knowledge generator; when dancing, each person knows that everyone else is paying attention, because if a person were not, the pattern of movement would be immediately disrupted'.[74]

In *Honor, Symbols, and War*, Barry O'Neill advances another rationalist account of the role of culture in social interaction, though this time more squarely focused on international relations. On first inspection, O'Neill's account seems at odds with Chwe's. Less focused on coordination problems, he is concerned primarily with the role of symbolic politics in the tensions and conflicts that characterize world politics. Political leaders, he contends, have an abiding interest in 'status regulators'; they 'worry about intangible goals like saving face and preserving national honour and prestige', and their pursuit of these goals generates conflict, even if success depends on social recognition.[75] Focusing on four such regulators – honour, social face, prestige, and moral authority – he shows how they depend on three kinds of cultural symbols: value, message, and focal symbols. What interests me here is how dependent O'Neill's account of status regulators is on common knowledge, and how his symbols, like Chwe's rituals, play a key role in generating such knowledge. For example, '[s]ocial face is the group's expectation about how it will treat the individual in direct interactions', and '[p]restige is the belief among the members that the person is admired – each one's belief that the rest of the group believes that the individual possesses the desirable trait'.[76] To maintain social face and enhance prestige, O'Neill argues, political leaders manipulate symbols, a primary purpose of which is the construction of common knowledge. 'Focal symbols', for example, 'are

[73] Ibid.   [74] Ibid.
[75] Barry O'Neill, *Honor, Symbols, and War* (Ann Arbor: University of Michigan Press, 2001), p. xi.
[76] Ibid., p. xii.

events, often not deliberate acts by any agent, that induce observers to adopt a common judgement about what move they will make in an important situation'.[77]

Culture, Coordination, and International Order

As the previous discussion shows, rational choice theory has a distinctive, well-honed account of culture. It has an explanation of cultural phenomena, such as norms and rituals. 'Thick' versions admit cultural values and beliefs at the level of individuals' preferences. And culture is given a key role in facilitating social coordination, providing common knowledge that informs individuals' mutual expectations. Culture is not, therefore, anathema to rational choice.

How it is imagined and integrated, however, is circumscribed by the theory's core ontological assumptions, making culture one thing and not another, with one causal role and not another. When rationalists are agnostic about the content of preferences, cultural purposes and understandings are easily accommodated. But these preferences are quarantined theoretically, leaving them only thinly cultural. Any connection they might have to individuals' identities – to their underlying conceptions of self – is bracketed, as is their relationship to, and dependence upon, broader intersubjective meanings. Cultural phenomena also enter rationalist theory as intervening variables, this time in the guise of social norms that help individuals select among multiple equilibria. The constitutive function of norms – how they structure the language games that render reality knowable, and how they inform individuals' role identities – is bracketed, though. Culture appears in its final rationalist form as common knowledge, but as we saw above, this is not the same as collective knowledge: both are intersubjective and structural, but common knowledge is coordinating and localized, whereas collective knowledge is constitutive and macro-social.

These criticisms have been well rehearsed, and while they bear noting here, they are not my principal concern. What interests me are the affinities between the 'culture as common knowledge' argument and the default conception of culture critiqued in Chapter 1. Recall that this conception weaves together four key ideas: that cultures

---

[77] Ibid.

are coherent entities; that they are products of their own endogenous processes; that culture and society are distinct, with the former enabling the latter; and that cultural diversity undermines social order. Unlike the understandings of culture found in realism, the English School, and constructivism, the 'culture as common knowledge' argument resonates with only some of these ideas. For instance, rationalists focus little on cultural entities like civilizations or nations, concentrating instead on particular cultural symbols or rituals. These might be the glue that holds together wider cultural communities, but this is not a primary rationalist concern. At other points, however, the 'culture as common knowledge' argument does resonate with the default conception. The idea that cultural practices generate the common knowledge essential for social coordination reproduces the culture/society distinction characteristic of the default conception, for example. The most striking affinity, however, concerns the underlying logic of the rationalist position. If social coordination depends on the common knowledge expressed in, and communicated by, cultural symbols and practices, then cultural diversity or heterogeneity can be expected to undermine coordination. Other sources of common knowledge might sustain coordination among small numbers of individuals – knowledge of each other's habits or predilections, for example – but if the logic holds, knowledge rooted in, and communicated by, common cultural values and practices is likely to be more important for large-scale social coordination.

It is here that the rationalist argument about culture, common knowledge, and social coordination converges, somewhat unexpectedly, with culturalist arguments about international order. Variously expressed in realism, the English School, and constructivism, these arguments assume some version of the default conception of culture, hold that international orders emerge in unitary cultural contexts, and think that diversity undermines order. For those holding such views, the 'culture and common knowledge' argument will be grist for the mill. Indeed, folk versions of the argument pepper the literature on international order. For example, Bull's argument about how a common civilization facilitates society among states can be read in this way. In addition to reinforcing common interests with common values, aspects of a common culture 'make for easier communication and closer awareness and understanding between one state and another, and thus facilitate the definition of common rules and the evolution of common institutions'.[78] Culture, it seems, enables the development of common knowledge, and this permits international social coordination. At least on this point, it seems, rationalism and the English School are in step, and rationalists might well argue that their theory provides the micro-foundations for Bull's intuitively correct, but undertheorized, observation.

It is unclear, however, whether rationalists would, or should, wish to be aligned with culturalist arguments about international order. There are two sets of issues here. First, as we saw in Chapter 1, the culturalist arguments are themselves deeply problematic. By treating cultures as homogeneous entities, they fly in the face of contemporary specialist understandings. And a wealth of new histories shows that the long-held assumption that international orders evolve in unitary cultural contexts is a myth: heterogeneity has been the norm. Second, as discussed above, rationalists have a thinner and more localized view of culture than the culturalists. Where the latter see culture as comprising a sufficient depth and density of values and practices to constitute political orders – shaping conceptions of right and institutional imaginations – rationalists use the term 'culture' to describe far more prosaic, often issue-specific – forms of common knowledge, and never cast this knowledge as constitutive. When culture is introduced as a source of common knowledge, it is in the form of discrete meanings and practices, symbols, and rituals. In fact, when O'Neill takes these arguments into the international arena, the picture he paints is one of symbolic complexity and political contestation.

There is, however, another way to enlist rationalist ideas to better understand the relationship between culture and international order. A culturalist seeking to enlist these ideas would start by positing a common, foundational culture and then use it to explain international social coordination. It is more productive, I argue in Chapter 6, to start from the other direction: from the challenge of international order building in culturally heterogeneous contexts. Order building involves a whole host of things, but two are engineering and legitimating forms of social coordination conducive to systemic rule. Cultural heterogeneity poses a structural challenge for such projects, though. Heterogeneous cultural environments contain a plethora of tangled meanings and practices that can be harnessed to all manner of political ends, by all manner of political actors. Order builders thus have a powerful incentive to organize culture, to craft intersubjective knowledge by accentuating some meanings and practices over others, and obscuring some cultural differences while highlighting others. Rationalist arguments about culture, common knowledge, and social coordination capture an important dimension of this. By organizing culture, and hence common knowledge, order builders augment their capacities for social and political coordination. However, the imperative to organize culture has a dimension that rationalists underappreciate. Social and political coordination in heterogeneous cultural contexts isn't just about orchestrating requisite forms of common knowledge. The collective knowledge that constitutes cultural identities – civilizational, religious, ethnic – is entwined with the common knowledge needed for coordination. Rational choice arguments about culture and coordination offer a powerful insight into the organization of culture, but shared knowledge needs to be understood more broadly, to encompass the constitutive aspect of collective knowledge. When the Qing emperors sought to organize culture through the Eight Banners and Lifanyuan systems, they were at once seeking to control axes of political coordination *and* trying to define legitimate cultural identifications. Like order builders in other contexts, I argue in Chapter 6, they did this by institutionalizing diversity regimes that simultaneously configured political authority and licensed certain axes of difference.[79]

Ironically, it is when rationalists come closest to the default conception of culture and to essentialist arguments about social order that they highlight the imperative political elites face to organize culture. In his recent book, *Rational Lives*, Dennis Chong seeks a rationalist explanation for '*value formation and change, group identification, and conflict over social norms and lifestyles*'.[80] His understanding of culture is as close to the default conception as one will find in rationalist thought:

A culture comprises an array of social and political institutions and shared values and traditions that allow people to enjoy a meaningful life.

---

[79] An initial elaboration of this argument is found in Reus-Smit, 'Cultural Diversity and International Order', 875–876.
[80] Dennis Chong, *Rational Lives: Norms and Values in Politics and Society* (Chicago, IL: University of Chicago Press, 2014), p. 4. Emphasis in original.

People define their conception of the good life and pursue their interests within the bounds of their cultural institutions; they have limited perspectives, which means that their choices do not take account of the set of all possible cultures.[81]

For Chong, social coordination is easier in societies with a single culture than in culturally diverse societies. In the former, '[c]oordination around common identifications and norms creates collective power that benefits individual group members', whereas in the latter '[c]ompeting norms and social conventions create coordination problems in the form of higher transaction costs. Heterogeneous conventions make it more difficult for people to communicate with one another and to engage in social interaction.'[82] Chong seems to treat culturally homogeneous societies as the norm – or at least an analytical baseline. What matters for our purposes is the emphasis he places on elite cultural orchestration in diverse societies. Sometimes elites accentuate existing cultural differences as they 'mobilize the public for collective goals by taking advantage of existing group identifications and values'.[83] At other times they try to bridge differences by appealing to 'more neutral principles and ideological values in order to broaden their coalitions'.[84]

Conclusion

Constructivists and English School theorists wear culture on their sleeves. For both, cultural phenomena – from collective mentalities to social norms – are fundamental to world politics, shaping everything from the spatial organization of political authority to the issue-specific conduct of states. For rationalists, by contrast, culture is a second-order concern, neither integral to their basic theory nor an explanatory priority. But just like realists, they have been drawn onto the cultural terrain, albeit for different reasons (and arguably to a more limited extent). In their efforts to explain cooperation under anarchy, they have fashioned a distinctive account of social norms. In response to criticisms that they assume individuals to be self-interested materialists, they have opened preferences to an infinite variety of goals and beliefs, any number of which could be cultural. And in theorizing how

[81] Ibid., p. 213.   [82] Ibid., pp. 215–216.   [83] Ibid., p. 8.   [84] Ibid., p. 9.

individuals solve coordination problems, they have opened the door to culture in the form of common knowledge.

We have already seen how these engagements with culture are conditioned by rational choice's basic ontological assumptions: social norms are admitted as intervening or dependent variables, cultural preferences are bracketed from their intersubjective sources, and culture as common knowledge has coordinating but not constitutive power. What contribution, though, can such an approach make to understanding the relationship between cultural diversity and international order, the primary concern of this project?

I can see three possible options, only the last of which is promising. The first would begin with individuals' cultural preferences – acknowledging that these might be highly varied, even contradictory – and then treat international order as an institutional equilibrium. This has the advantage of taking cultural heterogeneity seriously, even if the intersubjective dimensions of culture are bracketed. It confronts two problems, though. It is, first, an enormous leap from individual-level cultural preferences to the international institutional order, and any attempt to treat states as individuals with cultural preferences would essentialize culture at the national level, introducing once again the default conception of culture. Added to this, my previous work has shown how rationalist accounts of institutional practices fundamental to international order face multiple equilibria problems, and treating preferences as diverse, culturally or otherwise, will do little to resolve these.[85] The second option would take the opposite tack, assuming that international order cannot exist without mutual expectations, that such expectations depend on common knowledge, and that at the international level this can come only from a common cultural substratum. This would, however, simply reproduce in rationalist language the flawed Wightian thesis that order arises only in unitary cultural contexts and diversity is corrosive of order. This leaves us with one remaining option, already sketched above. That is to start with the challenge of constructing and legitimating international orders in heterogeneous contexts, focusing on how order builders organize cultural diversity, in part to enable forms of social coordination conducive to

---

[85] Reus-Smit, *Moral Purpose*, pp. 159–162.

systemic rule.[86] This has the virtue of enlisting the rationalist idea about culture, common knowledge, and social coordination, but in a way that is compatible with the two key insights about culture in recent anthropology and sociology (discussed in Chapter 1): that culture is inherently diverse, often contradictory, and that institutions play a key role in patterning and structuring culture. I further develop these ideas in Chapter 6.

[86] In his comments on earlier drafts of this chapter, Duncan Snidal suggested a fourth option: 'Mutual expectations, common knowledge and common culture lie at the state strata (sovereignty, self-determination etc.) and different substrata cultures only have to be homogenized insofar as this top strata impinges on the substrata. The impingement might be a lot (e.g., if economic or human rights norms are strong in state strata) but even then would not require full convergence – and the extent of convergence would depend on decisions at the state strata.' I have not taken up this suggestion for two reasons. First, the organization of culture that attends order building need not entail homogenization, only the authorization of axes of difference. Second, in the approach I map out in Chapter 6, the option Snidal suggests is in fact one kind of diversity regime, one institutionalized, in part, in the modern order only after the 1970s.

6 | The Organization of Diversity

International relations is a field that thrives on division. Indeed, our *modus operandi* – our approach to the advancement of knowledge – is to differentiate perspectives, and then place them in gladiatorial competition or artful combination to render world politics intelligible. Yet there are surprising points of convergence, at least among mainstream schools of thought. One of these concerns the nature of culture. IR is not known for its cultural sensibilities, and much of the field shies away from sustained engagement with the concept. It is something IR scholars refer to surprisingly often, though. As previous chapters have shown, not only do likely suspects, like constructivists and the English School, talk about culture, so too do realists and rationalists. More interestingly, despite coming at culture from different directions, integrating it in different ways, and locating it within their own distinctive fields of debate, they all settle on some version of the default conception. When culture is not atomized – disaggregated into discrete norms or practices – it is conceived as a coherent whole: a clearly differentiated, well-integrated, socially constitutive system of meaning and practice. We see this in Kissinger's and Wight's arguments about foundational civilizations; in Ruggie's, Phillips's, and my own arguments about deep normative structures; and in Chwe's and Chong's arguments about culture, common knowledge, and social coordination. A conception of culture long abandoned in specialist disciplines thus lives on in IR, a discipline whose global remit might have engendered greater sensitivity to cultural complexity.

IR's default conception of culture is problematic not only because it is inconsistent with decades of specialist research and theory but because it encourages two analytically unhelpful tendencies. It encourages us, first, to treat cultural formations – ethnicities, nations, civilizations, religions, etc. – as though they were natural forms, not historically contingent constructs. Second, and following from this, it obscures the politics of culture: how cultural meanings and practices are

187

constantly amplified or silenced, mobilized or suppressed. So long as this politics is obscured, we have no way of grasping the processes through which cultural formations are produced and reproduced, or comprehending the relationship between these processes and the constitution, institutionalization, and exercise of political power.

These tendencies have impeded or distorted understanding in many areas. Among other things, they have informed the reification and homogenization of religions,[1] they have blinded us to the complex relationship between gender and national culture,[2] and they have allowed the personification of 'the West', obscuring the energetic cultural politics required to sustain such a transnational imagined community.[3]

My concern here, however, is with the effects of the default conception and its attendant analytical tendencies on how we think about cultural diversity and international order. As we have seen, neither materialists or pluralists lose much sleep over this relationship: the former because culture doesn't matter; the latter because sovereignty has rendered culture a domestic affair. The prevailing view among others, however, is that international orders emerge in unitary cultural contexts and diversity undermines order. Widespread as this view is – both within the academy and among policymakers – it is utterly dependent on the veracity of the default conception of culture. If there is no such thing as a unitary cultural context – bounded, integrated, and coherent – then international orders cannot have emerged in such contexts. And if cultural diversity is the norm, then the relationship between diversity and order must be far more complex than commonly appreciated, as borne out in new histories of a wide range of international orders. Whether we are talking about the Roman Empire, early modern Europe, Qing China, the Ottoman Empire, or the modern order from the nineteenth century, two things stand out: all of these orders evolved in heterogeneous cultural

---

[1] Shakman Hurd, *Beyond Religious Freedom.*
[2] Abu-Lughod, *Writing Women's Worlds*; and Sally Engle Merry, *Gender Violence: A Cultural Perspective* (Malden, MA: Wiley-Blackwell, 2009).
[3] Peter J. Katzenstein (ed.), *Anglo-America and Its Discontents* (London: Routledge, 2012); Jacinta O'Hagan, *Conceptualizing the West in International Relations* (Houndmills: Palgrave, 2002); Srdjan Vucetic, *The Anglosphere: A Genealogy of a Racialized Identity in International Relations* (Stanford, CA: Stanford University Press, 2011).

contexts, and managing, ruling, or governing diversity was a key imperative of order building.

If the default conception of culture is unsustainable, along with the views of international order it encourages, how should we think about the relationship between cultural diversity and international order? This final chapter advances a new perspective, one that builds on specialist understandings of culture to better comprehend not only how diversity affects order but how order in turn conditions diversity.[4] International orders, I shall argue, are best conceived as systemic configurations of political authority, comprised of multiple units, organized according to some principle of differentiation: sovereignty, heteronomy, suzerainty, empire, or some combination. Scholars commonly stress the uneven distribution of material resources in which orders emerge, but orders also evolve in highly diverse cultural conditions. Together these pose profound legitimation challenges for order builders. Material might has to be converted into political authority, and extant diversity has to be converted into authorized forms of difference. To meet these challenges, order builders construct 'diversity regimes': system-wide norms and practices that simultaneously configure authority and organize diversity. The Treaties of Westphalia instituted such a regime, as did the nineteenth-century 'standard of civilization'. Understood in this way, diversity affects international order as a structural condition that generates governance imperatives, directly affecting an order's institutional architecture. This architecture has its own structuring effects, though: organizing cultural diversity in distinctive ways. Because of their legitimation role, diversity regimes help stabilize international orders. But because they license some forms of difference over others, they create social and political hierarchies, hierarchies that fuel struggles for recognition as material and cultural conditions change.

The following discussion is divided into two main sections. The first section makes the case for my distinctive conception of international order and introduces a selection of recent histories that emphasize the complex relationship between order and diversity. My purpose here is not to provide a systematic empirical defence of my argument (which I leave for Volume III), but rather to give readers good historical

---

[4] This perspective further develops an argument first rehearsed in Reus-Smit, 'Cultural Diversity and International Order'.

reasons to believe that such an argument is needed. The second section develops this argument in detail, beginning with the existential reality of cultural diversity and finishing with the cultural dynamics of international change.

International Order

Concepts

Two conceptual distinctions are important in any discussion of international order. The first concerns the different ways IR scholars use the term 'order'. As discussed in Chapter 3, sometimes we use it as a synonym for stability: 'There is order among the great powers.' At other times we use it when referring to an arrangement of states: 'The modern order differs from the absolutist.' These different meanings are thought to be related in the sense that the arrangement of states is said to affect international stability. The second distinction concerns the origins of international order, understood as an arrangement of states. A minority of scholars sees international order as a simple by-product of interstate competition, an 'unintended consequence of great-power security competition, not the result of states acting together to organize peace'.[5] More commonly, international orders are seen as intentional, as reflecting or embodying the values and objectives of either dominant states or the broader society of states.[6] In the following discussion, I am concerned with international order as an arrangement of states, and I join those who see orders as purposeful institutional configurations, at least partly the product of design.

The most influential elaboration of this view is provided by Bull, whose ideas undergird many accounts of international order. For Bull, an 'order' is a purposive arrangement of units: books on a library shelf, patients in a waiting room, seating in the UN General Assembly. An international order, it follows, is a purposive arrangement of sovereign states. It is a 'pattern of activity', founded on the principle of sovereignty and ordered by institutions such as diplomacy and international law. And its purpose is to uphold and advance

---

[5] Mearsheimer, *Tragedy of Great Power Politics*, p. 49.

[6] For a discussion of these two conceptions, see Randall L. Schweller, 'The Problem of International Order Revisited', *International Security*, 26.1 (2001), 161–186.

'the elementary or primary goals of the society of states',[7] the most important of which are protecting the territorial independence of individual states, limiting interstate violence, and preserving international society. International orders, Bull argues, are not the same as world orders, which he defines as 'patterns or dispositions of human activity that sustain the elementary or primary goals of social life among mankind as a whole'.[8] Against realists, Bull holds that international order is a recurrent feature of international life. But against cosmopolitans, he is sceptical about world order, stressing its moral primacy but seeing it as aspirational.

This conception of international order echoes throughout the literature. John Ikenberry defines international orders as 'the governing arrangements among a group of states, including its basic rules, principles, and institutions'.[9] These arrangements serve, at a minimum, to preserve security and systemic stability, but more recently 'states engaged in order building have also gone beyond this and attempted to establish a wider array of political and economic rules and principles of order'.[10] Janice Bially Mattern writes from a more critical perspective, but ends up at a very similar conception. International order, she argues, is 'a relationship among specific states that produces and reinforces shared understandings and expectations and behaviors with respect to one another'.[11] Evelyn Goh's recent study of order in East Asia builds explicitly on Bull's conception: 'International order is a pattern or arrangement that sustains the primary goals of the society of states.'[12]

International orders, so conceived, can be thinner or thicker, animated by more or less ambitious purposes, and evincing more or less elaborate institutions. To capture this variation, Hurrell distinguishes between three ideal types. The first is pluralist, 'made up of separate,

---

[7] Bull, *Anarchical Society*, p. 8.   [8] Ibid., p. 20.
[9] G. John Ikenberry, *After Victory: Institutions, Strategic Restraint, and the Building of Order after Major Wars* (Princeton, NJ: Princeton University Press, 2001), p. 45.
[10] G. John Ikenberry, *Liberal Leviathan: The Origins, Crisis, and Transformation of the American World Order* (Princeton, NJ: Princeton University Press, 2011), p. 11.
[11] Janice Bially Mattern, *Ordering International Politics: Identity, Crisis, and Representational Force* (New York: Routledge, 2005), p. 30.
[12] Evelyn Goh, *The Struggle for Order: Hegemony, Hierarchy, and Transition in Post–Cold War East Asia* (Oxford: Oxford University Press, 2013), p. 7.

sovereign states which are, in turn, linked through various kinds of political practices and institutionalized structures'.[13] The goals of such an order are to minimize conflict and foster elementary cooperation. The second type is solidarist. While still an order of sovereign states, this involves 'both limits on the freedom of states to resort to war and the creation of international rules that affected the domestic structures and organization of states, that invested individuals and groups within states with rights and duties, and that sought to embody some notion of a general common good'.[14] The third type identified by Hurrell decentres sovereign states, moving much closer to Bull's conception of world order. 'Tied closely to processes of social and economic globalization, this view sees traditional interstate governance as increasingly subsumed within a broader process in which there is a steady erosion of old distinctions between the domestic and the international, between public and private international law, and between public and private spheres generally.'[15]

For Ikenberry, the liberal international order combines both the first and second types. Its foundations are 'Westphalian': it is an order of sovereign states, led by great powers, conditioned by the balance of power, and founded on the principles of sovereignty, territorial integrity, and non-intervention.[16] After the Second World War, the United States led an ambitious elaboration of this order, promoting ever more elaborate forms of multilateral governance, covering everything from collective security and free trade to human rights. This 'liberal' order, Ikenberry holds, is 'open and loosely rule-based. Openness is manifest when states trade and exchange on the basis of mutual gain. Rules and institutions operate as mechanisms of governance – and they are at least partially autonomous from the exercise of state power.'[17] The Westphalia and liberal elements of the order converge in its hegemonic nature. This is an order that the United States built, that reflects its liberal values, and that has depended on American power, however benign and legitimate that might be.

Though widely employed, the Bullian conception of international order as a purposive arrangement of sovereign states has two significant limitations. First, and most importantly for our purposes, it

[13] Andrew Hurrell, *On Global Order: Power, Values, and the Constitution of International Society* (Oxford: Oxford University Press, 2007), p. 3.
[14] Ibid., p. 5.   [15] Ibid., pp. 6–7.   [16] Ikenberry, *Liberal Leviathan*, p. 51.
[17] Ibid., p. 18.

understands the 'arrangement' of states narrowly, as the architecture of institutions existing between sovereign states. But as we saw in Chapter 4, Ruggie points to a deeper, more fundamental arrangement that undergirds these institutions: the definition and differentiation of territorial sovereign states as the principal units of political authority. The prevailing conception of international order takes this arrangement for granted – international orders are, by definition, orders of sovereign states. Yet as Ruggie argues, not all international orders have been sovereign, and shifts in principles of differentiation have been a key axis of international change (as evident in the transition from medieval *heteronomy* to modern *sovereignty*).[18] Second, in distinguishing between international and world order, and international and world society, Bull obscures the crucial role that world social forces have played in shaping international orders. This is indicative of a broader tendency in IR to privilege endogenous international processes, at best acknowledging the relevance of domestic political change (such as Europe's nineteenth-century liberal-constitutionalist revolutions). But as I have shown elsewhere, fundamental transformations in international order, such as the rise of today's universal system of sovereign states, have been driven, in large measure, by world social forces: by polities excluded from the order, denied recognition, and by transnational political movements.[19]

I am concerned here with the first of these limitations: the definitional inability of the Bullian conception to accommodate non-sovereign international orders. Analytically, this conception renders only the smallest number of cases intelligible: China in the warring states period (475–221 BC), the Indian subcontinent at the time of Kautilya (371–283 BC), possibly the city-state systems of Ancient Greek and Renaissance Italy, and the global sovereign order after 1970. The early modern European order, and the modern order prior to the 1960s, fit only with difficulty, as they were hybrid orders, based on the paired organizing principles of sovereignty in the core and imperial rule over the periphery. If we want a conception of international order with broader analytical reach – that can comprehend not only non-sovereign

---

[18] See Ruggie, 'Continuity and Transformation'; and Ruggie, 'Territoriality and Beyond'.
[19] Reus-Smit, *Individual Rights*, pp. 198–201.

orders but also transitions from one kind to another – we need to remove the assumption of sovereignty from the definition. Several scholars have made this move. Gilpin is clear that international systems (which he also terms international orders) vary in the nature of their constituent units – from city-states and empires to sovereign states – and that shifts from one kind of order to another require a special designation: 'systems change'.[20] More recently, in order to compare Latin Christendom and the Sinosphere, Phillips defines international orders expansively, as 'the constellation of constitutional norms and fundamental institutions through which co-operation is cultivated and conflict contained between different political communities'.[21]

While these conceptions correctly jettison the assumption of sovereignty, broadening their analytical range to include orders comprising different kinds of units, they dance around the central issue. The most basic thing all political orders do is define and distribute legitimate power, or political authority. Sovereign states, for example, centralize and bound authority territorially, and within this general model, autocracies and democracies define and distribute authority differently. As many scholars have observed, though, the authority of political units is constituted not only by internal forces and processes but also by the wider order in which units are embedded. It is often argued, for example, that sovereignty is a social status, ordained by the society of states. The same can be said, however, for the units that comprised Europe's medieval heteronomous order, from the burgeoning towns and local lords to the papacy and the Holy Roman emperor, and also for the emperor and tributaries of the Chinese order. In each case, their political authority, varied and differently differentiated, has been constituted by the international orders in which they have been embedded. Placing this front and centre, I thus define such orders as systemic configurations of political authority, comprising multiple units of authority, arranged according to some principle of differentiation: sovereignty, heteronomy, suzerainty, empire, or some combination thereof.[22] The last of these elements is crucial, as it is what distinguishes one kind of order from another.

[20] Gilpin, *War and Change*, pp. 39–40.
[21] Phillips, *War, Religion and Empire*, p. 5.
[22] I have been developing this conception in a number of previous publications, including Christian Reus-Smit, 'The Liberal International Order Reconsidered',

Some might object to the term inter*national* being used to describe orders not made up of sovereign states. My response is simple. Concepts stand or fall according to how useful they are: how much or how little they illuminate, and how much or how little they help comprehension. If we limit the concept of international orders to systems of sovereign states, and are thoroughly consistent in this, then the concept illuminates and explicates much less than is commonly assumed. Defining it narrowly not only excludes most historical orders; it excludes most of what we routinely term 'the modern international order'. Until the 1970s, this order was not arranged solely according to the principle of sovereignty: it was a hybrid order that for five centuries conjoined sovereignty and empire, both within and beyond the European core. When a concept narrows the universe of cases so dramatically it becomes unhelpful, and a conception with greater analytical reach is warranted. The challenge, of course, is to give such a conception clear boundaries, and to specify within it key axes of variation. Defining international orders as systemic configurations of political authority does the first of these; allowing for variation in principles of differentiation does the second.

Because international orders define and distribute political authority, they are institutions: systems of norms and practices that define legitimate political agency and the bounds of rightful political action. Their institutional architectures are complex and multilayered, however. As noted in Chapter 4, I have previously identified three different levels of international institutions.[23] The most readily apparent are the functional, issue-specific institutions political units create to solve particular problems or realize particular ends. In the modern international order these are commonly termed 'regimes'. Although these are the most studied international institutions, at least on the modern setting, they are but expressions of deeper institutional practices, or fundamental institutions, that actors routinely employ to facilitate coexistence and collaboration. Since the nineteenth century, two interrelated practices have been favoured: positive international law and multilateralism. These are rooted in yet a deeper level of institutions, however, which I term 'constitutional structures'. The norms and practices that

in Rebekka Friedman, Kevork Oskanian, and Ramon Pacheco-Pardo (eds.), *After Liberalism* (London: Palgrave, 2013), p. 169; and Reus-Smit, 'Cultural Diversity and International Order', p. 855.
[23] Reus-Smit, *Moral Purpose of the State*, pp. 12–15.

comprise these structures define the most basic elements of an order: the units of legitimate authority and how they stand in relation to one another. There is broad agreement that in today's international order the norm of sovereignty performs this role. I have argued, however, that organizing principles like this are always sustained by hegemonic ideas about the moral purpose served by privileged forms of political organization – sovereignty, heteronomy, and empire as not self-sustaining values. While originally developed to understand the institutional architectures of sovereign orders, this typology of institutions has since been applied, in modified forms, to a range of differently configured orders, most notably the Chinese.[24]

Before proceeding, a word on orders, communicative action, and practices is warranted. In Chapter 4 I identified two strands of constructivist thought that point to more complex understandings of culture than those found in the norms and institutional structure projects. The first is the emphasis in linguistic and communicative action theories on the constitution of social life through a multiplicity of word games, mobilized through argument, both of which suggest a highly complex cultural terrain. As in my previous work, I see communicative action as central to the production and reproduction of international orders. And just as such action helps generate other dimensions of an order's institutional architecture, I see it as central to the development of the diversity regimes I explain below. Practice theorists are correct, however, that institutions do not just arise or evolve through rational construction or communicative action; they are also products of unintentional practices, of accreted ways of doing. This is as true of diversity regimes as it is of other ordering institutions, and I am careful to define these regimes as distinctive sets of norms *and* practices. I part company with practice theorists on two issues, however. As explained in Chapter 4, in emphasizing the constitutive power of practices, they risk unnecessarily discounting conscious institutional design, which I hold has been a crucial element in the development of all historical orders (as well as their distinctive diversity regimes). Second, some practice theorists suggest that in social contexts where

[24] See, for example, Yongjin Zhang, 'System, Empire and State in Chinese International Relations', *Review of International Relations*, 27.5 (2001), 43–63; Yongjin Zhang and Barry Buzan, 'The Tributary System as International Society in Theory and Practice', *Chinese Journal of International Relations*, 5.1 (2012), 3–36.

there is a multiplicity of practices, there must also be multiple social orders.[25] They are likely to be uncomfortable, therefore, with my references to *the* modern order, *the* Qing order, *the* Ottoman order, etc. I stand by this move, though. While international orders are embodied in, and sustained by, clusters of practices, and while they can have various regional or local suborders nested within them, they are also the macro-institutional frameworks defining and distributing political authority. At any historical point in time, and in any geographical context, there will tend, therefore, to be one overarching international *political* order, even if such orders are always contested and vary in coherence.

Histories

International orders are the largest scale configurations of political authority humans have created, spanning vast geographical areas and incorporating numerous local polities, at times nested in distinctive regional suborders. Two myths persist about the place of culture in such configurations. The first, with which we are now well acquainted, sees international orders as culturally dependent, emerging in homogeneous cultural contexts, instantiating a coherent set of cultural values and practices, and sustained only so long as cultural unity persists. The second, expressed most confidently by contemporary liberals and pluralists of the English School, holds that particular kinds of institutions neutralize culture, effectively removing it as a politically salient factor. For liberals, this is a virtue of 'open and rules-based' liberal institutions; for pluralists it is an accomplishment of sovereignty, nonintervention, and self-determination. Both of these claims are historically unsustainable. The histories of diverse international orders show the heterogeneous cultural contexts in which they have commonly

---

[25] In elaborating his theory of cognitive evolution, Emanuel Adler provides the most sustained and sophisticated expression of this view. He writes that '[c]ognitive evolution theory suggests a concept of multiple international social orders, which I define as fields, configurations, or "landscapes" of international practices, background knowledge, and communities of practice, whose *epistemic practical authority* assigns functions and statuses, and which, straddling a spectrum between interconnectedness and disassociation, arrange, organize, stabilize, and manage international social life'. Emanuel Adler, *A Social Theory of Cognitive Evolution: Change, Stability, and International Social Orders* (Cambridge: Cambridge University Press, forthcoming), p. 5 (manuscript).

emerged, and in each case how institutions have served not to neutral-ize culture but to define and organize it.

The early modern European order is a case in point. For culturalists, this is an order with deep cultural roots. Yet these authors obscure the heterogeneity of European culture and overstate its distinctiveness. We saw in Chapter 3, for example, that Wight anchors European international society in Western Christendom, attributing to this civilizational constellation the political sensibility needed for society among states – an orientation to the 'golden mean' – and belief in natural law, which he considered the surest foundation of the law of nations. Western Christendom was hardly a coherent cultural forma-tion, though. The boundaries with Byzantine Christianity were blurred and contested, and Catholic ascendancy in the West was an ongoing political project, in which heretical Christian beliefs were energetically suppressed, and Muslim and Jewish communities were periodically 'cleansed'. The terminal failure of this project was the Protestant Reformation, which divided Christians over the most basic questions of faith, belying once and for all any claims to the cultural unity or coherence of Western Christendom. There are, of course, culturalists who admit the religious ruptures of the Reformation, but emphasize other elements of European cultural distinctiveness. As we saw in Chapter 2, Kissinger claims that Europeans had a unique understand-ing of reality that enabled them to institute sovereign states as a temporal solution to religious divisions. How unique such an under-standing was to Europeans is entirely questionable, though. Equally temporal, if substantively different, solutions to religious divisions were instituted in other non-Western orders, most notably in the nearby Ottoman Empire.

Pluralists are correct that the Treaties of Westphalia instituted new norms and practices that resolved a century or more of religious conflict. Yet these norms are consistently misrepresented and misinter-preted. They are thought to have been an exercise in secular pluralism, in which princes were recognized as sovereign and given the right to define religion within their territories, thus relegating issues of religion to the newly constituted domestic realm. The Peace created a society of states, Jackson argues, that 'expresses the morality of difference',[26] or in Kissinger's words, 'it reserved judgement on the absolute in

---

[26] Ibid., p. 168.

favour of the practical and ecumenical'.[27] This was far from the case, however. The Westphalian settlement was an act of politico-cultural construction, in which a reconfiguration of political authority was inextricably connected to a particular construction of cultural difference.[28] The treaties were a significant step in the creation of a nascent order of sovereign states, but they also organized cultural diversity in a particular way. Not only did they privilege religion as the dominant cultural category; they recognized only some religious identities: Catholics, Lutherans, and Calvinists were authorized, but heretical Christian sects, Muslims, and Jews were not. The new configuration of political authority was also related to legitimate forms of difference in a distinctive way. It is often asserted that the Treaties simply endorsed the so-called Augsburg Principle of *cuis regio, eius religio*, which granted princes the right to define religion within their territories. In reality, however, the Treaties' success depended on them violating this principle. Instead of giving princes unfettered religious rights, they severely circumscribed these rights, granting Catholic and Protestant minorities significant protections and forbidding the forced conversion of populations.

The Ottoman order also emerged in a highly diverse cultural environment, and it too developed institutions for organizing this diversity. The Mediterranean Basin, across which the Empire spread, 'did not easily fit any particular category exclusively; it was not just Ottoman, Turkish, or Islamic. It was all these combined with Roman and Byzantine, Balkan, and Turco-Mongol institutions and practices'.[29] The international order that emerged in this heterogeneous environment was thus 'an amalgam of many cultures and traditions'.[30] While Islam enjoyed a privileged place in this amalgam – as both imperial faith and principal source of political legitimacy – its place was artfully bounded and delimited. Not only did the early Ottomans practice a 'heterodox form of Islam'; they innovated structurally, separating 'church and state' by asserting the Sultan's supreme legislative power,

---

[27] Ibid, pp. 3–4.
[28] For an extended discussion, see Reus-Smit, *Individual Rights*, pp. 97–102.
[29] Karen Barkey, *Empire of Difference: The Ottomans in Comparative Perspective* (Cambridge: Cambridge University Press, 2008), p. 8.
[30] Daniel Goffman, *The Ottoman Empire and Early Modern Europe* (Cambridge: Cambridge University Press, 2002), p. 8.

quite separate from shariah.[31] The most distinctive feature of Ottoman rule, however, was their delegation of authority to the Empire's diverse religious communities. This was an Empire with attenuated governance capacities, in which for most subjects 'direct contact with the sultan's government was an unusual event apart from paying taxes and supplying recruits'.[32] Non-Muslim communities were connected to the empire by delegated legal powers, which granted these communities considerable autonomy while at the same time enmeshing them in the legal hierarchies of the Empire:

In family and religious matters, Christians of various rites, Jews, and other non-Muslim subjects were under the legal authority of their own communities' leaders. What linked these groups and their different legal practices to the sultan's overarching authority was a personal and official tie. Chief rabbis, metropolitans of the Greek Orthodox church, and leaders of Armenian Orthodoxy and of other Christian groups held their offices as recipients of sultanic warrants. In return for their service to the sultan they were exempted from taxation and received rights to various revenues and resources.[33]

Violence and coercion were also part of the Ottoman's repertoire of integrative practices; the military enslavement of Christian boys in the elite Janissaries is a prime example.[34] Yet the formal institutionalization of authorized religious difference was important not just to the formal organization of the Empire, but also to the legitimation practices of successive dynasties.[35] Moreover, the Ottomans exploited the relative tolerance of their order to attract persecuted religious minorities, most notably when Ferdinand and Isabella expelled Spain's Muslim and Jewish communities.[36]

The construction and reconstruction of successive Chinese international orders – expanding and contracting with the rise and fall of imperial dynasties – took place across a highly diverse cultural terrain.

---

[31] Karen Barkey, 'Political Legitimacy and Islam in the Ottoman Empire: Lessons Learned', *Philosophy and Social Criticism*, 40.4–5 (2017), 473.

[32] Jane Burbank and Frederick Cooper, *Empires in World History: Power and the Politics of Difference* (Princeton, NJ: Princeton University Press, 2010), p. 140.

[33] Ibid.   [34] Geoffrey Goodwin, *The Janissaries* (London: Saqi Books, 2006).

[35] Ayse Zarakol, 'Ottoman Lessons for Cultural Diversity in International Relations', in Andrew Phillips and Christian Reus-Smit (eds.), *Diversity and Its Discontents* (Cambridge: Cambridge University Press, forthcoming).

[36] Heather Rae, *State Identities and the Homogenization of Peoples* (Cambridge: Cambridge University Press, 2002), pp. 55–82.

This was especially the case for the Qing Empire (1644–1912). After decades of territorial conquests, the Manchus consolidated an order roughly coterminous with that of modern China, expanding the boundaries of the Ming Empire to include the culturally diverse peoples of Manchuria, Mongolia, Tibet, and Xinjiang. The axes of diversity in this new order were multiple. The Manchus themselves were an alien dynasty, former 'barbarians' whose legitimacy depended on crafting a new imperial cultural identity from extant cultural resources. Added to this, the inner Asian regions they annexed were culturally complex and fluid. As in many early modern regions across the globe, Pamela Kyle Crossley observes, inner Asia had cultural formations 'in which economic livelihoods, religions, languages, and in many cases gene pools were distributed according to the common routes of commerce, war, and pilgrimage and mixed as the flow of goods and peoples determined'.[37]

To construct a legitimate political order in this context, the early Qing emperors built an institutional architecture that simultaneously engaged and reconstituted this diversity. Formal institutions like the Eight Banners system, which tied Manchu, Han, and Mongol ethnicities to the organization of military units, and the Lifanyuan system, which governed ethnic groups in Inner Asia, institutionalized cultural difference at the heart of the imperial administration. Conventional interpretations suggest that these institutions built on preexisting cultural identities.[38] Others have shown, however, that the Qing's practices actually constituted such identities. Imperial legitimacy depended on Emperor's capacity to narrate his relationship to subject communities, and as Crossley explains, '[s]ome constituencies had to be laden with codified distinctions to become objects to which the emperorship addressed itself, and to function as presences in the imperial narrative; those less amenable to such representation were liable to be shrunken or obliterated'.[39] The complexity of the cultural landscape encountered

---

[37] Pamela Kyle Crossley, *A Translucent Mirror: History and Identity in Qing Imperial Ideology* (Berkeley: University of California Press, 1999), p. 31.

[38] A recent example of this tendency is Chia Ning, 'Lifanyuan and the Management of Population Diversity in Early Qing (1636–1795)', Max Planck Institute for Social Anthropology, Working Paper 139 (2012).

[39] Crossley, *A Translucent Mirror*, p. 44. Crossley uses the term 'constituencies' in preference to 'peoples', because with the latter term 'there is the hazard that some readers could be led to believe that there was always a reliable historical or cultural content in these constructions' (p. 44).

202 On Cultural Diversity

by the Qing, and their efforts to order this diversity, cast serious doubt, Andrew Phillips argues, on recent portrayals of the Sinosphere as a realm of Confucian cultural affinity.[40] These three international orders – the early modern European, the Ottoman, and the Qing – were the principal antecedents of the modern international order. During the nineteenth century, Europe's absolutist society of states was convulsed by liberal-constitutionalist revolutions, and the Portuguese and Spanish empires collapsed, adding a host of new republics to international society. Shortly thereafter, a new wave of imperialism brought huge swaths of Africa, Asia, and the Pacific under European rule or domination. Yet this age of imperialism was relatively short lived. By the end of the First World War, the Austro-Hungarian, German, and Ottoman empires were gone, and the last Qing dynasty had fallen to republican revolutionaries, beginning China's long road from empire to sovereign state. By the 1970s Europe's remaining empires had collapsed, with post-1945 struggles for decolonization assailing multiple empires simultaneously, and, most significantly, terminally delegitimizing the institution of empire itself. The net result was the world's first universal system of sovereign states.[41]

While the modern order is often cast as 'Western', the cultural terrain in which it evolved was from the outset highly diverse. As we have seen, the early modern European order was born of religious turmoil, and by the nineteenth century ethno-nationalism had emerged as a new axis of cultural division. The early British, Dutch, Portuguese, and Spanish empires spread over a vast cultural mosaic, and even settler colonies, which ostensibly transplanted European societies, developed their own cultural complexions, affecting in far-reaching ways how they engaged with European international society.[42] The late nineteenth-century acceleration of imperialism in Asia, Africa, and

[40] Andrew Phillips, 'Contesting the Confucian Peace: Civilization, Barbarism, and International Hierarchy in East Asia', *European Journal of International Relations*, online at https://doi.org/10.1177/1354066117716265.
[41] I tell the story of the development of this universal system of states in my *Individual Rights*, arguing that successive waves of imperial collapse were driven, in significant measure, by struggles for individual rights.
[42] Latin America's colonial elite, for example, developed very different understandings of race from their Iberian counterparts, informing deep divisions over individual political representation, divisions that fuelled anticolonial sentiment. See Reus-Smit, *Individual Rights*, pp. 135–144.

the Pacific drew more and more non-European peoples under European control. Polities that were not colonized – such as China, Japan, and Siam – were eventually admitted to the society of states, gaining formal but second-class sovereign rights. With the collapse of the Ottoman Empire after the First World War, the evolving order gained a number of new sovereign states and imperial mandates, and incorporated an Islamic world marked by its own internal divisions and overlaying a rich matrix of other cultural identities. Post-1945 decolonization added to this cultural complexity not by bringing new identities, meanings, and practices into the modern order, as imperialism had already brought these into its ambit. Rather, by replacing empires with sovereign states, decolonization created new institutional frameworks in which difference could be articulated and structured.

Like its antecedents, the evolution of the modern international order has been punctuated by repeated attempts to organize cultural diversity. At the turn of the twentieth century, a standard of civilization was codified in international law to manage the heightened diversity that accompanied accelerated imperialism. And to manage intra-European diversity, ethnically defined nations were given a right to self-determination. After the Second World War, this understanding of legitimate statehood was jettisoned, as it was thought to have licensed Nazism and other xenophobic nationalisms. Standards of civilization were still invoked, though, to police the movement of colonial peoples toward independence. Only after the 1970s were they delegitimized, replaced by an emphasis on universal sovereign rights and domestic multiculturalism as the best means to manage global diversity.[43]

Ordering Difference

These snapshots of key historical orders highlight two things: the heterogeneous cultural contexts in which these orders have emerged and the development, in each and every case, of institutions to manage, govern, or rule this diversity. These facts resonate with insights from contemporary anthropology and sociology discussed in Chapter 1, particularly the inherent diversity of all cultural formations, and the

---

[43] Reus-Smit, 'Cultural Diversity and International Order', p. 878.

role social institutions play in structuring and patterning cultural meanings and practices. In what follows, I build on these historical and theoretical insights to advance a new perspective on cultural diversity and international order.[44] I do this in four steps, beginning with the deep existential context in which international orders emerge, through the institutional consequences of managing unequal material power and articulations of cultural difference, to sources of crisis and change.

Existential Diversity

Culture matters. Humans live in webs of intersubjective meanings, expressed through, embedded within, and reproduced by language, images, bodies, artefacts, and practices. These meanings are constitutive, shaping identities and interests, and they are strategic resources that actors mobilize in pursuit of diverse ends and purposes. Constructivists and rationalists are, in this sense, both correct. What culture is not, though, is coherent, integrated, and bounded. Indeed, instead of talking about culture as though it coalesces into neatly defined, easily differentiated wholes – a world of cultural billiard balls – we should assume as our starting assumption that culture is always heterogeneous. The Comaroffs' characterization of culture, discussed in Chapter 1, bears repeating: 'Culture always contains within it polyvalent, potentially contestable meanings, images, and actions ... Some of these, at any moment in time, will be woven into more or less tightly integrated, relatively explicit world views; others may be heavily contested, the stuff of counterideologies and "subcultures"; yet others may become more or less unfixed, relatively freefloating, and indeterminate in their value and meaning.'[45]

The 'strange multiplicity' of culture, as Tully terms it, has many axes and multiple expressions.[46] Three are particularly noteworthy, though. The first is the multiplicity of social identification. The literature on multiculturalism highlights the coexistence of multiple

---

[44] My discussion here draws on an earlier articulation of this argument in Reus-Smit, 'Cultural Diversity and International Order'.

[45] Comaroff and Comaroff, *Ethnography and the Historical Imagination*, p. 27.

[46] Tully, *Strange Multiplicity*, p. 11.

communities of religious, linguistic, and ethnic identification within national societies.[47] Yet patterns of identification are greatly complicated by cross-cutting identifications. While individuals often have distinctive religious, linguistic, or ethnic identities, they also have other meaningful identities: national, transnational, professional, familial, class, gender, etc. Individuals move in and out of such identities according to social context, and learn how to narrate, in socially intelligible ways, these fluid complexes of identities. This multiplicity, and its contextual fluidity, has been highly consequential politically. In the sixteenth century, when Europeans encountered the New World, they identified as Christians, but when they faced each other in Europe it was as Catholics and Protestants, and increasingly as French, English, Spanish, etc.[48]

Cultural multiplicity is also manifest in the complexity of meanings. In all social contexts, culture sends mixed messages. Individuals do not encounter a simple cultural script, or a neatly ordered repertoire of practices. Instead, they navigate complex, often conflicting, meanings. Within sovereign states, the meanings mobilized in the service of national unity coexist, often uncomfortably, with contrasting cosmopolitan, regional, ethnic, class, and gendered meanings, and cross-cutting politico-cultural meanings frequently betray markedly different conceptions of the scope and purpose of political authority. Most globalizing societies evince complex mixes of 'traditional', 'modern', and/or 'postmodern' cultural meanings, generating contestation at multiple levels, from the family to issues of public policy. At the international level, Stephen Krasner rightly points to the existence of multiple, often contradictory, norms.[49] Elsewhere I argue that he misreads the political implications of such complexity. He claims that it privileges consequentialist strategic action, but fails to grasp what it is about norms that make them strategically useful. He also thinks that normative complexity facilitates the exercise of political power, but

[47] See, for example, Will Kymlicka, *Multicultural Citizenship* (Oxford: Clarendon Press, 1995), and *Multicultural Odysseys* (Oxford: Oxford University Press, 2007).
[48] For an excellent discussion of these complex patterns of identification, see Heather Rae, 'Patterns of Identification on the Cusp of Globalization', in Tim Dunne and Christian Reus-Smit (eds.), *The Globalization of International Society* (Oxford: Oxford University Press, 2017), pp. 63–81.
[49] Stephen D. Krasner, *Sovereignty: Organized Hypocrisy* (Princeton, NJ: Princeton University Press, 1999), p. 51.

does not see how such complexity frustrates the control of meanings and allows materially weak actors to innovate in the cracks and contradictions of an order, often with transformative effects.[50] These problems aside, though, Krasner's starting proposition that world politics takes place in the context of diverse cultural meanings is broadly correct.

The third axis of cultural multiplicity stems from the variability of actors' interpretations. Not only do cultural environments comprise multiple, often conflicting meanings; individuals interpret these meanings differently. Meaning indeterminacy is a feature of all norms, values, and practices, and this allows individuals to read them very differently. Even in the realm of law, where norms are often formalized and subject to authoritative interpretation, it is widely accepted that legal meanings – norms, rules, and principles – are inherently indeterminate, leaving considerable scope for interpretation. This stems in part from the 'semantic openness of legal speech' (words and phrases can be open to diverse interpretation), and in part from the contestable histories that produced this speech in the first place.[51] Outside the realm of law, prominent examples of meaning indeterminacy abound. Religious meanings are a prime example. Religious doctrine, codified or not, is invariably subject to diverse interpretation, at times producing deep confessional schisms. If religious meanings were amenable to only one interpretation, there would have been no Reformation in Christianity and no Sunni/Shia divide in Islam.

If these and other dimensions of multiplicity greatly complicate the topography of culture, that topography is always patterned. As explained in Chapter 1, culture is more than a random collection of atomized symbols, meanings, and practices. These are always structured in particular ways, producing more or less stable identifications, routinized ways of doing, and distinctive styles of discursive and ritual engagement. Even culture's contradictions bind as much as they divide.

---

[50] Christian Reus-Smit, 'Protean Power and Revolutions in Rights', in Peter J. Katzenstein and Lucia A. Seybert (eds.), *Power in Uncertainty: Exploring the Unexpected in World Politics* (Cambridge: Cambridge University Press, 2018), pp. 59–78.

[51] Martti Koskenniemi, *From Apologia to Utopia: The Structure of Legal Argument*, 2nd edn. (Cambridge: Cambridge University Press, 2005), pp. 590–596.

The inherently diverse, but nonetheless patterned, nature of culture has led some anthropologists and sociologists to call for a focus not on culture per se but on the organization of diversity. In Hannerz's words, what is needed is a 'distributive' theory of culture, the key to which is understanding how the 'social structure of persons and relationships channels the cultural flow'.[52] We saw in Chapter 1 that in trying to understand the effects of this social structure a wide range of anthropologists and sociologists have emphasized the role of social institutions. While these institutions are themselves cultural artefacts – emerging in particular cultural contexts, conditioned by procedural and substantive values, and often designed to secure distinct cultural ends – once established, once actors encounter them as social facts, they have an organizing effect on cultural meanings and practices. Examples of this are everywhere, from Swidler's study of how the legal institution of marriage conditions cultural understandings of love to the way that institutionalized national policies of assimilation and multiculturalism license some forms of ethnic identification over others.[53]

The institution of multiculturalism brings to the fore a key issue: how particular kinds of social institutions can seek to construct authorized forms of diversity out of extant cultural heterogeneity. There is no such thing as culture that is unconditioned by social institutions, but institutions are often constructed with the explicit intent of reordering the cultural universe. Assimilation and genocide are designed to extinguish diversity, but other kinds of institutions – such as multiculturalism – celebrate diversity. In doing so, however, they authorize certain forms of identification and expressions of difference. Berrey draws a useful distinction between diversity as heterogeneity, and diversity as an organizational ideal.[54] As we saw in Chapter 1, she shows that after the 1960s civil rights movement, corporations, universities, and government agencies institutionalized diversity policies. But instead of overcoming racial hierarchies, they simply reconfigured the racial order.[55]

---

[52] Hannerz, *Cultural Complexity*, p. 14.
[53] Kenan Malik, 'The Failure of Multiculturalism', *Foreign Affairs*, 94.2 (2015), 21–32.
[54] Berrey, *Enigma of Diversity*, pp. 25–27.   [55] Ibid., p. 15.

Material Power, Cultural Diversity, and Legitimacy

International orders, I argued earlier, are systemic configurations of political authority, comprised of multiple units of authority, arranged according to a principle of differentiation: sovereignty, suzerainty, heteronomy, or some combination thereof. Because they are configurations of political authority, not simply material power, their efficacy and stability depend, in significant measure, on the cultivation and maintenance of legitimacy, on the social perception that they are 'desirable, proper, appropriate within some socially constructed system of norms, values, beliefs, and definitions'.[56] We take this for granted in contemporary discussions of the modern 'liberal' international order, where questions of its continued legitimacy loom large. But legitimacy was no less important to the early modern European order, with its discourse of the divine right of kings; to the Ottoman order, and its artful balancing of Islamic and secular legitimations; or to Qing order, where the 'barbarian' Manchus had to establish their authority not only over former Ming territories but also over the newly conquered regions of Inner Asia.

All international orders face two key legitimation challenges. The first, and most commonly observed, is to convert an unequal distribution of material capabilities into a configuration of political authority: might has to be translated into right. Why this is necessary has been explained many times, with the most common argument emphasizing the efficacy of legitimate rule. As Edmund Burke put it, 'the use of force is but *temporary*. It may subdue for a moment, but it does not remove the necessity of subduing again; and a nation is not governed, which is to be perpetually conquered.'[57] When rule is legitimate – when political authority replaces sheer domination – not only do the costs of rule decline, as the need for coercion and bribery diminishes, but political orders reap the benefits of voluntary compliance and support.[58] There is considerable debate about the precise relationship between material

---

[56] Mark Suchman, 'Managing Legitimacy: Strategic and Institutional Approaches', *Academy of Management Review*, 30.3 (1995), 574.

[57] Edmund Burke, 'Conciliation with the Colonies', in E. J. Payne (ed.), *Burke: Selected Works*, vol. 1 (Clark, NJ: Lawbook Exchange, 2005), p. 177.

[58] For a more extended discussion of the efficacy of legitimate rule, see Christian Reus-Smit, 'International Crises of Legitimacy', *International Politics*, 44.2–3 (2007), 163.

might and legitimacy, with the more dogmatic realists arguing that material power breeds its own legitimacy. The problem is, though, that social perceptions of political legitimacy are always formed with reference to prevailing norms and values. And while materially powerful actors can (and do) seek to narrate these to license their rule, this is not a matter of simple control. Harnessing established norms and values involves more than rhetorical enlistment; it requires actors to adapt themselves and their purposes to these meanings, all in a context where other actors are able to craft their own relations between political authority and available normative resources.[59]

The second legitimation challenge, so far largely ignored, is to organize cultural diversity: to take extant cultural heterogeneity, create authorized forms and expressions of difference, and order them hierarchically. This is essential to legitimation for three reasons. The first is control. In culturally heterogeneous environments, multiple opportunities exist for the construction of social identities, the mobilization of meanings, the exploitation of extant practices, and the use of these to legitimize diverse political projects. While such environments defy complete control, order builders have a powerful incentive to institutionalize preferred configurations of meanings and identities, engineer consent for these configurations, and limit the scope for cultural innovation. The second reason concerns self-location: the placing of oneself, as an order builder, within the cultural terrain one seeks to organize. When European rulers negotiated the Westphalian settlement, they not only reorganized the politico-cultural landscape, creating nascent sovereign states with defined relationships to authorize forms of religion; they located themselves, as new kinds of political actors, within that landscape. Ottoman and Qing emperors did precisely the same thing, organizing culture so that their own cultural identities were centrally, and indispensably, placed.

The third reason concerns social and political coordination. All political orders, international included, depend on the coordination of individuals' choices to realize common goals and avoid conflicts when interests diverge, all in ways consistent with the preferred form of rule. As we saw in Chapter 5, rationalists argue that social coordination

---

[59] On the need for actors to adapt to their own rhetoric, see Quentin Skinner, *Visions of Politics*, vol. 1: *Regarding Method* (Cambridge: Cambridge University Press, 2002), p. 155.

depends on common knowledge and that culture is a principal source of such knowledge. The problem for international order builders is that their cultural environments are highly diverse. They have a strong incentive, therefore, to organize these environments in ways that facilitate their desired forms of coordination, privileging certain meanings and practices to engineer the required shared knowledge. This is not just about the generation of common knowledge, which rationalists emphasize. Because international orders are developed in heterogeneous cultural contexts, social and political coordination requires the generation of collective knowledge: intersubjective understandings that constitute identities as well as coordinate action. In fact, in the development of international orders, the common and collective knowledge are often entwined: coordinating action requires the construction of identities, often cultural. The nineteenth-century 'standard of civilization' was an attempt to organize global cultural diversity, defining civilization and race as principal axes of cultural difference and ordering these differences hierarchically. Its codification into international law was not just about enforcement, though; it was about generating the shared knowledge (common and collective) needed for a distinct form of political coordination.[60]

Lest this sound too instrumental, as though order builders stand outside culture, organizing it solely for purposes of control, self-authorization, and coordination, how they pursue these ends is almost always informed by their preexisting cultural sensibilities and by how these relate to their conceptions of good and right. Europe's early modern rulers and the Ottoman sultans privileged religious difference when ordering their heterogeneous cultural environments, but they did this in very different ways. This is not just because they had different cultural resources to work with, or because decades of religious conflict mandated certain responses (as in the European case). It also reflected the nature and limits of their respective ecumenical sensibilities. Europe's rulers came to accept a circumscribed Christian pluralism, with

---

[60] See Brett Bowden, *The Empire of Civilization* (Chicago, IL: University of Chicago Press, 2009); Gerrit Gong, *The Standard of Civilization in International Society* (Oxford: Clarendon Press, 1984); Edward Keene, *Beyond the Anarchical Society* (Cambridge: Cambridge University Press, 2002); and Iver Neumann and Jennifer Welsh, 'The Other in European Self-Definition: An Addendum to the Literature on International Society', *Review of International Studies* 17.4 (1991), 327–348.

Judaism and Islam pushed to the margins. The Ottomans, by contrast, built an Islamic order that formally integrated quasi-autonomous Christian and Jewish communities, albeit hierarchically.

Diversity Regimes

To meet these legitimation challenges, international orders develop particular kinds of institutions, which I term 'diversity regimes'. Often the product of conscious design, but also evolving through piecemeal innovations, these are systems of rules, norms, and practices that simultaneously configure authority and organize diversity. Codified in legal instruments, embodied in formal institutions, and expressed and reproduced through informal understandings and social practices, these regimes do three things.

First, they legitimize certain units of political authority, and define how they stand in relation to one another. These might be sovereign states, standing in relations of formal equality (as in today's modern order). They might be an imperial household or metropolitan state hierarchically related to subordinate units that enjoy reserved but circumscribed legal and political authority (as the Ottoman and Qing orders). Or the units might vary greatly and have non-exclusive, over-lapping jurisdictions (as in Medieval Europe). Second, diversity regimes authorize certain categories of cultural difference, and within these categories, they order difference hierarchically. In the early modern European order, for example, religion was the recognized axis of difference, but Catholics, Lutherans, and Calvinists enjoyed rights denied to heretical Christian sects, Jews, and Muslims. While the Ottomans also privileged religious difference, this was not the case for the Qing order or the modern order in the early twentieth century. In both, ethnicity and civilization were the authorized axes of cultural diversity. Third, diversity regimes connect legitimate units of political authority with authorized categories of cultural difference. As we saw in the brief historical discussions above, in post-Westphalian Europe the sovereign state and Christianity were linked. In the Ottoman order, differential and hierarchically ordered political and legal authorities were the preserve of designated Islamic, Jewish, and Christian communities. In Qing China, the Eight Banners and Lifanyuan systems channeled imperial authority through authorized ethnicities, and civilizational discourses were mobilized to license suzerain rule of

neighbouring tributary states. In the modern international order, at
least three attempts have been made to coordinate authority and
difference. After the First World War, sovereignty in the European
core was seen as a right of ethnically defined nations, and imperial
rule over large swaths of the non-European world was justified on the
basis of civilizational differences. In the wake of the Holocaust, the
ethnic criterion for sovereignty was abandoned, and civic conceptions
of nationhood were privileged. Only after the 1970s, however, was
empire finally delegitimized a form of rule, in part because civilizational differences were no longer considered an appropriate basis on
which to distribute rights to self-determination.

Diversity regimes are not 'regimes' as commonly understood in
IR: issue-specific institutions around which actors' expectations converge.[61] As explained in Chapter 4 and reiterated above, it is useful to
distinguish between three levels of international institutions. The issue-
specific institutions that IR scholars commonly term 'regimes' are
instantiations of more 'fundamental' institutional practices, such as
multilateralism and international law. These are only possible, however, because deeper 'constitutional' institutions define the legitimate
political units in an order, how they are differentiated, and the moral
or ethical basis for such an arrangement.[62] How these different kinds
of institutions are manifest will vary from one kind of order to another:
different constitutional norms will license different kinds of political
units; different fundamental institutional practices will be privileged
over others; and variations in both of these will affect the kinds of
institutions actors develop to address particular issues. What matters
here, though, is that diversity regimes, as I speak of them, straddle
these institutional levels. By defining units of legitimate political
authority, authorizing forms of cultural difference, and relating these
to one another, diversity regimes are integral to an order's constitutional structure. In many cases, though, they also condition fundamental institutional practices. For example, the modern order's late
nineteenth-century diversity regime rested on the notorious standard
of civilization, which not only was codified in international law but, as

---

[61] Stephen D. Krasner (ed.), *International Regimes* (Ithaca, NY: Cornell University
Press, 1983), p. 27.
[62] Reus-Smit, *The Moral Purpose of the State*, pp. 12–15.

critics point out, also rendered international law an imperial project.[63] It is often in the rules, norms, and practices of issue-specific institutions, however, that diversity regimes are most tangible. Contemporary international norms prescribing multiculturalism within states, the UN's trusteeship system and the League of Nations' Mandate system, the European 'Minorities Treaties' after the First World War, the 'standard of civilization', and the articles on liberty of religious conscience in the Westphalian treaties all are manifestations and instantiations of prevailing diversity regimes.

Understanding the nature and significance of diversity regimes is currently impeded by two blind spots in the literature. First, there are some conceptions of international order that focus narrowly on the constraining or enabling effects of order, ignoring how orders constitute subjectivities. Structural realist accounts are a prime example: the existence of sovereign states is assumed, and the anarchic structure of the international system, along with the unequal distribution of material resources, empowers some while limiting the fortunes of others. Such accounts cannot see, let alone comprehend, institutions that constitute and arrange political units and cultural identities. There are conceptions of international order that do acknowledge the constitutive power of orders, but they tend to read this narrowly, as constituting rights-bearing powers. As we saw in Chapter 3, pluralists of the English School understand order in this way: the norms of international society constitute states with sovereign rights but no substantive cultural identities. Second, students of international order have so far neglected the recognition function of institutions. Culturalists – whether constructivist, English School, rationalist, or realist – see institutions as expressions of underlying cultural values, and pluralists, by contrast, think international institutions neutralize culture at the international level, pushing it into the domestic or private realms. These positions dominate current debate on the future of the modern international order in a multicultural world, but neither sees how institutions, in the form of diversity regimes, take extant cultural heterogeneity and construct authorized forms of difference. Nor do they see the central role such institutions have played across history and in multiple orders. Focusing on diversity regimes helps overcome

---

[63] See Antony Anghie, *Imperialism, Sovereignty, and the Making of International Law* (Cambridge: Cambridge University Press, 2007).

both of these blind spots, as they bring the constitutive power of international orders to the fore, and show how this power is grounded in the recognition function of institutions.

If all international orders have to configure political authority and organize cultural diversity, and to meet these ends they develop various kinds of diversity regimes, then the idea of a truly pluralist international order looks more like an ideal type than a historical form. The ideal imagines an order of sovereign states, in which norms of legal equality, non-intervention, and self-determination provide a framework for coexistence and coaction while protecting in domestic realms of autonomy the cultural diversity of sovereign peoples. As we have seen, this ideal is often tied to a distinct historical narrative, in which the traumas of Europe's religious wars impelled the construction of a pluralist order, and issues of culture and religion were relegated to the newly constituted domestic realm. Whatever the merits of this as an ideal, the accompanying historical narrative is more myth than reality. As we have seen, the Westphalian settlement was an exercise in politico-cultural engineering that accommodated certain forms of religious difference while suppressing others. And while the axes of authorized cultural difference have shifted – with religion, race, ethnicity, and civilization receiving more or less sanction – the evolving global order has never been culturally neutral. Even after the Second World War, when ethno-national criteria for self-determination were abandoned, and then in the wake of decolonization, when civilizational discourses could no longer sustain the institution of empire, a new regime emerged that combined universal sovereignty, civic nationalism, international norms of multiculturalism, and human rights. This is as much a diversity regime as any of those that structured previous historical orders; it remains, in essence, a system of norms and practices that simultaneously configures political authority and organizes diversity. And, like previous ones, it too can be contested.

Two things require noting before we proceed. First, just as diversity regimes straddle different levels of institutions – issue specific, fundamental, and constitutional – in sovereign orders, where there are putative international and domestic realms, diversity regimes always reach from the former into the latter. Whether it is the specification of rules governing liberty of religious conscience in the Treaties of Westphalia, the minority treaties after the First World War, or contemporary international norms protecting the civic and cultural rights of individuals, defining the parameters of legitimate cultural politics within states has always been part of managing cultural diversity internationally. Second, saying that all international orders develop diversity regimes, and that this always involves privileging and hierarchizing certain forms and expressions of difference over others, does not mean that these regimes are normatively equal, or that we cannot make judgements about their relative openness, tolerance, and fairness. Diversity regimes that promote civic nationalism and individual rights are clearly preferable to those that permit ethnic cleansing, even if they reduce space for the expression of particular kinds of cultural identities and values. The key point here is that any reasonable normative evaluation of different historical diversity regimes has to start with the recognition that all international orders have developed such regimes, that all have involved the construction and ranking of legitimate (and illegitimate) difference, and that the much vaunted pluralist international order is an ideal, not a historical comparator.

Sources of Change

Diversity regimes always bear the mark of conscious design, even if their evolution is affected by incremental innovations, piecemeal adjustments, the gradual accretion of social practices, and the playing-out of the contradictions that characterize any institutional formation. At key moments of conscious construction, order builders create diversity regimes in response to particular configurations of unequally distributed material capabilities and articulations of cultural difference, trying to forge a stable configuration of political authority and to define the terms of legitimate cultural identification and expression. Once established, diversity regimes have a structural quality, confronting actors as social facts that constitute political and cultural subjectivities and define the parameters of legitimate action. This gives them considerable stability, as over time the rules, norms, and practices that configure authority and construct diversity are reproduced by the very subjectivities they constitute. Diversity regimes face two pressures for change, however: shifts in the underlying distribution of material capabilities and new cultural claims, often animated by grievances against the hierarchies and exclusions of prevailing and past regimes.

The first of these features prominently in the literature on international change. Structural realists go furthest, casting international relations as a struggle for power, treating power as a simple expression of material capabilities, and defining systemic change as a shift in the distribution of such capabilities. Unsurprisingly, this is not my position. Rather, I align with those who acknowledge the importance of changing material conditions, as these have enabling and constraining effects on action, but who deny that these are, in themselves, determining. Social meanings, structures of knowledge, patterns of identification, discursive practices, and even rational choice all affect what actors make of their material environments. We see this in non-realist arguments about hegemony, where the distribution of capabilities may equip a dominant state, but where hegemonic status depends on social recognition, and where the character of hegemonic rule is conditioned by the hegemon's corporate and social identities.[64] More importantly, perhaps, we see it in claims that current shifts in material power are not themselves determining the contours of a new order, but that they are prompting a renegotiation of roles, rights, and responsibilities – of political authority, in short. For example, John Ikenberry admits that the material balance of power is shifting to the East, but holds that the institutions of the 'liberal' order are flexible enough to accommodate such changes. If there is a crisis today, he argues, it is a crisis of authority, driven by contests 'over the distribution of roles, rights, and authority'.[65] Evelyn Goh has a similar view of the East Asian regional order. Since the end of the Cold War, she writes, this order 'has been critically constituted by the "clash of meanings" over the changing patterns of unequal power, and the struggle for regional order has been about mediating between these competing meanings and claims to achieve a new regional social compact'.[66]

The second pressure for change has received little attention, largely because of a failure to recognize how international orders are structured by diversity regimes. Because diversity regimes authorize and order certain forms of cultural difference and relate these to legitimate units of political authority, they create social hierarchies and patterns

---

[64] For two different versions of this argument, see Ruggie, 'Multilateralism: The Anatomy of an Institution'; and Ikenberry, *Liberal Leviathan*.

[65] Ikenberry, *Liberal Leviathan*, p. xii.

[66] Evelyn Goh, *The Struggle for Order: Hegemony, Hierarchy, and Transition in Post–Cold War East Asia* (Oxford: Oxford University Press, 2013), p. 11.

of inclusion and exclusion. The diversity regime of the late nineteenth and early twentieth centuries privileged civilizational difference at the global level and primordial conceptions of ethnicity within Europe, tying the first to empire and the second to the nation-state. The resulting hierarchies were manifest in the subordination of 'barbarian' and 'savage' peoples in Asia, Africa, and the Pacific and in the pernicious distinction between 'state people' and 'minorities' in Europe, which in Hannah Arendt's words, 'handed out rule to some and servitude to others'.[67] Like all hierarchies, those produced by diversity regimes are stabilized by a combination of material inducements and intersubjective understandings about the order's legitimacy and the appropriateness of its constituent role identities. Such hierarchies also generate grievances, however: grievances rooted in unequal recognition.

To the extent that humans have any basic interests, social recognition is fundamental. If social identities are understood as 'sets of meanings that an actor attributes to itself *while taking into account the perspectives of others*,'[68] then actors' senses of self are dependent on social recognition. The individual self cannot develop without such recognition, as this is what enables individuals to understand what it is that makes them distinctive as human subjects, and that as such subjects, they are valued.[69] This need for recognition is a potent source of political struggle. Denial or withdrawal of recognition – which Axel Honneth terms 'disrespect' – threatens basic self-understandings and esteem, fuelling anger and humiliation.[70] Only when these feelings are generalizable, however – when a group of individuals, through communication, are able to experience them in common – can they animate collective action. Denials of 'legal' and 'achievement' recognition are particularly important here. The former refers to an individual's status as a rights-bearing member of a community; the latter to the degree to which their qualities, capacities, and achievements are thought 'to realize culturally defined values'.[71] In both cases, lack of recognition

---

[67] Hannah Arendt, *The Origins of Totalitarianism* (New York: Harvest Books, 1975), p. 270.

[68] Alexander Wendt, 'Collective Identity Formation and the International State', *American Political Science Review*, 88.2 (1994), 385.

[69] Axel Honneth, *The Struggle for Recognition: The Moral Grammar of Social Conflicts* (Cambridge, MA: MIT Press, 1995), pp. 89–90.

[70] Ibid., p. 131.   [71] Ibid., p. 122.

is generalizable, as the denial of rights, and the denigration or devaluing of social roles, commonly apply to classes of actors (workers, women, untouchables, barbarians, savages, etc.).

By constructing diversity regimes in particular ways – authorizing certain forms of difference, ordering them hierarchically, and relating them to units of political authority – diversity regimes are institutionalized forms of recognition: they recognize cultural identities, constituting them in the process, and allocating them rights and entitlements. At the same time, however, they are institutionalized forms of disrespect. From extant cultural heterogeneity, they privilege some axes of cultural difference and expression while marginalizing others. The diversity regime constructed at Westphalia did this, and so too did the Ottoman Millet system and Qing China's Eight Banners and Lifanyuan systems. As they ordained certain identities, beliefs, and practices as legitimate, they cast others as beyond the pale. Diversity regimes are thus Janusfaced. Because they are institutionalized forms of recognition, they help legitimate rule under conditions of cultural heterogeneity. But because they produce social and political hierarchies, they all have the hardwired potential for alienation, humiliation, stigmatization, and, in turn, political resistance and mobilization'.[72]

If international orders are systemic configurations of political authority, then the modern order prior to the 1970s was a hybrid, licensing sovereignty in the core and empire over the periphery. Elsewhere I argue that the long transition from this world to today's universal system of states can be understood as a shift from one recognition order to another.[73] The empires that enmeshed much of the non-European world were hierarchies, distributing social and political entitlements unequally between the metropole and its colonies, and between imperial citizens and subjects. These hierarchies collapsed in a series of great imperial implosions, concluding with post-1945 decolonization and demise of the institution of empire itself. The most important of these implosions – which saw, among other things, the collapse of the Holy Roman, Portuguese, Spanish, and British empires – were driven, I argue, by struggles on the part of colonial subjects for the recognition of individual rights. A traditional recognition order,

---

[72] On the nature and dynamics of stigmatization in world politics, see Ayse Zarakol, *After Defeat: How the East Learned to Live with the West* (Cambridge: Cambridge University Press, 2011).

[73] Reus-Smit, *Individual Rights*, pp. 59–66.

which distributed entitlements unequally on the basis of social position within imperial hierarchies, was eventually supplanted by an order that cast the self-determination of colonized peoples as a necessary condition for the enjoyment of individual rights.[74] When I first advanced this argument, the idea of diversity regimes was some way over the horizon. It is now clear, however, that the hybrid order was sustained by an evolving diversity regime, one that bound a particular configuration of political authority to a civilizational ordering of diversity. Moreover, the struggles for individual rights I detailed can be seen as political responses to the grievances generated by imperial hierarchies and exclusions.

Domestic Analogues

If readers find the idea of diversity regimes hard to grasp, very similar – and far more familiar – processes have long been at work within sovereign states. There too the nature of political orders has been shaped by the imperatives to configure political authority and organize cultural diversity, and to meet these imperatives states have constructed all manner of diversity regimes. From cultural and physical genocide, through assimilation to a dominant culture or 'melting' to produce a new hybrid, to various policies of multiculturalism, states have sought to organize cultural difference and tie this organization to structures of political authority. That we rightly reach different normative conclusions about these policies should not blind us to the fact that all are diversity regimes. To facilitate rule, they all take extant cultural heterogeneity and create authorized forms of difference. This is true even of multiculturalism, arguably one of the most pluralistic and tolerant of regimes. Multiculturalism as a description of lived diversity – the multiculturalism I experienced growing up in inner-city Melbourne in the 1970s – is not the same as multiculturalism as a public policy: a policy instituted in Australia from the late 1970s onward. Whatever the merits of such policies, and I take them to be many, they nonetheless 'seek to institutionalize diversity by putting people into ethnic and cultural boxes ... and defining their needs and rights accordingly'.[75] In doing so they reconstruct the cultural order, authorizing some axes of difference while occluding or suppressing others. This in turn creates institutional incentives for individuals to

[74] Ibid., pp. 35–67.   [75] Malik, 'The Failure of Multiculturalism', pp. 21–22.

craft their cultural identities, practices, and discourses in particular ways, and for cultural groups to coalesce and mobilize around authorized forms of difference.

A key proposition of this book, and the volumes that follow, is that the institutional ordering of culture that we see so readily within states also occurs in international orders. The Westphalia settlement, the Ottoman Millet system, Qing China's Lifanyuan system, and the nineteenth-century standard of civilization all are international analogues of assimilation and multiculturalism. International orders necessarily configure political authority differently from more localized forms of political order – sovereign states or others. And the complexity of the cultural contexts in which they emerge is of an altogether different magnitude. The same underlying logic is at work, though. In contexts of unequal material capabilities and extant cultural heterogeneity, order builders face two legitimation challenges: to configure political authority and to organize cultural diversity. To meet these challenges, they construct diversity regimes. These are not simply analogues of domestic regimes, however. As already noted, in sovereign orders, with notionally distinct international and domestic realms, international diversity regimes often mandate particular kinds of domestic regimes. For example, the post-Versailles reordering of Europe granted self-determination to ethnically defined nations, but in an unsuccessful attempt to prevent ethnic cleansing, a raft of treaties compromised sovereignty by requiring protections for minorities. International and domestic diversity regimes have also been connected through isomorphic processes. In addition to international diversity regimes proscribing certain domestic regimes, socialization across an order can encourage the spread of institutional practices. Multiculturalism is a case in point. Since the 1970s international norms have encouraged states to institute multicultural policies, and this has been reinforced by the transnational mobilization of human rights norms.[76] States have also learnt multiculturalism from other states, however. Australian multicultural policy, for example, was strongly influenced by Canadian initiatives.[77]

---

[76] See Kymlicka, *Multicultural Odysseys.*

[77] See Gwenda Tavan, *The Long, Slow Death of White Australia* (Melbourne: Scribe, 2005); and Louis Pauly and Christian Reus-Smit, 'Negotiating Anglo-America: Australia, Canada, and the United States', in Katzenstein (ed.), *Anglo-America and Its Discontents*, pp. 127–152.

Conclusion

In culturalist accounts of international order, whether they come from classical realists, the English School, or constructivists, culture is conceived as a deep constitutive structure and international institutions are seen as cultural artefacts: with cultural meanings affecting their form, and cultural consensus ensuring a baseline of support (in addition to any practical or functional imperatives that might sustain commitment and compliance). The argument presented here flips much of this on its head. Instead of seeing culture as a coherent deep structure, I see it as a realm of great variety, complexity, and contradiction. This heterogeneous cultural universe has structural effects, though. Order builders encounter it as a social reality, a reality that can generate all manner of identifications, mobilizations of meaning, and repertoires of practice, amenable to all kinds of political enlistment. Culture thus appears as a particular kind of governance challenge, affecting international order through the diversity regimes that order builders create in response. Institutions, in this account, remain cultural artefacts, in the sense that institutional design is always culturally inflected: order builders never stand outside culture, and their choices are bounded by what is imaginable and enabled by what is justifiable. Yet the relationship between international institutions and culture cuts the other way as well. Institutions, in the form of diversity regimes, organize diversity: they authorize some axes of difference over others, and link these to prevailing configurations of political authority. None of this means that cultural meanings, practices, and discourses lack constitutive effects, conditioning actor's identities, informing their interests, and shaping repertoires of legitimate action. What it means, though, is that these constitutive effects are not products of a coherent deep culture. In any social setting, identities, interests, and practices exhibit great variety, and this variety is more comprehensible if we understand the constitutive environment itself as inherently diverse, even if this diversity is always institutionally structured.

Conclusion

The modern international order is undergoing a far-reaching transformation. Reconfigurations of power are occurring at multiple levels. New great powers are rising; transnational insurgents are innovating new forms of organized violence, challenging established ideas and practices of national, regional, and global security; and new political constellations within liberal democracies are contesting existing structures of political authority and prevailing modes of global governance. This transformation is not just about power; it is also about culture. Shifting power configurations are entwined with new or reemergent expressions of cultural difference. Western states, struggling with a resurgence of ethno-nationalism, challenges to multiculturalism, and the rise of the far right, share the stage with powers such as China, which are narrating their civilizational heritages to boost domestic legitimacy and global standing. And transnational violence is being justified in the name not of national liberation or familiar political ideologies, but of religious identity, belief, and grievance.

Understanding how new expressions of cultural difference, entangled with shifting configurations of power, will affect the peace, stability, and development of the modern international order is thus crucially important. Yet, as we have seen in previous chapters, IR is poorly equipped to address this issue. Culture is either something we ignore – preferring to concentrate on material power and the rational pursuit of interests – or something we invoke but misunderstand. One of the contributions of this book is to show just how widespread such invocations and misunderstandings are, echoing not just through the critical margins of the field, or through sociological strands of the mainstream (such as constructivism and the English School), but also through realism and rational choice theory. What is striking, though, is how, within the mainstream, ostensibly different schools of thought understand culture in broadly the same way, a way long abandoned in specialist fields like anthropology, cultural studies, and sociology.

Where these fields treat culture as inherently diverse, and have long rejected the idea of cultures as singular, purposive entities, IR scholars persist in seeing them as coherent, integrated, bounded, and constitutive systems of meanings and practices, whether they are talking about strategic cultures, ethnicities, nations, or civilizations. This has implications in any number of areas, but especially for how IR currently debates the impact of cultural diversity on the future of the modern international order. If we are not insisting that the pluralism of this order, or its open and rules-based nature, tames cultural differences, we claim that it is rooted in Western civilization, and is now threatened by heightened cultural diversity. But if cultural formations are always heterogeneous, then civilizational arguments such as these appear less and less compelling. Not only does Western civilization lose its purported coherence, but cultural diversity, in one form or another, looks more like a constant in the evolution of the modern order.

Academic IR is not alone in invoking anachronistic conceptions of culture or in drawing unsustainable conclusions about cultural diversity and international order. Indeed, very similar assumptions and claims permeate contemporary public debate. The culturalist anxieties of Western leaders about the future of the modern order is palpable. We see it in their frequent expressions of commitment to the 'rules-based order', and their imploring of China to be a responsible power that plays by the existing rules. The fear that Martin Jacques might be right – that China is a 'civilizational power' that will seek to remake the international order in its own image – is never far from the surface.[1] Former Australian prime minister Kevin Rudd put it clearly, though: 'Very soon we will find ourselves at a point in history when, for the first time since George III, a non-Western, non-democratic state will be the largest economy in the world. If this is the case, how will China exercise its power in the future international order? Will it accept the culture, norms and structure of the postwar order? Or will China seek to change it?'[2] The anxiety is also evident in urgent calls for the renovation of the modern order in the face of cultural division.

---

[1] Martin Jacques, *When China Rules the World: The End of Western World and the Birth of a New Global Order*, 2nd edn. (Harmondsworth: Penguin, 2012).

[2] Kevin Rudd, 'The West Isn't Ready for the Rise of China', *New Statesman*, 2012. www.newstatesman.com/politics/international-politics/2012/07/kevin-rudd-west-isnt-ready-rise-china.

The world faces a critical choice, President Barack Obama told the UN Security Council in 2014: 'We can renew the international system that has enabled so much progress, or we can allow ourselves to be pulled back into the undertow of instability ... And it is no exaggeration to say that humanity's future depends on us uniting against those who would divide us along the fault lines of tribe, sect, race, or religion.'[3] Perhaps the starkest expression of cultural anxiety is found in President Donald Trump's calls for the defence of Western civilization. 'The fundamental question of our time', he told a Polish audience, 'is whether the West has the will to survive. Do we have the confidence in our values to defend them at all cost? Do we have enough respect for our citizens to project our borders? Do we have the desire and the courage to preserve our civilization in the face of those who would subvert or destroy it?'[4] Here the threat is not only from without; it is from civilizational decay within: a version of the apostasy Wight saw eroding Christian international society (discussed in Chapter 3).

The default conception of culture undergirds all of these expressions of anxiety. Western civilization is treated as an unproblematic cultural entity, the modern order is assumed to be a Western cultural artefact, China is imagined as an alien cultural actor, and cultural dissolution or fragmentation is seen as a threat to the order. This book has shown how deeply problematic such ideas are, but also how pervasive they are in IR theory, a body of knowledge that should inform more sophisticated public understandings of cultural diversity and international order. History shows the dangers of misunderstanding this relationship all too clearly. After the First World War it was thought that partitioning Europe into ethnically defined nation-states would foster peace – a project animated by the default conception of culture, and one that proved tragically misguided.

In Chapter 6 I proposed a different way of thinking about cultural diversity and international order, one that better reflects specialist

---

[3] President Barak Obama, 'President Obama's UN Speech: Defending World Order', 24 September 2014. https://obamawhitehouse.archives.gov/the-press-office/2014/09/24/remarks-president-obama-address-united-nations-general-assembly. Accessed 29 December 2017.

[4] President Donald J. Trump, 'Remarks by President Trump to the People of Poland, July 6, 2017', p. 12. www.whitehouse.gov/the-press-office/2017/07/06/remarks-president-trump-people-poland-july-6-2017. Accessed 11 December 2017.

understandings of culture, that is cognisant of recent histories that emphasize the heterogeneous contexts in which international orders emerge, and that makes sense of the persistent efforts of order builders to organize cultural diversity. I began in the opposite place to culturalists: by assuming that orders emerge in culturally diverse, not homogeneous, contexts. The question then is what this diversity means for the development of international orders, understood as systemic configurations of political authority. The answer lies in the dual legitimation challenges faced by order builders: to convert unequal material capabilities into political authority, and to translate extant cultural heterogeneity into authorized diversity. These challenges are near impossible to meet individually, as the effective recognition of some axes of cultural difference over others invariably involves the differential allocation of political authority; the intimate connection between the Westphalian allocation of sovereign rights and the recognition of select Christian confessions is a case in point. To meet these paired challenges, I suggest that order builders construct diversity regimes, system-wide norms and practices that simultaneously define legitimate units of political authority and how they are differentiated; recognize certain axes of cultural difference; and specify how authority and difference relate. Not only does this render intelligible much of what order builders institute – from the Westphalian settlement to the Ottoman Millet and Qing Lifanyuan systems – it sheds light on an important dimension of international change. While diversity regimes recognize and empower certain forms and expressions of difference, they also create social and political hierarchies, and generate patterns of inclusion and exclusion. These structures of inequality are fertile terrain for grievances, and when material and ideational conditions change, they can fuel struggles for recognition and the reconfiguration of political authority (e.g. post-1945 decolonization) or, more minimally, emotionally energize the pursuit of other objectives (China's repeated references to its 'century of humiliation', for example).

In the following pages I explore two implications of this argument. The first section considers what it means for thinking about cultural diversity and the future of the modern international order. If the cultural conditions in which this order has evolved have been highly diverse, and if the imperative to organize diversity has affected the order's institutional architecture, are the terms of current debates correct? I suggest not. Instead of assuming that the Western order will fall in the face of sudden onset diversity, or confidently asserting that its pluralist institutions will continue to accommodate states of diverse cultural backgrounds, we should be probing the nature of the prevailing diversity regime, and asking whether it can accommodate new conjunctions of power and articulations of difference. The second section explores the normative implications of my argument. As noted in Chapter 1, so much of our normative theorizing in IR has been pulled between two poles: between a cosmopolitanism (or universalism) that discounts the moral significance of cultural differences and a communitarianism (or relativism) that treats discrete cultural communities as the sources of 'thick' moral values and robust obligations. What happens to this debate, though, if culture matters (contra the cosmopolitans), but its diversity is not that of cultural billiard balls (contra the communitarians)? And what if the global cultural terrain is polyvalent, but institutionally structured? Taking these issues seriously, I suggest, requires an institutional turn in normative IR theory, a turn political theorists took two decades ago.

The Modern International Order

Current debates about cultural diversity and the future of the modern international order are polarized between two positions: one culturalist, the other institutionalist. Both assume that the order is an order of sovereign states, both assume that it is Western in origin, and both accept that change is in the air. They differ, however, over how thickly cultural the order is, and over the relationship between culture and international institutions. Together, these differences lead to very different views about the likely impact of heightened cultural diversity.

Culturalists, whom we have already met in previous chapters, see the modern order as culturally thick. Not only is it Western in origin (which could just mean that it is a rational institution first constructed in Europe); it instantiates Western values, advances Western interests, and depends on Western cultural consensus for its success and stability. International institutions, on this view, are cultural artefacts: good and desirable, but artefacts nonetheless. Cultural diversity is a problem from this perspective, as it fractures the order's cultural foundations. It is also a recent problem, a novel challenge thrown up by the shift in power from West to East. Unlike other power transitions in the last three hundred years, therefore, this one packs a double whammy: the ranks of the great powers are changing, with all the instability this normally entails, and the cultural universe on which ordered interstate relations depend is fragmenting.

Institutionalists also see the modern order as culturally conditioned, but in a far thinner sense. On one view, which we encountered in Chapter 3, European rulers, exhausted by religious wars, bequeathed to the world a pluralist society of states. Born of pragmatism, this order was enabled nonetheless by a distinctive set of cultural ideas, from pre-territorial conceptions of sovereignty to Protestant reconceptualizations of temporal/sacral relations.[5] On another view, the modern international order is a liberal construction of the nineteenth and twentieth centuries, and embodies the values of core liberal states. 'Through the Victorian era and into the twentieth century', John Ikenberry writes, 'the fortunes of liberal democratic states flourished – and with the growth and expansion of this liberal core of states and its organizing principles, world politics increasingly took a liberal internationalist cast'.[6] While the cultural dimensions of the modern order are acknowledged in both of these arguments, what distinguishes them is their ultimate discounting of culture. As we saw in Chapter 3, institutionalists of the first kind, like Jackson, hold that norms of sovereign equality, non-intervention, and self-determination neutralize culture, quarantining it to life within the state. Institutionalists of the second kind hold a similar view, but this time it is the open and rules-based institutions of the post-1945 liberal order that do the work. These institutions have an unprecedented capacity to accommodate states and peoples of diverse cultures, with diverse goals. The order's 'sprawling landscape of rules, institutions, and networks provides newer entrants into the system with opportunities for status, authority, and a share in the governance of the order. Access points and mechanisms for political communication and reciprocal influence abound.'[7]

From the perspective advanced here, this debate is problematic in at least four respects. First, both positions assume that we are talking about an international order of sovereign states. But, as I argue in Chapter 6, defining international orders so narrowly gives us very little analytical purchase, as there are so few historical exemplars. Most importantly, until the 1970s the modern international order was a

---

[5] Jackson, *The Global Covenant*, pp. 156–161.
[6] Ikenberry, *Liberal Leviathan*, pp. 15–16.   [7] Ibid., p. 345.

hybrid. In the European core it distributed political authority on the principle of sovereignty, but over the imperial periphery it did so on the principle of empire. As Edward Keene explains, the Europeans adopted 'one kind of relationship, equality and mutual dependence, as the norm in their dealings with each other, and another, imperial paramountcy, as normal in their relations with non-Europeans'.[8]

Second, as we saw in Chapter 6, this order evolved in a highly diverse cultural context. Schisms over the most fundamental questions of Christian faith, identity-transforming encounters between European and New World others, the fragmentary dynamics of the Age of Nationalism, the sweep across new cultural terrain that attended the nineteenth-century acceleration of European imperialism, and the gradual admission of non-European states to a globalizing international society all belie the idea that cultural diversity is something new, an unfamiliar condition of twenty-first-century world politics.

Third, neither the culturalists nor the institutionalists fully appreciate that a central dynamic of the modern international order is the politics of membership, a politics infused with cultural preconceptions and prejudices. Because international orders define legitimate units of political authority and specify their respective rights and obligations, their core business is recognition. Furthermore, in highly diverse cultural contexts, such recognition is always informed by cultural assessments, from the most discriminatory to the most ecumenical. Institutionalists, like Ikenberry, have little to say about this politics. They assume a system of states, dwell little on its incorporative dynamics, and beyond highlighting the leadership of liberal states, leave questions of culture aside. The other kind of institutionalist – the English School pluralist – acknowledges the politics of recognition that attended decolonization, but treats this as rational process of integration, in which non-European peoples came to accept the rules and norms of the expanding society of states.[9] The politics of culture that was integral to this is largely occluded. For many culturalists writing on the future of the modern order, the membership politics that shaped the order's evolution gets little attention. Earlier culturalists like Wight,

---

[8] Keene, *Beyond the Anarchical* Society, p. 6.
[9] For a critique of these arguments, see Christian Reus-Smit and Tim Dunne, 'The Globalization of International Society', in Dunne and Reus-Smit (eds.), *The Globalization of International Society* (Oxford: Oxford University Press, 2017), pp. 18–42.

by contrast, were very much attuned to this, worrying in particular about the corrosive effects of decolonization. What they share in common, however, is blindness to the cultural politics of membership within Western international society: that politics is something that occurs between the West and the rest.

Last, culturalists and institutionalists ignore the recognition function of international institutions. The former, as we have seen, treat institutions as cultural artefacts: instantiations of particular cultural values and practices, designed to further culturally inflected interests. The latter see institutions as neutralizing culture, as removing it from the public realm or relegating it to the domestic arena. Neither see how institutions – from sovereignty and international law to suzerainty and the Millet system – have defined and structured cultural diversity, licensing some axes of difference over others.

Together, these limitations in the culturalist and institutionalist positions lead to the incorrect framing of contemporary debates about cultural diversity and international order. For culturalists, the question today is whether an essentially Western order will be undermined by the new diversity of the system. Will it be overturned by an ascendant China that seeks an order that better reflects its cultural values? Or will it decline as diversity undermines the cultural consensus needed to sustain modern norms and practices? For the most part, culturalists predict a negative outcome, already foretelling the order's demise. Institutionalists are far more positive. For them, the question is whether the pluralist or open and rules-based institutions of the modern order can accommodate states of diverse cultural backgrounds, just as liberal democracies accommodate individuals with diverse purposes. The answer, in this case, is generally positive. Even if the distribution of authority within the order shifts, the order itself is flexible enough to accommodate present changes.

If the argument presented here is correct, then the key questions are somewhat different. To begin with, if cultural diversity has been a constant in the history of the modern international order, and if it has posed governance challenges that have led to the construction of a series of diversity regimes, then diversity, in its many forms and expressions, has had a deeply constitutive effect. This is not to say, of course, that expressions of cultural difference cannot have profoundly negative effects, as Nazism alone more than demonstrates. But in each of the orders discussed here, including the modern one, cultural complexity has been the background condition, and institutions defining and ordering authorized axes of cultural difference have been the result. The question today, therefore, is not whether a Western order can survive sudden-onset diversity, or whether pluralist or liberal institutions can neutralize such diversity; it is whether the global diversity regime instituted after decolonization can accommodate new conjunctions of power and articulations of cultural difference. This poses three questions that I pursue in the two volumes that will follow this one: What is the nature of the prevailing diversity regime? How are shifting configurations of power and new expressions of cultural difference interacting? And does the prevailing diversity regime have the adaptive capacities to accommodate these emerging conjunctions of power and difference?

Addressing these questions is beyond the scope of this Conclusion, but two observations are warranted. First, post-1945 decolonization entailed a global reconfiguration of political authority from a world of sovereign-imperial complexes to universal sovereignty. Associated with this was the discrediting of civilizational criteria of recognition and the privileging of civic forms of nationalism, promoted through international norms of multiculturalism and human rights. In any attempt to detail the prevailing diversity regime, these will almost certainly be components. Second, in recent years three kinds of cultural claims have reemerged with new vigour: civilizational, ethno-national, and religious. There are many things to note about these claims, not the least their expression across the order: East and West, North and South, in liberal and authoritarian states. What interests me here, though, is that each of these claims was authorized in a previous diversity regime: religion at Westphalia, civilization and ethno-nationalism after Versailles. It is their rejection, however, that in part defines the post-decolonization regime. When assessing the adaptive capacities of this regime, therefore, a key question is the degree to which it can accommodate such claims.

Normative Implications

The preceding chapters have focused on pathologies in empirical IR theory, and the alternative I propose is empirical-theoretic as well. Yet the critique I level at IR's existing understandings of culture, and my own emphasis on the organization of diversity, have significant normative implications. I have argued elsewhere that all normative theorizing, whether about world politics or not, builds on empirical assumptions. If the central question for such theory is 'How should we act?' then answers demand more than logically robust moral principles: they require assumptions about the contexts of action – the nature of agency, the scope of social interaction and attachment, and the possibilities of change.[10] In normative IR theory by far the most prominent of these assumptions have concerned culture. Do cultural identifications, meanings, and attachments define our moral horizons, the nature of our sensibilities and obligations? Even those who deny the significance of culture rarely do it by philosophical fiat alone; they anchor their philosophical claims in empirical propositions, like the fact of practical global interdependence.

For a long time debates in normative IR theory were polarized between communitarian and cosmopolitan positions, both of which rested on cultural assumptions. Cosmopolitans hold that some moral values are human, not particularistic, and that there are moral obligations that transcend cultural, social, and political boundaries. Sometimes these arguments rest on claims about the nature of all humans as moral beings, and sometimes on the global moral community produced by transnational interconnections and dependencies.[11] Either way, humanity is considered a coherent moral unit. Communitarians, by contrast, argue that any values or obligations that extend to all of humanity are necessarily thin. Real communities, bound together by substantive cultural meanings and practices, are the sources of real moral values and commitments. Thick community breeds thick morality.[12]

Both sides of this debate are unsustainable. While there might be good reasons to believe that there are values that should be considered

---

[10] For an extended discussion, see Christian Reus-Smit, 'Constructivism and the Structure of Ethical Reasoning', in Richard M. Price (ed.), *Moral Limit and Possibility in World Politics* (Cambridge: Cambridge University Press, 2008), pp. 53–82. Also see Eckersley and Brown, 'International Political Theory in the Real World'.

[11] A classic example of the former is Henry Shue, *Basic Rights: Subsistence, Affluence, and US Foreign Policy*, 2nd edn. (Princeton, NJ: Princeton University Press, 1996); and of the latter, Charles Beitz, *Political Theory and International Relations* (Princeton, NJ: Princeton University Press, 1979).

[12] See Michael Walzer, *Thick and Thin: Moral Argument at Home and Abroad* (Notre Dame, IN: University of Notre Dame Press, 1994).

universal, and that humans have non-trivial moral obligations to one another, these reasons cannot be that culture, and cultural diversity, are irrelevant. Constructivists, and those on whom they draw, have shown persuasively that actors' interests – and hence their values – are shaped by their social identities, which are constituted by inter-subjective meanings and practices. Culture thus affects values, and in fundamental ways. This is far from a victory for communitarians, though. Communitarians imagine cultures as coherent, integrated, and bounded – as entities to which individuals belong. But as this book has argued, culture is inherently diverse, often contradictory. As Seyla Benhabib explains, communitarianism is based on 'a poor sociology. Very often, cultures are presented as hermetic and sealed wholes; the internal contradictions and debates within cultures are flattened out; the different conceptual and normative options which are available to participants of a given culture and society are ignored.'[13]

As we saw in Chapter 1, much of this has already been acknow-ledged in the field we now term 'international political theory'. Cosmo-politans are acknowledging the importance of local societal contexts for the incubation and cultivation of values, including cosmopolitan ones. And communitarians are admitting greater cultural complexity, no longer assuming that civilizations are integral wholes, or that cultural community is coextensive with the boundaries of the sovereign state. In the middle ground between these less categorical positions several strands of scholarship have sought to reconcile universalism with cultural or value diversity. One strand seeks to ground universal-ist claims in the points of normative consensus that exist between otherwise diverse states. Mervin Frost's early work is emblematic of this approach, as is Charles Beitz's more recent account of human rights.[14] A second strand seeks to recast cosmopolitanism in dialogical or communicative terms, where the universal value at work is not substantive but procedural: individuals, brought together through global webs of interdependence, have a moral obligation to resolve

---

[13] Seyla Benhabib, 'Cultural Complexity, Moral Interdependence, and the Global Dialogical Community', in Martha Nussbaum and Jonathan Glover (eds.), *Women, Culture, and Development* (Oxford: Oxford University Press, 1995), p. 240.

[14] Mervin Frost, *Ethics in International Relations: A Constitutive Theory* (Cambridge: Cambridge University Press, 1996); and Charles R. Beitz, *The Idea of Human Rights* (Oxford: Oxford University Press, 2009).

conflicts of value through unforced dialogue between all affected.[15] A third, and final, strand seeks to show the long evolution of diverse human societies toward the development of universalist moral conventions, providing empirical foundations for cosmopolitan moral arguments. Linklater's ambitious multivolume project on global harm conventions is perhaps the best example.[16]

Each of these projects attempts to reconcile a revised moral universalism with the cultural diversity of humanity without falling into the old communitarian trap of reifying cultures. Here is not the place for sustained engagement with their relative strengths and weaknesses, but one thing stands out. The argument advanced in this book highlights two features of the relationship between culture and international order: that culture is inherently diverse and this diversity cannot be reduced to reified cultural billiard balls (nations, civilizations, etc.), and that international orders organize diversity, taking extant heterogeneity and creating authorized forms and expressions of difference. The above strands of scholarship address the first of these features but neglect the second. The first two accept the complexity of the global cultural terrain, looking for cosmopolitan points of consensus or dialogical potentialities, but ignoring how ordering institutions structure diversity, producing systemic patterns of inclusion and exclusion. Linklater is different. He has long been concerned with patterns of inclusion and exclusion, and the harm conventions he examines are, in essence, institutional forms of moral recognition. He is also interested in how the conventions that evolve in different kinds of orders – from empires to societies of states – are often centrally concerned with minimizing violence and other harms in transcultural contexts. His main interest, however, is with how long-term civilizing processes expand domains of harm protection, simultaneously extending the bounds of moral community. His focus is not on how, or why, the institutions of international orders organize cultural diversity, or what this means for the production and reproduction of social and political hierarchies.

---

[15] See, for example, Seyla Benhabib, *The Claims of Culture: Equality and Diversity in the Global Era* (Princeton, NJ: Princeton University Press, 2002); and Richard Shapcott, *Justice, Community and Dialogue in International Relations* (Cambridge: Cambridge University Press, 2001).

[16] Linklater, *The Problem of Harm*; and Linklater, *Violence and Civilization*.

If this analysis is correct, an institutional turn is needed in normative IR theory, a turn political theory made two decades ago. This is not to suggest that normative international theory has said nothing about institutions; there is work on a host of different issues, from the ethics of global financial institutions to the normative legitimacy of UN Security Council decisions. What is missing, though, is normative consideration of the regimes that organize global cultural diversity. As we saw in Chapter 1, political theorists were quick to accept that culture is always varied, tangled, and riddled with contradictions. They did so for a particular purpose, though: to evaluate normatively the policies and practices that states were instituting to organize cultural diversity, principally, varied forms of multiculturalism. This is what animated early works like Tully's *Strange Multiplicity* and, more recently, studies such as Alan Patten's *Equal Recognition*.[17] There is currently no international analogue of this work, largely because of the general failure to recognize that the organization of diversity is a feature of *all* political orders, international as well as national. Yet the diversity regimes that structure international orders generate inequality as much as recognition, and thus warrant normative evaluation as much as their national counterparts. It is beyond the scope of this book to embark on such evaluation, especially because it cannot proceed without the more detailed understanding of the modern diversity regime and its historical antecedents, which will be detailed in subsequent volumes. Three sets of questions would seem important to such a project, however. What is the nature of the contemporary diversity regime, what politico-cultural hierarchies does it generate, how do these relate to other axes of inequality, and how does all of this compare with past diversity regimes (in the modern order, and in other orders)? What normative criteria should we use to evaluate the current diversity regime and to assess its merits relative to those in the past (the stability of the order, its degree of tolerance, or its effect on material well-being, for example)? And, finally, what if any aspects of the contemporary diversity regime deserve moral and political defence, and what aspects demand change?

---

[17] Tully, *Strange* Multiplicity; Alan Patten, *Equal Recognition: The Moral Foundations of Minority Rights* (Princeton, NJ: Princeton University Press, 2014).

Global International Relations

In his presidential address to the International Studies Association, Amitav Acharya put plainly what we have all known but failed to own: that 'the discipline of International Relations (IR) does not reflect the voices, experiences, knowledge claims, and contributions of the vast majority of the societies and states in the world, and often marginalizes those outside the core countries of the West'.[18] He called for a disciplinary overhaul, for a 'global IR' that would shed its blinkers, open its ears, and start learning from the ideas and experiences of the hitherto marginalized majority, an IR 'that transcends the divide between the West and the Rest'.[19] This call has inspired (and empowered) a new wave of scholarship that is broadening our conceptual repertoire, reformulating our theories, and challenging some of our most basic empirical assumptions.

This book and the trilogy's other two volumes are a contribution to this project. By drawing, however lightly in the first instance, on the histories of the Ottoman and Qing orders, as well as the early modern European and modern orders, it adds to the 'comparative historiography of international systems and orders' that Acharya recommended.[20] Its main contribution runs far deeper, though. By defining cultural diversity as the norm in the development of international orders, it challenges the culturalist assumption that diversity is a problem that attends the rise of 'the rest': first through decolonization, and now with the shift in power to the East. Added to this, by highlighting the practices of organizing culture that have structured Eastern as well as Western orders, it enables us to see that these are not the preserve of one kind of order, and allows us to draw comparisons between the diversity regimes of different historical orders. The benefits of such comparisons are not just empirical; they are also normative. As we have seen, diverse thinkers – from Kissinger to Jackson – hold that the pluralist international order Europe bequeathed to the world is 'the most articulate institutional arrangement' yet devised for the political coexistence of peoples of diverse cultures.[21] How would we know, though, without any historical comparisons? Is it really true that the

---

[18] Amitav Acharya, 'Global International Relations (IR) and Regional Worlds', *International Studies Quarterly*, 58.4 (2014), 647.
[19] Ibid.   [20] Ibid., p. 652.   [21] Jackson, *The Global Covenant*, p. 181.

supposedly pluralist order created after Westphalia was better than the diversity regimes that were instituted in the Ottoman Empire, and on what basis would we make such a judgement? The perspective advanced here, and developed in the next two volumes, opens the door not only to questions such as these but, it is hoped, to answers as well.

Bibliography

Abbott, Kenneth W. and Snidal, Duncan, 'Hard and Soft Law in International Governance', *International Organization*, 54.3 (2000), 421–456.

Abbott, Kenneth W., Keohane, Robert O., Moravcsik, Andrew, Slaughter, Anne-Marie, and Snidal, Duncan, 'The Concept of Legalization', *International Organization*, 54.3 (2000), 401–419.

Abu-Lughod, Lila, *Writing Women's Worlds: Bedouin Stories* (Berkeley: University of California Press, 1993).

Acharya, Amitav, 'How Ideas Spread: Whose Norms Matter? Norm Localization and Institutional Change in Asian Regionalism', *International Organization*, 58.2 (2004), 239–275.

Whose Ideas Matter?: Agency and Power in Asian Regionalism (Ithaca, NY: Cornell University Press, 2009).

Civilizations in Embrace: The Spread of Ideas and the Transformation of Power; India and Southeast Asia in the Classical Age (Singapore: Institute for Southeast Asian Studies, 2012).

'Global International Relations (IR) and Regional Worlds', *International Studies Quarterly*, 58.4 (2014), 647–659.

Adler, Emanuel, 'Seizing the Middle Ground: Constructivism in World Politics', *European Journal of International Relations*, 3.3 (1997), 319–363.

A Social Theory of Cognitive Evolution: Change, Stability, and International Social Orders (Cambridge: Cambridge University Press, forthcoming).

Adler, Emanuel and Pouliot, Vincent, 'International Practices', *International Theory*, 3.1 (2011), 1–36.

(eds.), *International Practices* (Cambridge: Cambridge University Press, 2011).

'International Practices: Introduction and Framework', in Emanuel Adler and Vincent Pouliot (eds.), *International Practices* (Cambridge: Cambridge University Press, 2011), pp. 3–35.

Anghie, Antony, *Imperialism, Sovereignty, and the Making of International Law* (Cambridge: Cambridge University Press, 2007).

Arendt, Hannah, *The Origins of Totalitarianism* (New York: Harvest Books, 1975).

Aumann, Robert J., 'Agreeing to Disagree', *Annals of Statistics*, 4.6 (1976), 1236–1239.

Axelrod, Robert, *The Evolution of Cooperation* (Harmondsworth: Penguin, 1990).

Bain, William, 'Rival Traditions of Natural Law: Martin Wight and the Theory of International Society', *International History Review*, 36.5 (2014), 943–960.

Baldwin, David A., *Power and International Relations: A Conceptual Approach* (Princeton, NJ: Princeton University Press, 2016).

Barkawi, Tarak, *Orientalism and War* (Oxford: Oxford University Press, 2013).

Barkey, Karen, *Empire of Difference: The Ottomans in Comparative Perspective* (Cambridge: Cambridge University Press, 2008).

'Political Legitimacy and Islam in the Ottoman Empire: Lessons Learned', *Philosophy and Social Criticism*, 40.4–5 (2017), 469–477.

Barkin, Samuel, *Realist Constructivism* (Cambridge: Cambridge University Press, 2010).

Becker, Gary, *The Economic Approach to Human Behavior* (Chicago, IL: University of Chicago Press, 1976).

Beitz, Charles, *Political Theory and International Relations* (Princeton, NJ: Princeton University Press, 1979).

The Idea of Human Rights (Oxford: Oxford University Press, 2009).

Benedict, Ruth, *Patterns of Culture* (Boston: Houghton Mifflin, 1959).

Benhabib, Seyla, 'Cultural Complexity, Moral Interdependence, and the Global Dialogical Community', in Martha Nussbaum and Jonathan Glover (eds.), *Women, Culture, and Development* (Oxford: Oxford University Press, 1995), pp. 235–258.

The Claims of Culture: Equality and Diversity in the Global Era (Princeton, NJ: Princeton University Press, 2002).

Berger, Peter L. and Luckman, Thomas, *The Social Construction of Reality: A Treatise in the Sociology of Knowledge* (New York: Anchor Books, 1966).

Berrey, Ellen, *The Enigma of Diversity: The Language of Race and the Limits of Racial Justice* (Chicago, IL: University of Chicago Press, 2015).

Betts, Alexander and Orchard, Phil, 'Introduction: The Normative Institutionalization-Implementation Gap', in Alexander Betts and Phil Orchard (eds.), *Implementation and World Politics: How International Norms Change Practice* (Oxford: Oxford University Press, 2013), pp. 1–28.

Bhabha, Homi K., *The Location of Culture* (London: Routledge, 2004).

Bially Mattern, Janice, *Ordering International Politics: Identity, Crisis, and Representational Force* (New York: Routledge, 2005).

Bially Mattern, Janice and Zarakol, Ayse, 'Hierarchies in World Politics', *International Organization*, 70.3 (2016), 623–654.

Blaikie, Norman, *Approaches to Social Inquiry* (Cambridge: Polity Press, 1993).

Blumer, Herbert, *Symbolic Interactionism: Perspective and Method* (Berkeley: University of California Press, 1986).

Boas, Franz, *Race, Language, and Culture* (Chicago, IL: University of Chicago Press, 1940).

Boli, John, Meyer, John, and Thomas, George, 'Ontology and Rationalization in the Western Cultural Account', in George Thomas et al. (eds.), *Institutional Structure: Constituting State, Society, and the Individual* (London: Sage, 1989), pp. 12–37.

Booth, Ken, *Strategy and Ethnocentrism* (New York: Holmes and Meier, 1979).

Boudon, Raymond, 'Beyond Rational Choice Theory', *Annual Review of Sociology*, 29 (2003), 179–196.

'Rational Choice Theory', in Bryan Turner (ed.), *The New Blackwell Companion to Social Theory* (Oxford: Basil Blackwell, 2009), pp. 179–196.

Bowden, Brett, *The Empire of Civilization* (Chicago, IL: University of Chicago Press, 2009).

Bozeman, Adda, *The Future of Law in a Multicultural World* (Princeton, NJ: Princeton University Press, 1971).

'The International Order in a Multicultural World', in Hedley Bull and Adam Watson (eds.), *The Expansion of International Society* (Oxford: Oxford University Press, 1984), pp. 387–406.

Brown, Chris, *Practical Judgment in International Relations* (London: Routledge, 2010).

Brown, Chris and Eckersley, Robyn, 'International Political Theory in the Real World', in Chris Brown and Robyn Eckersley (eds.), *The Oxford Handbook of International Political Theory* (Oxford: Oxford University Press, 2018), pp. 3–20.

Bueger, Christian, 'Pathways to Practice: Praxiology and International Politics', *European Political Science Review*, 6.3 (2014), 383–406.

Bukovansky, Mlada, *Legitimacy and Power Politics: The American and French Revolutions in International Political Culture* (Princeton, NJ: Princeton University Press, 2002).

Bull, Hedley, *Justice in International Relations: 1983–84 Hagey Lectures* (Waterloo: University of Waterloo Press, 1984).

The Anarchical Society: A Study of Order in World Politics (New York: Columbia University Press, 1977).

'The Emergence of a Universal International Society', in Hedley Bull and Adam Watson (eds.), *The Expansion of International Society* (Oxford: Clarendon Press, 1985), pp. 118–126.

'The Importance of Grotius in the Study of International Relations', in Bull, Kingsbury, and Roberts (eds.), *Hugo Grotius and International Relations* (Oxford: Clarendon Press, 1992), pp. 65–93.

'The Grotian Conception of International Society', in Kai Alderson and Andrew Hurrell (eds.), *Hedley Bull on International Society* (Basingstoke: Macmillan, 2000), pp. 95–118.

'Natural Law and International Relations', in Kai Alderson and Andrew Hurrell (eds.), *Hedley Bull on International Society* (Basingstoke: Macmillan, 2000), pp. 157–169.

Bull, Hedley and Watson, Adam (eds.), *The Expansion of International Society* (Oxford: Oxford University Press, 1984).

'Introduction', in Hedley Bull and Adam Watson (eds.), *The Expansion of International Society* (Oxford: Oxford University Press, 1984), pp. 1–9.

Burbank, Jane and Cooper, Frederick, *Empires in World History: Power and the Politics of Difference* (Princeton, NJ: Princeton University Press, 2010).

Burke, Edmund, 'Conciliation with the Colonies', in Edward John Payne (ed.), *Burke: Selected Works*, vol. 1 (Clark, NJ: Lawbook Exchange, 2005), pp. 161–307.

Burley, Anne-Marie, 'Regulating the World: Multilateralism, International Law, and the Projection of the New Deal Regulatory State', in John Gerard Ruggie (ed.), *Multilateralism Matters: The Theory and Praxis of an Institutional Form* (New York: Columbia University Press, 1993), pp. 125–156.

Buzan, Barry, 'Culture and International Society', *International Affairs*, 86.1 (2010), 1–25.

From International to World Society: English School Theory and the Social Structure of Globalisation (Cambridge: Cambridge University Press, 2004).

An Introduction to the English School of International Relations: The Societal Approach (Cambridge: Polity Press, 2014).

Cameron, Euan, *The European Reformation*, 2nd edn. (Oxford: Oxford University Press, 2012).

Chan, Stephan, *Plural International Relations in a Divided World* (Cambridge: Polity Press, 2017).

Chong, Dennis, *Rational Lives: Norms and Values in Politics and Society* (Chicago, IL: University of Chicago Press, 2014).

Chowdhry, Geeta and Nair, Sheila, 'Introduction: Power in a Postcolonial World: Race, Gender, and Class in International Relations', in Geeta Chowdhry and Sheila Nair (eds.), *Power, Postcolonialism and International Relations* (London: Routledge, 2002), pp. 1–32.

Christensen, Thomas J., *Useful Adversaries: Grand Strategy, Domestic Mobilization, and Sino-American Conflict, 1947–1958* (Princeton, NJ: Princeton University Press, 1996).

Chwe, Michael Suk-Young, *Rational Ritual: Culture, Coordination, and Common Knowledge* (Princeton, NJ: Princeton University Press, 2001).

Clark, Ian, *Hegemony in International Society* (Oxford: Oxford University Press, 2011).

Clifford, James, *The Predicament of Culture* (Cambridge, MA: Harvard University Press, 1988).

Coady, C. A. J., 'The Moral Reality in Realism', *Journal of Applied Philosophy*, 22.2 (2005), 121–136.

Coleman, James S., *Foundations of Social Theory* (Cambridge, MA: Harvard University Press, 1990).

Comaroff, John and Comaroff, Jean, *Ethnography and the Historical Imagination* (Boulder, CO: Westview Press, 1992).

Crawford, Neta, *Argument and Change in World Politics: Ethics, Decolonization, and Humanitarian Intervention* (Cambridge: Cambridge University Press, 2002).

Crossley, Pamela Kyle, *A Translucent Mirror: History and Identity in Qing Imperial Ideology* (Berkeley: University of California Press, 2002).

de Mesquita, Bruce Bueno, *The War Trap* (New Haven, CT: Yale University Press, 1981).

'Ruminations on Challenges to Prediction with Rational Choice Models', *Rationality and Society*, 15.1 (2003), 136–147.

Devetak, Richard, Dunne, Tim, and Nurhayati, Ririn Tri, 'Bandung 60 Years On: Revolt and Resilience in International Society', *Australian Journal of International Affairs*, 70.4 (2016), 358–373.

Donnelly, Jack, *Realism and International Relations* (Cambridge: Cambridge University Press, 2000).

Doty, Roxanne Lynn, *Imperial Encounters: The Politics of Representation in North-South Relations* (Minneapolis: University of Minnesota Press, 1996).

Dowding, Keith, 'Rational Choice Theory', in Mark Bevir (ed.), *The Sage Handbook of Governance* (London: Sage, 2011), pp. 36–50.

Drieschova, Alena, 'Peirce's Semeiotics: A Methodology for Bridging the Material-Ideational Divide in IR Scholarship', *International Theory*, 9.1 (2017), 33–66.

Dunne, Tim, *Inventing International Society: A History of the English School* (Basingstoke: Macmillan, 1998).

Dunne, Tim and Reus-Smit, Christian (eds.), *The Globalization of International Society* (Oxford: Oxford University Press, 2017).

Durkheim, Emile, *The Rules of Sociological Method* (New York: Free Press, 1982).

The Division of Labor in Society (New York: Free Press, 1997).

Eagleton, Terry, *Culture* (New Haven, CT: Yale University Press, 2016).

Eckersley, Robyn, 'From Cosmopolitan Nationalism to Cosmopolitan Democracy', *Review of International Studies*, 33.4 (2007), 675–692.

Elster, Jon, 'Introduction', in Jon Elster (ed.), *Rational Choice* (New York: New York University Press, 1986), pp. 1–33.

'Rationality and Social Norms', *European Journal of Sociology*, 32.1 (1991), 109–129.

Epp, Roger, 'The English School on the Frontiers of International Society: A Hermeneutic Recollection', *Review of International Studies*, 24.5 (1998), 47–63.

Eriksson, Lina, *Rational Choice Theory: Potential and Limits* (Houndmills: Palgrave Macmillan, 2011).

Erksine, Toni, *Embedded Cosmopolitanism* (Oxford: Oxford University Press, 2008).

Fearon, James and Wendt, Alexander, 'Rationalism v. Constructivism: A Skeptical View', in Walter Carlsnaes, Thomas Risse, and Beth Simmons (eds.), *Handbook of International Relations* (London: Sage, 2002), pp. 52–72.

Featherstone, Mike (ed.), *Global Culture* (London: Sage, 1990).

Ferejohn, John A., 'Rationality and Interpretation: Parliamentary Elections in Early Stuart England', Working Paper No. 44, Centre for Law and Economic Studies, Columbia University School of Law (2000).

Finnemore, Martha, *National Interests and International Society* (Ithaca, NY: Cornell University Press, 1996).

Finnemore, Martha and Sikkink, Kathryn, 'International Norm Dynamics and Political Change', *International Organization*, 52.4 (1998), 887–917.

Foote, Nelson, 'Identification as the Basis for a Theory of Motivation', *American Sociological Review*, 16.1 (1951), 4–21.

Foucault, Michele, *The Order of Things: An Archaeology of the Human Sciences* (New York: Vintage Books, 1973).

Frost, Mervyn, *Ethics in International Relations: A Constitutive Theory* (Cambridge: Cambridge University Press, 1996).

Geertz, Clifford, *The Interpretation of Cultures: Selected Essays by Clifford Geertz* (New York: Basic Books, 1973).

Giddens, Anthony, *The Constitution of Society: Outline of a Theory of Structuration* (Berkeley: University of California Press, 1984).

Gilpin, Robert, *War and Change in World Politics* (Cambridge: Cambridge University Press, 1981).

Glaser, Charles, *Rational Theory of International Politics* (Princeton, NJ: Princeton University Press, 2010).

Goffman, Daniel, *The Ottoman Empire and Early Modern Europe* (Cambridge: Cambridge University Press, 2002).

Goh, Evelyn, *The Struggle for Order: Hegemony, Hierarchy, and Transition in Post–Cold War East Asia* (Oxford: Oxford University Press, 2013).

Goldthorpe, John H., 'Rational Action Theory for Sociology', *British Journal of Sociology*, 49.2 (1998), 167–192.

Gong, Gerrit W., 'China's Entry into International Society', in Hedley Bull and Adam Watson (eds.), *The Expansion of International Society* (Oxford: Oxford University Press, 1984), pp. 171–183.

Gong, Gong, *The Standard of Civilization in International Society* (Oxford: Clarendon Press, 1984).

Goodwin, Geoffrey, *The Janissaries* (London: Saqi Books, 2006).

Gray, Colin S., 'National Styles in Strategy: The American Example', *International Security*, 6.2 (1981), 21–47.

Nuclear Strategy and National Style (Lanham, MD: Hamilton Press, 1986).

'Strategic Culture as Context: The First Generation Strikes Back', *Review of International Studies*, 25.1 (1999), 49–69.

Green, Donald P. and Shapiro, Ian, *The Pathologies of Rational Choice: A Critique of Applications in Political Science* (New Haven, CT: Yale University Press, 1994).

Gupta, Akhil and Ferguson, James, 'Beyond "Culture": Space, Identity, and the Politics of Difference', *Cultural Anthropology*, 7.1 (1992), 6–23.

Guzzini, Stefano, 'The Enduring Dilemmas of Realism in International Relations', *European Journal of International Relations*, 10.4 (2004), 533–568.

Habermas, Jürgen, *Theory of Communicative Action* (Boston: Beacon Press, 1984).

Moral Consciousness and Communicative Action (Cambridge, MA: MIT Press, 1990).

Hafner-Burton, Emilie M., Haggard, Stephan, Lake, David A., and Victor, David G., 'The Behavioral Revolution and International Relations', *International Organization*, 71.S1 (2017), S1–S31.

Hall, Ian, *The International Thought of Martin Wight* (Basingstoke: Palgrave, 2006).

'Martin Wight, Western Values, and the Whig Tradition of International Thought', *International History Review*, 36.5 (2014), 961–981.

'The "Revolt against the West" Revisited', in Tim Dunne and Christian Reus-Smit (eds.), *The Globalization of International Society* (Oxford: Oxford University Press, 2017), pp. 345–361.

Hannerz, Ulf, *Cultural Complexity: Studies in the Social Organization of Meaning* (New York: Columbia University Press, 1992).

Hansen, Lene, *Security as Practice: Discourse Analysis and the Bosnian War* (London: Routledge, 2006).

'The Politics of Securitization and the Muhammad Cartoon Crisis: A Post-Structural Perspective', *Security Dialogue*, 45.4–5 (2011), 357–369.

Harsanyi, John C., 'Rational Choice Models of Political Behavior vs. Functionalist and Conformist Theories', *World Politics*, 21.4 (1969), 513–538.

Hart, H. L. A., *The Concept of Law*, 2nd edn. (Oxford: Clarendon Press, 1994).

Hartz, Louis, *The Founding of New Societies* (New York: Houghton, Mifflin, Harcourt, 1969).

Hay, Colin, 'Political Ontology', in Robert E. Goodin (ed.), *The Oxford Handbook of Political Science* (Oxford: Oxford University Press, 2011), pp. 460–477.

Hechter, Michael and Kanazawa, Satoshi, 'Sociological Rational Choice Theory', *Annual Review of Sociology*, 23 (1997), 191–214.

Hermann, Richard K., 'How Attachments to the Nation Shape Beliefs about the World: A Theory of Motivated Reasoning', *International Organization*, 71.S1 (2017), S61–S84.

Hobson, John, *The Eastern Origins of Western Civilization* (Cambridge: Cambridge University Press, 2004).

Hollis, Martin, *Models of Man: Philosophical Thoughts on Social Action* (Cambridge: Cambridge University Press, 1977).

Honneth, Axel, *The Struggle for Recognition: The Moral Grammar of Social Conflicts* (Cambridge, MA: MIT Press, 1995).

Hudson, Valerie M., *Culture and Foreign Policy* (Boulder, CO: Lynne Rienner, 1997).

Huntington, Samuel, 'The Clash of Civilizations?', *Foreign Affairs*, 72.3 (1993), 22–49.

Hurrell, Andrew, *On Global Order: Power, Values, and the Constitution of International Society* (Oxford: Oxford University Press, 2007).

Hutchison, Emma, *Affective Communities in World Politics: Collective Emotions after Trauma* (Cambridge: Cambridge University Press, 2016).

Ikenberry, G. John, *After Victory: Institutions, Strategic Restraint, and the Building of Order after Major Wars* (Princeton, NJ: Princeton University Press, 2001).

Liberal Leviathan: The Origins, Crisis, and Transformation of the American World Order (Princeton, NJ: Princeton University Press, 2011).

Iriye, Akira, *Cultural Internationalism and World Order* (Baltimore, MD: Johns Hopkins University Press, 1997).

Jackson, Patrick Thaddeus (ed.), 'Bridging the Gap: Toward a Realist-Constructivist Dialogue', *International Studies Review*, 6.2 (2004), 337–352.

Jackson, Robert, *Quasi-States: Sovereignty, International Relations and the Third World* (Cambridge: Cambridge University Press, 1990).

The Global Covenant: Human Conduct in a World of States (Oxford: Oxford University Press, 2000).

'From Colonialism to Theology: Encounters with Martin Wight's International Thought', *International Affairs*, 84.2 (2008), 351–364.

Jacques, Martin, *When China Rules the World: The End of Western World and the Birth of a New Global Order*, 2nd edn. (Harmondsworth: Penguin, 2012).

Jeffery, Renee, 'Australian Realism and International Relations: John Anderson and Hedley Bull on Ethics, Religion, and Society', *International Politics*, 45.1 (2008), 52–71.

Jepperson, Ronald L., Wendt, Alexander, and Katzenstein, Peter J., 'Norms, Identity, and Culture in National Security', in Peter J. Katzenstein (ed.), *The Culture of National Security: Norms and Identity in World Politics* (New York: Columbia University Press, 1996), pp. 33–75.

Jerolmack, Colin and Porpora, Douglas, 'Religion, Rationality and Experience: A Response to the New Rational Choice Theory of Religion', *Sociological Theory*, 22.1 (2004), 140–160.

Jervis, Robert, *Perception and Misperception in International Politics* (Princeton, NJ: Princeton University Press, 1976).

Johannessen, Kjell, 'The Concept of Practice in Wittgenstein's Later Philosophy', *Inquiry*, 31.3 (1988), 357–369.

Johnston, Alastair Iain, *Cultural Realism: Strategic Culture and Grand Strategy in Chinese History* (Princeton, NJ: Princeton University Press, 1995).

Kaplan, Morton, *System and Process in International Politics* (New York: Wiley, 1957).

Katzenstein, Peter J. (ed.), *Anglo-America and Its Discontents* (London: Routledge, 2012).

'International Relations Theory and the Analysis of Change', in Ernst-Otto Czempiel and James N. Rosenau (eds.), *Global Changes and*

Theoretical Challenges (Lexington, MA: Lexington Books, 1989), pp. 291–304.

(ed.), *The Culture of National Security: Norms and Identity in World Politics* (New York: Columbia University Press, 1996).

Culture Norms and National Security: Police and Military in Postwar Japan (Ithaca, NY: Cornell University Press, 1996).

'Introduction: Alternative Perspectives on National Security', in Peter J. Katzenstein (ed.), *The Culture of National Security* (New York: Columbia University Press, 1996), 1–32.

'A World of Plural and Pluralist Civilizations: Multiple Actors, Traditions, and Practices', in Peter J. Katzenstein (ed.), *Civilizations in World Politics* (London: Routledge, 2010), pp. 1–40.

'Many Wests and Polymorphic Globalism', in Peter J. Katzenstein (ed.), *Anglo-America and Its Discontents: Civilizational Identities beyond East and West* (London: Routledge, 2012), pp. 207–247.

'The West as Anglo-America', in Peter J. Katzenstein (ed.), *Anglo-America and Its Discontents: Civilizational Identities beyond East and West* (London: Routledge, 2012), pp. 1–30.

Katzenstein, Peter J., and Seybert, Lucia (eds.), *Protean Power: Exploring the Uncertain and Unexpected in World Politics* (Cambridge: Cambridge University Press, 2018).

Keal, Paul, *European Conquest and the Rights of Indigenous Peoples* (Cambridge: Cambridge University Press, 2003).

Keene, Edward, *Beyond the Anarchical Society* (Cambridge: Cambridge University Press, 2002).

Keir, Elizabeth, *Imagining War: French and British Military Doctrine between the Wars* (Princeton, NJ: Princeton University Press, 1999).

Keohane, Robert O., 'The Demand for International Regimes', in Stephen D. Krasner (ed.), *International Regimes* (Ithaca, NY: Cornell University Press, 1983), pp. 141–172.

After Hegemony: Cooperation and Discord in the World Political Economy (Princeton, NJ: Princeton University Press, 1984).

Kissinger, Henry, *A World Restored: Metternich, Castlereagh and the Problems of Peace: 1812–1822* (Boston: Houghton Mifflin, 1957).

World Order: Reflections on the Character of Nations and the Course of History (London: Allen Lane, 2014).

Klein, Bradley, 'Hegemony and Strategic Culture: American Power Projection and Alliance Defence Politics', *Review of International Studies*, 14.2 (1988), 133–148.

Klotz, Audie, *Norms in International Relations* (Ithaca, NY: Cornell University Press, 1996).

Koskenniemi, Martti, *From Apologia to Utopia: The Structure of Legal Argument*, 2nd edn. (Cambridge: Cambridge University Press, 2005), pp. 590–596.

Krasner, Stephen D., 'Structural Causes and Regime Consequences: Regimes as Intervening Variables', *International Organization*, 36.2 (1982), 185–205.

(ed.), *International Regimes* (Ithaca, NY: Cornell University Press, 1983).

Sovereignty: Organized Hypocrisy (Princeton, NJ: Princeton University Press, 1999).

Kratochwil, Friedrich, 'Regimes and the "Science" of Politics: A Reappraisal', *Millennium: Journal of International Studies*, 17.2 (1988), 263–284.

Rules, Norms, and Decisions: On the Conditions of Practical and Legal Reasoning in International Relations and Domestic Affairs (Cambridge: Cambridge University Press, 1989).

'Constructivism: What It Is (Not) and How It Matters', in Donatella Della Porta and Michael Keating (eds.), *Approaches and Methodologies in the Social Sciences* (Cambridge: Cambridge University Press, 2008), pp. 80–98.

'Sociological Approaches', in Christian Reus-Smit and Duncan Snidal (eds.), *The Oxford Handbook of International Relations* (Oxford: Oxford University Press, 2008), pp. 444–461.

Kratochwil, Friedrich and Ruggie, John Gerard, 'A State of the Art on an Art of the State', *International Organization*, 40.4 (1986), 753–775.

Kroeber, A. L. and Kluckhohn, Clyde, *Culture: A Critical Review of Concepts and Definitions* (Cambridge, MA: Peabody Museum, Harvard University, 1952).

Kroeber, A. L. and Parsons, Talcott, 'The Concepts of Culture and of Social System', *American Sociological Review*, 23.5 (1958), 582–583.

Kupchan, Charles A., *No One's World: The West, the Rising Rest, and the Coming Global Turn* (New York: Oxford University Press, 2012).

Kuper, Adam, *Culture: The Anthropologists Account* (Cambridge, MA: Harvard University Press, 1999).

Kymlicka, Will, *Multicultural Citizenship* (Oxford: Clarendon Press, 1995).

Multicultural Odysseys (Oxford: Oxford University Press, 2007).

Lapid, Yosef, 'Culture's Ship: Returns and Departures in International Relations Theory', in Yosef Lapid and Friedrich V. Kratochwil (eds.), *The Return of Culture and Identity in IR Theory* (Boulder, CO: Lynne Rienner, 1996), pp. 3–20.

Leander, Anna, 'Practices (Re)producing Order: Understanding the Role of Business in Global Security Governance', in M. Ougaard and A. Leander (eds.), *Business and Global Governance* (New York: Routledge, 2009), pp. 57–77.

Lebow, Richard Ned, *A Cultural Theory of International Relations* (Cambridge: Cambridge University Press, 2008).

Legro, Jeffrey W., *Cooperation under Fire: Anglo-German Restraint during World War II* (Ithaca, NY: Cornell University Press, 1995).

Legro, Jeffrey W. and Moravcsik, Andrew, 'Is Anybody Still a Realist?', *International Security*, 24.2 (1999), 5–55.

Lesser, Alexander, 'Social Fields and the Evolution of Society', *Southwestern Journal of Anthropology*, 17.1 (1961), 40–48.

Levi, Margaret, 'Reconsiderations of Rational Choice in Comparative and Historical Analysis', in Mark Irving Lichbach et al. (eds.), *Comparative Politics: Rationality, Culture, and Structure* (Cambridge: Cambridge University Press, 2009), pp. 117–133.

Levy, Jack S., 'An Introduction to Prospect Theory', *Political Psychology*, 13.2 (1992), 171–186.

Linklater, Andrew, *The Problem of Harm in World Politics* (Cambridge: Cambridge University Press, 2011).

Violence and Civilization in the Western States-Systems (Cambridge: Cambridge University Press, 2017).

Linklater, Andrew, and Suganami, Hidemi, *The English School of International Relations* (Cambridge: Cambridge University Press, 2006).

List, Christian and Spiekermann, Kai, 'Methodological Individualism and Holism in Political Science: A Reconciliation', *American Political Science Review*, 107.4 (November 2013), 629–643.

Little, Richard, 'The English School's Contribution to the Study of International Relations', *European Journal of International Relations*, 6.3 (2000), 395–422.

Lowe, Lisa, *The Intimacies of Four Continents* (Durham, NC: Duke University Press, 2015).

Luce, Duncan and Raiffa, Howard, *Games and Decisions: Introduction and Critical Survey* (New York: Wiley, 1957).

Malik, Kenan, 'The Failure of Multiculturalism', *Foreign Affairs*, 94.2 (2015), 21–22.

Martin, Lisa, 'The Rational State Choice of Multilateralism', in John Gerard Ruggie (ed.), *Multilateralism Matters: The Theory and Praxis of an Institutional Form* (New York: Columbia University Press, 1993), pp. 91–121.

Mearsheimer, John J., *The Tragedy of Great Power Politics* (New York: Norton, 2001).

Merry, Sally Engle, 'Changing Rights, Changing Culture', in Jane K. Cowan, Marie-Benedicte Dembour, and Richard A. Wilson (eds.), *Culture and Rights: Anthropological Perspectives* (Cambridge: Cambridge University Press, 2001), pp. 31–55.

Gender Violence: A Cultural Perspective (Malden, MA: Wiley-Blackwell, 2009).

Mitzen, Jennifer, 'Anchoring Europe's Civilizing Identity: Habits, Capabilities and Ontological Security', *Journal of European Public Policy*, 13.2 (2006), 270–285.

Morgan, Lewis H., *Ancient Society* (New York: Henry Holt and Company, 1877).

Morgenthau, Hans J., *Politics among Nations: The Struggle for Power and Peace*, 6th edn. (New York: McGraw Hill, 1985).

Morton, Samuel George, *Crania Americana* (Philadelphia: J. Dobson, 1839).

Nardin, Terry, *Law, Morality, and Relations of States* (Princeton, NJ: Princeton University Press, 1983).

Neumann, Iver B., *Uses of the Other: 'The East' in European Identity Formation* (Minneapolis: University of Minnesota Press, 1998).

'Returning Practice to the Linguistic Turn: The Case of Diplomacy', *Millennium: Journal of International Studies*, 31.3 (2002), 627–651.

At Home with the Diplomats (Ithaca, NY: Cornell University Press, 2012).

Neumann, Iver B. and Welsh, Jennifer M., 'The Other in European Self-Definition: An Addendum to the Literature on International Society', *Review of International Studies* 17.4 (1991), 327–348.

Ning, Chia, 'Lifanyuan and the Management of Population Diversity in Early Qing (1636–1795)', Max Planck Institute for Social Anthropology, Working Paper 139 (2012).

Norton, Anne, *95 Theses on Politics, Culture, and Method* (New Haven, CT: Yale University Press, 2004).

O'Hagan, Jacinta, 'Conflict, Convergence or Co-Existence: The Relevance of Culture in Reframing World Order', *Transnational International Law and Contemporary Problems*, 9.1 (1999), 537–567.

Conceptualizing the West in International Relations (Houndmills: Palgrave, 2002).

O'Neill, Barry, *Honor, Symbols, and War* (Ann Arbor: University of Michigan Press, 2001).

Onuf, Nicholas Greenwood, *World of Our Making: Rules and Rule in Social Theory and International Relations* (New York: Routledge, 2012).

'Constructivism at the Crossroads; or, the Problem of Moderate-Sized Dry Goods', *International Political Sociology*, 10.2 (2016), 115–132.

Ostrom, Elinor, *Governing the Commons: The Evolution of Institutions for Collective Action* (Cambridge: Cambridge University Press, 1990).

Oxford Dictionary of English, 3rd edn. (Oxford: Oxford University Press, 2010).

Parsons, Talcott, *The Social System* (London: Routledge, 1991).

Pauly, Louis, and Reus-Smit, Christian, 'Negotiating Anglo-America: Austra-
    lia, Canada, and the United States', in Peter J. Katzenstein (ed.), *Anglo-
    America and Its Discontents* (London: Routledge, 2012), pp. 127–152.
Percy, Sarah and Sandholtz, Wayne, 'Do Norms Really Die?' (unpublished
    paper).
Pettit, Phillip, '*Virtus Normativa*: Rational Choice Perspectives', *Ethics*,
    100.4 (1990), 725–755.
Pettit, Philip, 'Institutional Design and Rational Choice', in Robert Goodin
    (ed.), *The Theory of Institutional Design* (Cambridge: Cambridge Uni-
    versity Press, 1996), pp. 54–89.
Phillips, Andrew, *War, Religion, and Empire: The Transformation of Orders*
    (Cambridge: Cambridge University Press, 2011).
    'Contesting the Confucian Peace: Civilization, Barbarism, and Inter-
    national Hierarchy in East Asia', *European Journal of International
    Relations*, online at https://doi.org/10.1177/1354066117716265.
Philpott, Daniel, *Revolutions in Sovereignty* (Princeton, NJ: Princeton
    University Press, 2001).
Posen, Barry R., 'Nationalism, the Mass Army, and Military Power',
    International Security, 18.2 (1993), 80–124.
Pouliot, Vincent, *International Security in Practice: The Politics of NATO–
    Russia Diplomacy* (Cambridge: Cambridge University Press, 2010).
Price, Richard, 'Reversing the Gun Sights: Transnational Civil Society Targets
    Land Mines', *International Organization*, 53.3 (1998), 613–644.
    (ed.), *Moral Limit and Possibility in World Politics* (Cambridge:
    Cambridge University Press, 2008).
Quackenbush, Stephen, 'The Rationality of Rational Choice Theory',
    International Interactions, 30.2 (2004), 87–107.
Rae, Heather, *State Identities and the Homogenization of Peoples*
    (Cambridge: Cambridge University Press, 2002).
    'Patterns of Identification on the Cusp of Globalization', in Tim Dunne
    and Christian Reus-Smit (eds.), *The Globalization of International Soci-
    ety* (Oxford: Oxford University Press, 2017), pp. 63–81.
Reus-Smit, Christian, 'The Constitutional Structure of International Society
    and the Nature of Fundamental Institutions', *International Organiza-
    tion*, 51.4 (1997), 555–589.
    The Moral Purpose of the State (Princeton, NJ: Princeton University Press,
    1999).
    'Human Rights and the Social Construction of Sovereignty', *Review of
    International Studies*, 27.4 (2001), 519–538.
    American Power and World Order (Cambridge: Polity Press, 2004).
    'International Crises of Legitimacy', *International Politics*, 44.2–3 (2007),
    157–174.

'The Concept of Intervention', *Review of International Studies*, 39.4 (2013), 1057–1076.

Individual Rights and the Making of the International System (Cambridge: Cambridge University Press, 2013).

'The Liberal International Order Reconsidered', in Rebekka Friedman, Kevork Oskanian, and Ramon Pacheco-Pardo (eds.), *After Liberalism* (London: Palgrave, 2013), pp. 167–186.

'International Law and the Mediation of Culture', *Ethics and International Affairs*, 28.1 (2014), 65–82.

'Cultural Diversity and International Order', *International Organization*, 71.4 (2017), 851–885.

'Protean Power and Revolutions in Rights', in Peter J. Katzenstein and Lucia Seybert (eds.), *Power in Uncertainty: Exploring the Unexpected in World Politics* (Cambridge: Cambridge University Press, 2018), pp. 59–78.

Risse, Thomas '"Let's Argue!": Communicative Action in World Politics', *International Organization*. 54.1 (2000), 1–39.

Risse, Thomas and Ropp, Stephen, 'Introduction and Overview', in Thomas Risse, Stephen Ropp, and Kathryn Sikkink (eds.), *The Persistent Power of Human Rights* (Cambridge: Cambridge University Press, 2013), pp. 3–25.

Risse, Thomas and Sikkink, Kathryn, 'The Socialization of International Human Rights Norms into Domestic Practices: Introduction', in Thomas Risse, Stephen Ropp, and Kathryn Sikkink (eds.), *The Power of Human Rights: International Norms and Domestic Change* (Cambridge: Cambridge University Press, 1999), pp. 1–38.

Ruggie, John Gerard, 'Continuity and Transformation in the World Polity: Toward a Neorealist Synthesis', *World Politics*, 35.2 (1983), 261–285.

'Multilateralism: The Anatomy of an Institution', in John Gerard Ruggie (ed.), *Multilateralism Matters: The Theory and Praxis of an Institutional Form* (New York: Columbia University Press, 1993), pp. 3–50.

'Territoriality and Beyond: Problematizing Modernity in International Relations', *International Organization*, 47.1 (1993), 139–174.

Winning the Peace: America and World Order in the New Era (New York: Columbia University Press, 1996).

'What Makes the World Hang Together? Neo-Utilitarianism and the Social Constructivist Challenge', *International Organization*, 54.4 (1998), 855–885.

Said, Edward W., *Culture and Imperialism* (New York: Alfred A. Knopf, 1993).

Sambanis, Nicholas, Skaperdas, Stergios, and Wohlforth, William C., 'Nation-Building through War', *American Political Science Review*, 109.2 (2015), 279–296.

Saurin, Julian, 'International Relations as Imperial Illusion; or, the Need to Decolonize IR', in Branwen Gruffydd Jones (ed.), *Decolonizing International Relations* (Lanham, MD: Rowman and Littlefield, 2006), pp. 23–42.

Schelling, Thomas C., *The Strategy of Conflict* (Cambridge, MA: Harvard University Press, 1980).

Schweller, Randall L., *Deadly Imbalances: Tripolarity and Hitler's Strategy of World Conquest* (New York: Columbia University Press, 1998).

'The Problem of International Order Revisited', *International Security*, 26.1 (2001), 161–186.

Shakman Hurd, Elizabeth, *Beyond Religious Freedom: The New Global Politics of Religion* (Princeton, NJ: Princeton University Press, 2015).

Shapcott, Richard, *Justice, Community and Dialogue in International Relations* (Cambridge: Cambridge University Press, 2001).

Shaw, George Bernard. *Pygmalion* (Harmondsworth: Penguin, 2001).

Simon, Herbert A., 'A Behavioral Model of Rational Choice', *Quarterly Journal of Economics*, 69.1 (1955), 99–118.

Skinner, Quentin, *Visions of Politics, vol. 1: Regarding Method* (Cambridge: Cambridge University Press, 2002).

Snidal, Duncan 'Rational Choice and International Relations', in Walter Carlsnaes, Thomas Risse, and Beth Simmons (eds.), *Handbook of International Relations*, 2nd edn. (London: Sage, 2013), pp. 85–111.

Snyder, Jack, *The Soviet Strategic Culture* (Santa Monica, CA: Rand Corporation, 1977).

Myths of Empire: Domestic Politics and International Ambition (Ithaca, NY: Cornell University Press, 1991).

Stark, Rodney and Bainbridge, William S., *A Theory of Religion* (New York: Peter Lang, 1987).

Stark, Rodney and Finke, Roger, *Acts of Faith: Explaining the Human Side of Religion* (Berkeley: University of California Press, 2000).

Stocking, George W., 'Franz Boas and the Culture Concept in Historical Perspective', *American Anthropologist*, 68.4 (1966), 867–882.

Stuart, Reginald C. and Silverman, Dan P., *War and American Thought* (Kent, OH: Kent State University Press, 1982).

Suchman, Mark, 'Managing Legitimacy: Strategic and Institutional Approaches', *Academy of Management Review*, 30.3 (1995), 571–610.

Sutch, Peter, 'The Slow Normalization of Normative Political Theory', in Chris Brown and Robyn Eckersley (eds.), *The Oxford Handbook of International Political Theory* (Oxford: Oxford University Press, 2018), pp. 35–47.

Suzuki, Shogo, Zhang, Yongjin, and Quirk, Joel, *International Orders in the Early Modern Period* (London: Routledge, 2014).

Swidler, Ann, 'Culture in Action: Symbols and Strategies', *American Sociological Review*, 5.2 (1986), 273–286.

Talk of Love: How Culture Matters (Chicago, IL: University of Chicago Press, 2001).

Tavan, Gwenda, *The Long, Slow Death of White Australia* (Melbourne: Scribe, 2005).

Taylor, Charles, *Sources of the Self* (Cambridge, MA: Harvard University Press, 1989).

Tickner, J. Ann, *Gender in International Relations* (New York: Columbia University Press, 1992).

Towns, Ann, *Women and States: Norms and Hierarchies in International Society* (Cambridge: Cambridge University Press, 2010).

'Contesting the Liberal Order: Gender and the Generation of Cultural Cleavages across "the West"' (unpublished manuscript).

Tully, James, *Strange Multiplicity: Constitutionalism in an Age of Diversity* (Cambridge: Cambridge University Press, 1995).

Tversky, Amos and Kahneman, Daniel, 'Rational Choice and the Framing of Decisions', *Journal of Business*, 59.4.2 (1986), S251–S278.

Tylor, Edward B., *Primitive Culture*, vol. 1 (Boston: Estes and Lauriat, 1874).

Vucetic, Srdjan, *The Anglosphere: A Genealogy of a Racialized Identity in International Relations* (Stanford, CA: Stanford University Press, 2011).

Waltz, Kenneth N., *Man, the State, and War: A Theoretical Analysis* (New York: Columbia University Press, 1959).

Theory of International Politics (New York: Random House, 1979).

Walzer, Michael, 'On the Role of Symbolism in Political Thought', *Political Science Quarterly*, 82.2 (1967), 191–204.

Watson, Adam, *The Evolution of International Society* (London: Routledge, 1992).

Weldes, Jutta, Laffey, Mark, Gusterson, Hugh, and Duvall, Raymond (eds.), *Cultures of Insecurity: States, Communities, and the Production of Danger* (Minneapolis: University of Minnesota Press, 1999).

Welsh, Jennifer M., 'A Normative Case for Pluralism: Reassessing Vincent's Views on Humanitarian Intervention', *International Affairs*, 78.5 (2011), 1193–1204.

Wendt, Alexander, 'The Agent–Structure Problem in International Relations Theory', *International Organization*, 41.3 (1987), 334–370.

'Anarchy Is What States Make of It: The Social Construction of Power Politics', *International Organization*, 46.2 (1992), 391–426.

'Collective Identity Formation and the International State', *American Political Science Review*, 88.2 (1994), 384–396.

Social Theory of International Politics (Cambridge: Cambridge University Press, 1999).

Wheeler, Nicholas J., *Saving Strangers: Humanitarian Intervention in International Society* (Oxford: Oxford University Press, 2002).

Wight, Martin, 'Western Values in International Relations', in Herbert Butterfield and Martin Wight (eds.), *Diplomatic Investigations: Essays in the Theory of International Politics* (London: George Allen and Unwin, 1966), pp. 89–131.

Systems of States (Leicester: University of Leicester Press, 1977).

Power Politics, 2nd ed. (Harmondsworth: Penguin, 1986).

'An Anatomy of International Thought', *Review of International Studies*, 13.3 (1987), 221–227.

International Theory: The Three Traditions (New York: Holmes and Meier, 1992).

'The Disunity of Mankind', *Millennium: Journal of International Studies*, 44.1 (2015), 129–133.

Williams, Michael, *The Realist Tradition and the Limits of International Relations* (Cambridge: Cambridge University Press, 2005).

Williams, Raymond, *Keywords: A Vocabulary of Culture and Society* (London: Fourth Estate, 2014).

Wittgenstein, Ludwig, *Philosophical Investigations*, 4th edn. (Oxford: Blackwell, 2009).

Wohlforth, William C. 'Realism and the End of the Cold War', *International Security*, 19.3 (1994–1995), 91–129.

'Realism', in Christian Reus-Smit and Duncan Snidal (eds.), *The Oxford Handbook of International Relations* (Oxford: Oxford University Press, 2008), pp. 131–149.

Wolf, Eric R., *Europe and the People without History* (Berkeley: University of California Press, 1982).

Zakaria, Fareed, *From Wealth to Power: The Unusual Origins of American's World Role* (Princeton, NJ: Princeton University Press, 1998).

Zarakol, Ayse, *After Defeat: How the East Learned to Live with the West* (Cambridge: Cambridge University Press, 2011).

(ed.), *Hierarchies in World Politics* (Cambridge: Cambridge University Press, 2017).

'Ottoman Lessons for Cultural Diversity in International Relations' (unpublished manuscript).

Zhang, Yongjin, 'System, Empire and State in Chinese International Relations', *Review of International Relations*, 27.5 (2001), 43–63.

Zhang, Yongjin and Buzan, Barry, 'The Tributary System as International Society in Theory and Practice', *Chinese Journal of International Relations*, 5.1 (2012), 3–36.

Zimmerman, Lisbeth, *Global Norms with a Local Face* (Cambridge: Cambridge University Press, 2017).

Index

Abu-Lughod, Lila, 31–32, 40
Acharya, Amitav, 139–140, 235–236
actors, 122–154, 167–170, 208–209
  interpretations of, 206–207
Adler, Emanuel, 122, 152–153, 197
agents, 161
American Revolution, 146–147
anarchy, 54–55, 63–66, 128–129,
  167–170
  Wendt on, 10, 50–51, 128–130
Anderson, John, 84–85, 98, 100–101
Anglo-American core, 46
anthropologists, 7–8, 20–36, 95–96
anti-colonial sentiment, 202
Arendt, Hannah, 217
Aristotle, 45
Asia, 140, 145–147, 200–202, 216
Augsburg Principle, 199
Aumann, R. J., 177
Axis powers, 94

Bain, William, 93
Baldwin, David, 55, 57
Bandung Conference (1955), 115
Bandung powers, 94
barbarians, 91, 200–202, 217
Barkin, Samuel, 55
Becker, Gary, 159, 162–164
Bedouin culture, 31–32, 40
Beitz, Charles, 232
beliefs, 161, 173–174
Benedict, Ruth, 23–25, 27–33, 38–39,
  70, 150–151
Benhabib, Seyla, 232
Berger, Peter L., 129
Berrey, Ellen, 35–36, 207
Betts, Alexander, 137–138
Bhabha, Homi, 41
Blaikie, Norman, 165
Blumer, Herbert, 129

Boas, Franz, 21–25, 30, 38
Boudon, Raymond, 162
boundaries, 40
boundedness, 30–33
Bourdieu, Pierre, 125
Bozeman, Adda, 95–96
British Committee on International
  Theory, 96–97
British Empire, 84
Brown, Chris, 43
Bukovansky, Mlada, 146–147
Bull, Hedley, 9–10, 84–85, 87–118
  on civilization, 181–182
  on international order, 190–194
Burke, Edmund, 208
Butterfield, Herbert, 95
Buzan, Barry, 87, 108–109, 114–116

capabilities, 56–60
Catholic minorities, 199
change, 141–153, 215–219
China, 222–223, 229–230
Chinese, 194–196. See also Qing
  Chinese
Chong, Dennis, 183–184
Christendom, 91, 145–147, 193–194,
  197–200
Christianity, 44, 94–95, 100–101, 206,
  211–212. See also natural law
Christians, 94, 200, 210–211, 225
Chwe, Michael, 178–180
civilizational constellations, 45
civilizational hierarchy, 38–39
civilizational power, 223
civilizations, 43–47, 72, 90–103, 128,
  181–182
  clash of, 43, 45–47, 72
  standard of, 3, 110, 189, 203, 210
  Western, 25, 38–40, 101–103,
  222–230